Pension Policy

Pension Policy

The Search for Better Solutions

John A. Turner

2010

W.E. Upjohn Institute for Employment Research
Kalamazoo, Michigan

Library of Congress Cataloging-in-Publication Data

Turner, John A. (John Andrew), 1949 July 9-
  Pension policy : the search for better solutions / John A. Turner.
    p. cm.
  Includes bibliographical references and index.
  ISBN-13: 978-0-88099-354-8 (pbk. : alk. paper)
  ISBN-10: 0-88099-354-5 (pbk. : alk. paper)
  ISBN-13: 978-0-88099-355-5 (hardcover : alk. paper)
  ISBN-10: 0-88099-355-3 (hardcover : alk. paper)
  1. Pensions—Government policy. 2. Defined benefit pension plans. 3. Annuities.
I. Title.
  HD7091.T86 2009
  331.25'2—dc22

                      2009037585

The facts presented in this study and the observations and viewpoints expressed are the sole responsibility of the author. They do not necessarily represent positions of the W.E. Upjohn Institute for Employment Research.

Cover design by Alcorn Publication Design.
Index prepared by Diane Worden.
Printed in the United States of America.
Printed on recycled paper.

Contents

Acknowledgments   ix

1 Introduction to Pension Policy   1
   An Introduction to Pensions   2
   Basic Issues in Pension Policy   4
   An Overview of the Book   11

2 Mandates: Pathways to Expanding Private Sector Provision   21
   Four Pathways to Pension Coverage—Degrees of Compulsion   22
   Voluntary Carve-Out Accounts   25
   Pension Privatization in OECD Countries   29
   Conclusion   31

3 Extending Pension Coverage   33
   Measures of Coverage   34
   Policies to Encourage Employers to Provide Pension Plans   37
   Policies to Encourage Workers to Participate   40
   Conclusion   52

4 Labor Market Policy: Portability and Retirement   55
   Portability   55
   Retirement   73
   Conclusion   81

5 Tax Policy: Influencing Coverage and the Structure of Pensions   83
   Overview   84
   Pension Tax Policy in OECD Countries   86
   Tax Policy Analysis   87
   Conclusion   98

6 Managing Pension Risk   101
   Risk in Pension Plans   102
   Risk in 401(k) Plans   104
   Risk in Defined Benefit Plans   109
   Conclusion   122

7   **Hybrid Plans: The Best of Both Worlds?**   125
     Types of Hybrid Plans   125
     Analysis of Risk-Bearing in Hybrid Plans   132
     Conclusion   134

8   **Financing Pensions for Adequacy and Security**   137
     Financing Issues Common to Defined Contribution and Defined   137
       Benefit Plans
     Defined Contribution Financing Issues   141
     Defined Benefit Financing Issues   154
     Conclusion   163

9   **Pension Benefit Policy: The Search for Lost Pensions and**   165
     Other Issues
     Defined Contribution Plans   165
     Defined Benefit Plans   169
     Issues Affecting Both Defined Contribution and Defined
       Benefit Plans   171
     Conclusion   179

10 **The Decline in Annuitization and How to Reverse It**   181
     Annuity Basics   182
     Annuitizing 401(k) Plans   183
     Annuity Options   194
     Income Redistribution   197
     Market Innovations: Longevity Insurance, Laddering, and Framing   199
     Conclusion   200

11 **Finding Better Solutions**   203
     Public Policy for 401(k) Plans   203
     Public Policy for Defined Benefit Plans   206
     Proposal: A New Type of Hybrid—the Life-Indexed DB   210
     Conclusion   212

References   213

The Author   227

Index   229

About the Institute   243

Tables

3.1   Reasons Why Workers Who Are Eligible to Participate in a   48
      Pension Plan Do Not Participate (%)

3.2   Reasons for Not Contributing to the Federal Thrift Savings   49
      Plan (%)

5.1   Tax Treatment of Employee Pension Contributions   91

5.2   Net Tax Cost per Dollar Contributed to a Pension, Different   96
      Countries, 2006

6.1   PBGC Single-Employer Trust Fund Financial Status, 2000–2007   115

7.1   Types of Hybrid Pension Plans   126

8.1   Mutual Fund Expenses, Selected Countries, 2002 (% assets)   153

10.1   Features of Annuities in Mandatory Individual Account   186
      Systems in Sweden, Chile, and the United Kingdom

10.2   Comparison of Monthly Annuity Benefits for a $100,000   189
      Account Balance with Unisex and Gender-Based Pricing,
      Benefits Taken at Age 62, 2007 ($)

10.3   Comparison of a Unisex Annuity Provided through the Thrift   189
      Savings Plan and a Gender-Based Annuity Provided to
      Individuals by the Same Insurance Company, 2007

Acknowledgments

This book was inspired by an Upjohn Institute book that I coauthored with Noriyasu Watanabe while on a Fulbright at the Institut de Recherches Economique et Sociale in Paris. That book, *Private Pension Policies in Industrialized Countries: A Comparative Analysis* (Turner and Watanabe 1995), focuses primarily on voluntarily provided defined benefit plans. The pension world has changed considerably since that book was published, with defined contribution pensions playing an increasingly dominant role. The current book examines a broad range of pension policy issues in the new environment.

I have greatly benefited from collaboration over many years with distinguished coauthors whose work with me I have cited, and to whom I express gratitude: Clive Bailey, Daniel Beller, David Blake, Ellen Bruce, Richard Burkhauser, Yung-Ping Chen, Lorna Dailey, Philip DeJong, William Even, Colin Gillion, Teresa Ghilarducci, Roy Guenther, Richard Hinz, Gerard Hughes, Mark Iwry, Sophie Korczyk, Denis Latulippe, Jules Lichtenstein, David McCarthy, Olivia Mitchell, Dana Muir, Leslie Muller, David Rajnes, Patricia Reagan, Martin Rein, Amy Shannon, Satyendra Verma, Noriyasu Watanabe, and Hazel Witte. I wish to thank members of the DB+ Initiative, and especially Karen Ferguson, with whom I worked to develop reforms to improve the U.S. pension system. I also wish to thank my wife, Kathy, and daughter, Sarah, for supporting my absences to write, attend conferences, and work abroad, and to thank my parents, Henry and Mary, for ultimately making everything possible.

1
Introduction to Pension Policy

The U.S. pension system needs fixing. While some of its problems are longstanding, the system overall is in decline. Projections of the future are not certainties, and some analysts differ, but it appears likely that the financial security of current workers when they retire will be less than that of current retirees. For workers relying on 401(k) plans (which were named after the Internal Revenue Code section that enabled them), dramatic declines in the financial markets around the world in 2008 turned retirement security formerly provided to long-tenure workers by defined benefit plans into a system of retirement roulette. Workers in 401(k) plans are gambling that they will not be retiring in a period of dramatic stock market declines, such as experienced in 2008.

By international standards, the U.S. pension system performs poorly. When measured in a comparable fashion, the U.S. poverty rate for people age 65 and older is more than twice as high as in other high-income countries (Pension Rights Center 2007). The move toward 401(k) plans has reduced the extent to which the pension system provides annuities and survivors benefits, reducing retirement income security. People who work for employers that offer 401(k) plans often do not participate, and when they do they tend to make poor financial decisions. Employers are abandoning defined benefit plans for workers while maintaining generous pensions for executives. People in defined benefit plans who are laid off suffer portability losses, while their employers' plans receive corresponding actuarial bonuses. Long-lived retirees in defined benefit plans have the real value of their benefits decimated by inflation, while long-lived retirees in defined contribution plans risk running out of money because of not having annuitized their account balances.

The pension system is supposed to provide secure and adequate retirement income. In both respects, the U.S. system needs better solutions. With the decline in defined benefit plans and the increasing reliance on 401(k) plans, future retirees will have less secure and less adequate retirement income than current retirees. While that outcome would not occur if all workers covered by 401(k) plans contributed to their plans consistently and made wise investment decisions, research

1

shows that many people do not contribute consistently and some do a poor job of managing their 401(k) plans.

Pension policy is complex. It involves issues relating to taxation, labor economics, finance and behavioral finance, law, actuarial science, business administration, and accounting. Drawing on these disciplines, but taking an economist's perspective, this book discusses pension policy for U.S. private sector employer-provided pension plans. In analyzing pension policy, it addresses two questions: 1) What is the pension policy problem? and 2) What are the possible solutions? The book's focus is the search for better solutions for pension policy.

The United States has a federal system of government, where states play an important role in the development of policies in some areas. The 50 states provide the opportunity for social experimentation on policy innovations at a smaller level than the national level. That possibility for experimentation, however, is not available in the pension system because federal law preempts state law on pension issues. For this reason, international experience is particularly important in studying innovations in pension policy. Thus, this book presents lessons for U.S. policy from the experience of other countries.

AN INTRODUCTION TO PENSIONS

The two main types of pension plans are defined benefit plans and defined contribution plans. Hybrid plans combine features of both. Defined benefit plans base benefits on a benefit formula that usually involves the worker's years of service and earnings. Examples of types of defined benefit plans include final salary plans, where the benefit is based on the average of the last few years of earnings, and career average plans, where the benefit is based on average earnings over the worker's career.

Defined contribution plans are retirement savings plans where the worker accumulates assets in an individual account. The most prominent U.S. example is 401(k) plans, where the worker generally must contribute to participate, and where the employer may contribute based on the worker's contribution. When this book refers to U.S. defined contribution plans, it generally is referring to 401(k) plans, since they have become nearly synonymous with defined contribution plans because of their prevalence. In 2005, there were $2.4 trillion in 401(k) plans and $0.4 trillion in non-401(k) defined contribution plans (USDOL 2008).[1]

When the landmark pension legislation, the Employee Retirement Income Security Act of 1974 (ERISA), was passed, pension coverage was primarily provided by defined benefit plans. In part because of the effects of that act and of subsequent legislation, pension participation has shifted away from defined benefit plans and toward defined contribution plans. According to the U.S. Department of Labor (USDOL), since 1984 more workers have been active participants in defined contribution plans than have been in defined benefit plans. By the early 2000s, considerably more than twice as many workers were active participants in defined contribution plans as were in defined benefit plans (USDOL 2008). The shift from defined benefit to defined contribution plans has meant the shift of investment risk from employers to employees, but it has reduced risks for job-changing or laid-off employees.

The 401(k) plan is usually participant-directed. That means that participants decide their investment, at least for the plan's assets that derive from the participant's own contributions. In 401(k) plans, employee choice plays a large role. Participation is typically voluntary. Employees who choose to participate also can choose, within limits, what percentage of salary to contribute. They choose investments from the options offered by the plan.

A more recent development in U.S. pensions is a hybrid plan called a cash balance plan. These plans are hybrids because they combine features of both defined benefit and defined contribution plans. To employees they have many features of defined contribution plans, while to employers they are funded like defined benefit plans. In 1995, 3 percent of defined benefit participants were in cash balance plans (Elliott and Moore 2000). A decade later, cash balance plans accounted for a quarter of defined benefit plan participants (USDOL 2008).

Legislation has created several new types of plans. The Pension Protection Act of 2006 introduced a new type of hybrid plan, one combining defined benefit and 401(k) features—the DB(k) plan. The legislation enabling that plan will take effect in 2010. Earlier legislation had created the Roth IRA and the Roth 401(k). With the two Roth plans, contributions are not tax-deductible, but benefits received at retirement are tax-free.

Other countries have also had major changes in pensions. In recent years, the United Kingdom, Ireland, Germany, Norway, and New Zealand have added employer mandates for pension provision, making employer mandates a major trend. The Netherlands and Iceland have introduced hybrid pension plans. Germany and Japan have introduced new types of defined contribution plans.

At the same time that these changes were occurring in the real world, economists have advanced the economic analysis of pensions. With the development of behavioral economics, we better understand the problems people encounter interacting with the pension system, particularly with 401(k) plans. The development of individual account plans has led to a more sophisticated analysis of those plans and to a new emphasis on understanding annuities.

BASIC ISSUES IN PENSION POLICY

To introduce pension policy, this section discusses nine issues that affect pension financing. Countries use a wide range of approaches in addressing the basic financing issues discussed in this chapter. The issues discussed here represent fundamental questions about retirement income financing that must be addressed in designing new pension systems or changing established ones.

Issue 1: Should the Private Pension System Be Voluntary or Mandatory?

A number of countries, including Australia, Switzerland, Sweden, Finland, France, Chile, Mexico, and the Netherlands, require most employees to be covered by a pension plan, either by law or by collective bargaining agreements. While U.S. employers have long provided pensions voluntarily, they also have a long tradition of staunchly opposing mandates. Nonetheless, the topic of extending coverage by mandate is perennial in the policy debate because of the failure of other approaches to cover more than half of the private sector workforce.

To encourage, rather than to mandate, workers to participate in pensions, the federal and state governments provide tax incentives, employers provide matching contributions to 401(k) plans, and, increasingly, employers that offer 401(k) plans are automatically enrolling new employees. The government has added the Saver's Credit to increase the incentive to participate for low-income workers. The Saver's Credit provides a tax credit to low-income workers with tax liability who participate in a pension plan.

Other countries have gone further, establishing a range of mandates with increasingly greater degrees of compulsion—mandates that employers provide plans (but that workers don't need to participate), mandates that employers offer matching contributions, mandates for automatic enrollment of employees with opt-out, and mandates that employees participate. In recent years, the United Kingdom, Ireland, Germany, Norway, and New Zealand have added employer mandates for pension provision, but with voluntary employee participation.

Mandates can differ in the way they treat employers and employees. In Australia, the mandate requires both that employers offer a plan and that employees participate. By contrast, the United Kingdom mandates that employers offer a plan, but participation by employees is voluntary. U.S. pension law does not require employers to offer a plan, but if they do, they must cover most full-time employees.

Mandates also differ in the extent to which they cover the workforce. Mandates on employers need to recognize that most employers are small employers employing a few people. Many are not even businesses, but are homeowners employing someone to take care of their children or clean their house. Mandates may exclude small employers who employ, for example, fewer than 10 employees, employees working in households, young employees, low-wage employees, and employees working fewer than a minimum number of hours or with short tenure. In countries where pension plans are voluntarily provided by employers, the government may set minimum standards as to which workers (or what percentage of the workforce of the employer sponsoring a plan) are included in the plan.

The United States and nearly all other countries have a mandatory, state-operated pension—social security. Some people argue that instead of mandating pensions, why not simply increase the generosity of social security. Social security, however, is not funded, while private pensions are.

Although mandates are capable of greatly increasing pension coverage, they do so at the cost of loss of individual choice. The United States has not mandated pensions, but it has moved toward greater degrees of encouragement.

Issue 2: If Private Pensions Are Voluntary, to What Extent Should the Government Encourage Them?

All countries with well-developed voluntary pension systems encourage pensions by providing preferential tax treatment. In Canada and the United States, pension plans receive tax preferences that allow money to accumulate tax-free. Countries, such as New Zealand, that have not provided tax preferences for pensions, but have treated them like other forms of savings, have had few employers provide pensions.

A progressive personal income tax provides greater tax incentive and greater tax subsidy to higher-income persons than to lower-income persons. This incentive is upside down. High-income persons are already more likely to save for retirement than are low-income persons. An alternative approach would be to provide everyone a limited tax credit for pension savings, which would provide the same marginal incentive to workers at different income levels. The tax treatment of pensions is considered in greater detail in Chapter 5.

Issue 3: Who Is Best Able to Bear the Inherent Financial and Demographic Risks in Pension Plans?

Pension plans can involve five types of actors: employees, labor unions, employers and employers' organizations, financial service providers, and government. Risks could be borne by any of these actors. The primary decision as to who bears risks is made when policymakers or the pension provider decides whether to offer defined benefit, defined contribution, or hybrid plans. With defined benefit plans, typically the provider bears the financial market risk, as well as the demographic risk that the participants will live longer on average than expected. However, in cases of bankruptcy of the sponsoring firm, the financial risk can be borne by workers. Countries where defined benefit plans predominate include Germany, Japan, Canada, Ireland, and the Netherlands. With defined contribution plans, the participant bears the financial market risk. If the plan does not provide annuitized benefits, the participant also bears the demographic risk that he or she will live longer than expected. Countries where defined contribution plans predominate include Australia and Sweden. The United States and the United Kingdom, and to a lesser degree Canada and Ireland, have seen a trend toward defined contribution plans.

With hybrid plans, the financial and demographic risks can be borne in different ways. For example, with cash balance plans, the participant may bear some financial market risk (as such risk affects the crediting rate provided by the plan) and may bear life expectancy when not annuitizing their account balance. Risk-bearing in pension plans is considered in more detail in Chapter 6, and hybrid plans are considered in Chapter 7.

Issue 4: Should the Government Mandate Insurance or Guarantees for Pension Benefits?

The government requires that benefits in some plans be guaranteed in Finland, Germany, Japan, Switzerland, the province of Ontario in Canada, the United Kingdom, and the United States. In Japan, Germany, the United Kingdom and the United States, mandatory pension benefit insurance for defined benefit plans is provided. This insurance covers the risk that the sponsoring firms will declare bankruptcy without having fully funded their pension plans. Chile, Argentina, Mexico, and Switzerland provide some form of insurance or guarantee of account balances in defined contribution plans. Pension insurance programs and guarantees are discussed in Chapter 6.

Issue 5: Who Should Pay for Pension Plans?

Ultimately, according to economic theory, regardless of whether the employer or employee makes the contribution, the employees bear the cost, either through reduced wages relative to what they would be without a pension plan or through direct contributions. This process is clearly visible in the trade-offs labor unions make in collective bargaining, but this tenet of economic theory is greeted with skepticism among noneconomists.

The question remains as to who should finance the pension plan. Should the funding come from employers, employees, or both? In the United States, funding for private sector defined benefit plans comes almost entirely from employers. In Canada, the United Kingdom, and most other countries with substantial numbers of defined benefit plans, employees contribute to those plans and receive a tax deduction for doing so. In some defined benefit plans in Canada, the employees' contribution rate has been increased as a response to the greater benefit costs resulting from longer life expectancy. In the United States, private sector employees do not receive a tax deduction for contributions to defined benefit plans, but they do receive a tax deduction for contributions to 401(k) plans.

The lack of tax deductibility of employee contributions to U.S. private sector defined benefit plans is an anomaly. It is not the case for employees in U.S. state and local government plans, and it is not the case for defined benefit plans in all other countries with significant numbers of those plans. The question of who should pay for pensions is considered in Chapter 8, including whether employee contributions to U.S. private sector defined benefit plans should be tax deductible.

Issue 6: To What Extent Should Pension Portfolios Be Regulated?

In the United Kingdom and the United States, defined benefit pension portfolios are governed by the mandate that the portfolios be prudently invested. Investments are not judged in isolation but within the context of their role in the pension portfolio. In the United Kingdom, no more than 5 percent of the defined benefit plans assets can be invested in the securities of the sponsoring employer. In the United States, the limit is 10 percent.

Problems with the investment of pension plans occur in the defined contribution sector. For example, employees of Enron lost millions of dollars when that company collapsed, because many employees were heavily invested in their employer's stock, counter to basic ideas of risk diversification.

Issue 7: What Types of Organizations Should Be Allowed to Sponsor Pension Plans?

In most countries with private pension systems, employers are allowed and encouraged to provide private pension plans. In many countries, multiemployer, industry, or union organizations are allowed to sponsor or cosponsor pension plans. These countries include the Netherlands, Japan, Canada, Germany, and the United States. Proposals for raising U.S. pension coverage have included some that would extend the role of multiemployer plans to efficiently provide pensions through economies of scale for employees who work for small employers.

Issue 8: What Types of Institutions Should Be Allowed to Manage Pension Funds?

In defined contribution plans, the employer has traditionally chosen the investments, but in 401(k) plans, generally the employer chooses the range of funds from which the employee can choose, and the employee makes the ultimate choice, at least with respect to the employee's contributions. Some defined benefit plans are jointly trusteed, with a committee of both employers and employees making the financial decisions. In many countries, including Canada and the United States, multiemployer groups jointly manage plans with labor unions.

In most countries, including the United States, Canada, and the United Kingdom, employers are allowed to manage pension plans. In Japan, however, pension plans must be managed by financial institutions external to the sponsoring company. In Japan, employers play little role, only serving as a collection agent for pension contributions, which are transmitted to a pension fund management company.

Other than employers and unions, a variety of financial institutions can manage pension funds. Pension fund management can be provided by life insurance companies, mutual funds, banks, or companies specially constituted to manage pension funds. The organizations can be profit-making entities or nonprofit entities. In Chile, only special institutions established specifically to manage pension funds are allowed to do so. In most countries, including Japan, Canada, the United Kingdom, and the United States, insurance companies and investment managers are allowed to manage pension funds. In Germany, banks play a major role in managing pension funds, while their role in the United States is limited to offering Individual Retirement Accounts (IRAs).

Pension fund management can be centralized in one or a few entities, or it can be decentralized. Within that framework, investment management can be done on an individual or a collective basis.

Issue 9: What Role Should Defined Benefit Plans, Defined Contribution Plans, and Hybrid Plans Play?

The role of defined benefit plans has declined in a number of countries, including the United States and the United Kingdom. Some commentators have argued that defined benefit plans are dinosaurs—they will eventually become extinct because of changes in the labor market environment. Workers are more mobile, and consequently they tend to favor defined contribution plans. However, the decline has been much more limited in Canada, Japan, and the Netherlands. Canada has a long-established policy of maintaining a level playing field as it relates to allowable contributions to defined contribution and defined benefit plans, which may have played a role in the limited decline of defined benefit plans.

A U.S. government policy, perhaps unintended, is the government's apparent encouragement of defined contribution plans over defined benefit plans. As an example of the stricter regulation of defined benefit plans than defined contribution plans, pension law requires defined benefit plans to provide annuities as the default option, requiring spousal consent if a different option is chosen. By contrast, 401(k) plans face no such requirements. The looser regulation of 401(k) plans may be an historical artifact resulting from the origins of 401(k) plans as secondary plans provided by employers that offered defined benefit plans.

Discouragement of defined benefit plans also may be an unintended consequence of policies that are designed to strengthen defined benefit plans but that also increase their costs. It may result in part from government policies designed to reduce the tax expenditure associated with defined benefit pensions by giving them tax preferences. It may be due to government policies that provide options to 401(k) plans, such as deductibility of employee contributions, that are not provided to defined benefit plans.

Both defined benefit plans and defined contribution plans impose risks on workers. In U.S. defined benefit plans, if a worker is laid off at age 50, his future pension benefit will be based on his wages at age 50. There will be no adjustment for inflation that occurs from that point up to the age when he will be eligible to receive benefits, which could be age 65. British workers are protected against this risk by mandatory price indexation of deferred vested benefits. Reforms may be warranted to provide further protection for workers who are laid off. This could be viewed as costly to employers, or it could be viewed as preventing employers from receiving an actuarial bonus, and thus an incentive, in defined benefit pension plans when they lay off workers.

In general, however, workers are better off when covered by both defined benefit plans and defined contribution plans. The two types of plans together, with their different patterns of risk-bearing, provide risk diversification. Hybrid plans blend the risk characteristics of defined benefit plans, generally imposing more risks on employees than traditional defined benefit plans but fewer risks than 401(k) plans. Hybrid plans are discussed further in Chapter 7.

AN OVERVIEW OF THE BOOK

This book focuses on current pension policy issues. It takes into account the major changes in the prevalence of pension plans of different types, in pension law, and in the economic analysis of pensions. The book approaches pension policy from different perspectives. One perspective is the international perspective, with a focus on lessons from international experience for U.S. pension policymakers. While attention is paid to the economic analysis of pensions, the book focuses on advancing our understanding of pension policy. The book's goal is to improve pension policy, and ultimately the lives of retirees, in the United States and elsewhere.

While the book covers a broad range of topics, pension plans and pension policy are both complex, and the coverage is not complete. Nonetheless, readers seeking an overall introduction to pension policy may read the book from cover to cover; other readers may find it more profitable to read particular chapters for a survey of policy issues of particular interest.

Policy issues addressed include the following four questions:

1) How can pension coverage be increased?

2) What can be done to save defined benefit plans?

3) How can annuitization be increased in defined contribution plans?

4) How should pension policy adjust to continuing increases in life expectancy?

"Mandates: Pathways to Expanding Private Sector Provision" (Chapter 2) analyzes issues relating to making private pensions mandatory, including by privatizing social security with individual accounts. It expands on the brief discussion of mandates in this chapter. A number of countries have mandated individual account plans that are managed by pension fund providers. Countries use mandatory individual accounts primarily in Latin America and Central and Eastern Europe, but Hong Kong and Sweden are other notable examples.

Some policy experts have discussed proposals mandating that employers withhold from payroll employee contributions, with automatic enrollment but worker opt-out, as an alternative to individual accounts being mandated through social security. While social security provides a uniform structure of benefits and contributions across the workforce, mandatory private pensions allow greater flexibility and diversity in the types of arrangements.

Administrative feasibility, meaning functionality at reasonable cost, is a key issue with mandates involving small employers. Many small employers do not have automated payroll systems, but instead write payroll checks by hand or pay in cash. For those employers, withholding pension contributions and transmitting them to a pension fund provider is administratively more costly than it is for large employers with automated payroll systems who can make electronic transfers of funds. For this reason, some employer mandates exempt employers below a certain size, such as 10 full-time employees. Administrative issues relating to employer mandates are discussed in Chapter 2.

"Extending Pension Coverage" (Chapter 3) analyzes a wide range of issues relating to pension coverage. It discusses measures of pension coverage in defined contribution plans. The standard measure of coverage overstates the percentage of workers accruing benefits based on their current work. A measure of pension coverage that requires that the worker actually be accruing pension benefits, rather than that the worker just have a 401(k) account, yields lower coverage than do traditional measures (Turner, Muller, and Verma 2003). The chapter also discusses the sensitivity of pension coverage to changes in income tax rates (Reagan and Turner 2000).

Pension coverage patterns differ if examined within the context of a family rather than an individual. Because fewer women are married than in the past, the rising pension coverage rate for women as workers is partially offset by declining pension coverage of women as spouses of men with coverage (Even and Turner 1999).

Only about half of all workers participate in any type of pension plan at a given point in time. Some workers do not contribute to a 401(k) plan even though their employer offers a matching contribution. The chapter discusses the role of inertia versus economic incentives as an explanation for why workers turn down pension coverage (Turner and Verma 2007). At least five reasons may explain nonparticipation by workers eligible to participate in a 401(k) plan. Besides the traditional economic reason of lack of economic incentives, four other reasons apply to workers who do not fit the classic definition of being well-informed and rational: 1) high discount rates causing them to place little value on future benefits, 2) lack of information, 3) lack of willpower to follow through on a decision, and 4) failure to make a decision because of passivity, ambivalence, and other similar behavioral factors. The last two reasons are often grouped together as inertia. Understanding the different reasons may aid in developing effective policies that would help workers achieve good pension outcomes.

"Labor Market Policy: Portability and Retirement" (Chapter 4) considers how pension plans—in this case particularly defined benefit plans—affect people who change jobs or are laid off. A worker laid off in his 50s will generally see the investments in his defined contribution plan continue to increase in value. However, his defined benefit plan will continuously decline in value because the nominal wages used to calculate his benefits will be eroded by inflation occurring between the point of layoff and the point of eligibility for benefits, which could be as late as age 65.

Many workers favor phased retirement as a way to gradually transition into retirement rather than a cliff-style retirement of going from full-time work to zero work (Latulippe and Turner 2000). Early retirement in certain physically demanding occupations is facilitated by pensions. Discussions of retirement age policy often focus on people with physically demanding jobs where postponed retirement would be difficult (Turner and Guenther 2005).

While it is often assumed that defined contribution plans do not affect retirement decisions, empirical evidence suggests that workers postpone retirement during economic downturns because of the associated decline in their account balances, possibly destabilizing labor markets by increasing supply at the same time that demand is reduced (Ghilarducci and Turner 2007).

"Tax Policy: Influencing Coverage and the Structure of Pensions" (Chapter 5) discusses the tax treatment of the tax basis in contributory pension plans. Tax basis will increasingly be an important issue for baby boomer retirees because it arises in IRAs and 401(k) plans when workers make nondeductible contributions. The tax basis is not indexed for inflation. Thus, its real value erodes over a worker's career because of inflation. Roth 401(k) plans provide eligible workers a choice as to the tax treatment of their pension contributions, in that they have taxable contributions but tax-free benefits. These plans thus do not have the problem of inflation eroding the tax basis or of the worker needing to provide years of contribution records to prove the tax status of withdrawals.

The tax code contains a number of penalties and requirements associated with fixed ages as they relate to pension plans. An example is the age of 70 ½, which is the age at which pension distributions must occur if the participant is no longer employed with the sponsoring employer. Employees who withdraw 401(k) plan money from their plans before age 59 ½ and are still working for the sponsoring employer must pay a 10 percent penalty, as well as paying income taxes. This chapter discusses the role of fixed ages in pension tax law and whether these ages should be raised or indexed as life expectancy increases.

"Managing Pension Risk" (Chapter 6) investigates a broad range of risks facing pension participants and plan sponsors. For workers having long careers with a single employer, defined benefit plans promise retirement benefits with substantially less risk than the retirement benefits promised by 401(k) plans. Defined benefit plans, however, can be risky for workers who change jobs or are laid off.

Sponsors of defined benefit plans face longevity risk relating to the longevity of their retirees. Both the cohort and idiosyncratic (individual) risks of increased life expectancy are borne by sponsors of defined benefit plans but are borne by individual participants in 401(k) plans. Cohort life expectancy risk is the risk that on average people in a cohort will live longer than expected. Idiosyncratic life expectancy risk is the risk that a particular individual will live longer than expected. While the idiosyncratic risks can easily be diversified away through risk pooling for a large number of people, pooling does not reduce the cohort risk. Cohort life expectancy risk can be borne by individuals at low cost, while it is expensive for plan sponsors. The opposite pattern holds for risk-bearing of idiosyncratic risk, which is expensive for individuals but not for plan sponsors because they can diversify it away.

The chapter also discusses the UK Pension Protection Fund (PPF), which is based on an attempt to learn from the U.S. experience with the Pension Benefit Guaranty Corporation (PBGC). After more than 30 years, the PBGC continues to face serious problems, including a large deficit.

"Hybrid Plans: The Best of Both Worlds?" (Chapter 7) focuses on the ways that pension plans can be structured to share risks between workers and employers. Hybrid defined benefit plans may be desirable as a way of preserving the positive aspects for workers of defined benefit plans while reducing the risks that employers face, such as investment risk and longevity risk.

While hybrid plans have features of both defined benefit and defined contribution plans, some are more like defined benefit plans in that they define benefits with a benefit formula; however, they do contain some defined contribution features. Hybrid plans that are essentially defined benefit plans with defined contribution features shift some of the risk traditionally borne by employers to workers. Hybrid pension plans that are basically defined contribution plans because the benefit is tied to the rate of return on an account balance usually add a rate of return guarantee (Turner and Rajnes 2003).

Cash balance plans are the best-known U.S. hybrid plans (Turner 2003a), but employers have also offered other types, such as pension equity plans. The new DB(k) plan can be offered starting in 2010.

The Netherlands has recently adopted hybrid plans with defined benefit plan benefit formulas, but in which the workers bear the investment and demographic risks through variable contribution rates that they pay. Iceland has mandatory plans that are hybrids, and the United Kingdom has some types of hybrid plans. The ABP plan in the Netherlands, which is a hybrid plan, is the largest plan in the world in terms of assets. These plans all shift cohort life expectancy risk to participants. In addition, a number of types of hybrid plans have been proposed, such as life expectancy–indexed defined benefit plans (Chapter 10 and Muir and Turner 2007). The chapter discusses reasons for the growing role of cash balance plans in the U.S. pension system (Lichtenstein and Turner 2005).

"Financing Pensions for Adequacy and Security" (Chapter 8) includes a discussion of the financial decisions made by participants in defined contribution plans. This chapter incorporates insights from behavioral finance concerning the errors participants make in managing their pension investments. Gender differences in pension investments are discussed (Hinz, McCarthy, and Turner 1997).

An assumption underlying the U.S. system of voluntary employee participation in defined contribution plans is that individuals make good financial decisions. A major weakness of this approach is that many individuals make poor financial decisions, especially when long planning horizons are involved, resulting in retirement income that is insufficient to maintain their preretirement living standards. Behavioral finance has documented these choices and how they result in outcomes that are unfavorable to workers in the long run. Behavioral finance theorists have used their insight into the roles that inertia and procrastination play in worker behavior to propose defaults that preserve worker choice while arguably achieving better long-run outcomes for many workers.

Once a worker has decided to participate in a 401(k) plan, the factor most affecting the amount of assets accumulated at retirement is how much the participant and employer contribute to the plan. Financial education can be used to influence the decisions participants make (McCarthy and Turner 2000). Defaults in defined contribution plans can have large effects on worker participation, but the degree to which these effects persist over long periods of time and the degree to which they work in different types of financial markets have not been investigated (Turner 2006). One default that has been proposed is a gradually increasing contribution rate.

The level and disclosure of fees in 401(k) plans is a multibillion dollar issue. Pension participants in 401(k) plans annually pay billions of dollars in fees. With defined benefit plans, the plans' expenses are borne by the sponsoring employer, but with defined contribution plans, most of the expenses are borne by the participants. Participants with substantial account balances can easily pay hundreds or even thousands of dollars in fees every year.

In spite of the large amounts of money involved, participants rarely know how much they are paying in fees, and thus are not able to make informed decisions between alternative options (Turner and Korczyk 2004). They are purchasing services without knowing the price. While transparency is a desirable attribute concerning fees, 401(k) fees are opaque. The topic is also important because of the size of the effect of apparently small fees on account balances. A fee of 1 percent can reduce the account balance of a 401(k) plan by 12 percent over a period of 20 years (Muller and Turner 2008).

While some researchers and organizations have focused on extending coverage or strengthening 401(k) plans, the policy community for the most part appears to have given up on saving defined benefit plans. However, policies might strengthen defined benefit plans and slow or reverse their decline. A strong retirement income system would ideally contain both defined benefit and defined contribution plans because both types provided together do a better job of helping workers deal with various risks than either do when provided alone.

"Pension Benefit Policy: The Search for Lost Pensions and Other Issues" (Chapter 9) notes that benefits can be provided to participants in defined contribution plans in five ways: 1) as annuities, 2) as lump sums, 3) as phased withdrawals, 4) as installment payments, and 5) as a series of ad hoc payments. Three issues concerning benefit receipt are as follows:

1) What happens to workers' accounts when they change jobs before retirement?

2) Are workers' accounts annuitized, taken as a lump sum, taken as a phased withdrawal, or taken in installments at retirement?

3) Are survivor benefits provided?

Pension law requires defined benefit plans to provide survivor benefits as an option. It does not require 401(k) plans that do not provide annuities as an option—which are most 401(k) plans—to provide survivor benefits.[2] Because of the complex issues associated with annuities, Chapter 10 is devoted to them. This chapter discusses the effect of the move toward defined contribution plans on the income inequality of pension beneficiaries.

Lost pensions are a problem for some job-changers. This problem is the focus of efforts by pension assistance programs and a program run by the PBGC, but it has received little attention from economists. The United Kingdom and Australia have gone far beyond the United States in developing policy to deal with this problem (Blake and Turner 2002). Pensions may be lost in the sense that job-leavers subsequently cannot find their former employer to claim benefits. That problem is especially likely to occur when the sponsoring firm has changed location or name, perhaps as a result of having been bought out.

"The Decline in Annuitization and How to Reverse It" (Chapter 10) is an important issue because annuities provided by pensions are decreasing. They are decreasing because of the decline in traditional defined benefit plans—historically a key source of low-cost guaranteed lifetime income—and the shift to cash balance plans. Cash balance plans are required to provide annuities, but perhaps because the benefit is expressed in terms of an account balance, workers typically take their benefits as lump sums. Annuities can be particularly valuable for women because women tend to outlive the men in their lives, and their risk of poverty at the end of life is greater than for men.

Annuities could potentially play an important role in 401(k) plans. While it has been expected that workers would increasingly annuitize their 401(k) plans with the decline in defined benefit plans, that has not occurred. Annuities have been analyzed extensively in the context of Social Security reform, and in the context of individually purchased annuities, but little attention has been paid to them in the context of the unisex requirement in the 401(k) plan setting. With unisex annuities, sometimes single men can receive higher benefits outside the pension plan than inside it. Thus, an unintended consequence of the unisex rulings by the Supreme Court may have been that the resulting adverse selection has caused most 401(k) plan sponsors not to offer annuities. Recently, some plan sponsors have begun offering annuities outside the plan through third-party providers. These annuities take into account the different mortality risks of men and women.

The concluding chapter, "Finding Better Solutions," (Chapter 11) discusses the main policy proposals for both 401(k) plans and defined benefit plans. In addition, with the goal of maintaining a role for defined benefit plans in the retirement income system, it proposes a new type of hybrid pension plan—the life-indexed DB plan—that preserves key aspects of defined benefit plans while shifting some risk and cost to workers.

Notes

1. Authors differ in the exact terminology they use to refer to different types of plans. In this paper, "pension plans" refers to both defined benefit and defined contribution plans. Because 401(k) plans so dominate the defined contribution plans in the United States, generally 401(k) plans are discussed.
2. Money purchase plans are required to provide annuities with joint and survivor benefits.

2

Mandates

Pathways to Expanding Private Sector Provision

How can pension coverage be expanded? How can retirement benefits and retirement savings be increased? How can the range of individual choice with respect to retirement income be enlarged? Roughly half of U.S. workers are covered by a pension, with older workers and higher income workers being more likely to be covered than their counterparts (Purcell 2006). Workers in small firms are much less likely to be covered than workers in large firms.[1]

Mandating private pensions (Ghilarducci 2008) or individual accounts as part of Social Security (President's Commission to Strengthen Social Security 2001) has been proposed as the answer to those questions. While the debate is heated at times, and apparently dormant at others, it is a continuing area of disagreement among pension experts. Mandating appeals to some people on both economic and ideological grounds. On economic grounds, they argue that mandatory individual accounts would increase savings. Some liberals favor mandating private pensions as the only way to extend pension coverage to most of the workforce. Some conservatives argue that mandatory individual accounts as a partial replacement for Social Security would enhance individual freedom, private property ownership, and personal responsibility while reducing the government's role in the economy (ibid.).

At the heart of the debate is whether mandates should supplement Social Security or partially replace it. Some people oppose mandates that replace Social Security, arguing that individual accounts may entail too much financial market risk, especially for financially vulnerable retirees (Gillion et al. 2000). Individual accounts that partially replace Social Security are also accompanied by high transition costs to pay the benefits already promised under the old Social Security system.

Individual accounts that are add-ons to Social Security, however, may be viewed differently because they retain Social Security as the traditional base of retirement income. They also do not require transition costs because they do not reduce the funds allocated to pay for Social Security benefits already promised. They result in higher contributions being paid by workers and employers to the retirement income system, but in some cases that may be desirable when inadequate resources are being set aside for future retirements.

FOUR PATHWAYS TO PENSION COVERAGE—DEGREES OF COMPULSION

Countries have developed a variety of policies to encourage the development of pension plans. These policies, however, can be grouped into four pathways to pension coverage that are differentiated by the degree of incentive or compulsion provided to workers to participate in the plan (Rein and Turner 2001). These pathways vary from 1) unrestrained choice for the worker (including whether to participate in a pension plan), to 2) a choice between two alternatives—participating in a government-provided pension versus a private-sector-provided one—to 3) a mandatory arrangement determined by collective bargaining between employers and trade unions, to 4) a government-imposed mandate. The focus of this chapter is on mandating, but by way of introduction all four approaches are compared.

Voluntary participation, with tax incentives. The pathway the United States uses to encourage employers to provide pension coverage is voluntary with tax incentives. Pension law does not require employers to provide pensions, and employees are not required to be covered. Regulations require an employer who offers a plan to cover a minimum percentage of full-time workers.

A weakness of this approach is that, practically without exception, countries that have used this approach have not raised pension coverage above 50 percent for private sector workers. With this approach, coverage rates tend to be relatively low among low-wage workers (Hinz and Turner 1998).

Labor contracting. A second pathway with an element of mandating is widespread labor contracting. In some countries where all or most of the labor force is covered by a collective bargaining agreement, a high percentage of the labor force has pension coverage through pension plans resulting from collective bargaining. Countries using this approach include France, the Netherlands, Denmark, Norway, and Sweden. This approach can only be used in countries where a high percentage of the labor force is covered by a union or where, as in the Netherlands, under labor law a collective bargaining agreement can be mandatorily extended to other firms in the same industry.

Contracting out. Contracting out involves requiring participation in a retirement income plan but permitting a choice between participating in social security or in an alternative private plan. With contracting out, the employer and workers reduce their contribution to social security if they participate in a private sector plan that provides benefits meeting at least minimum requirements. For those workers choosing to contract out, the reduced contribution to social security reduces the benefit the worker ultimately receives from social security, but the worker receives an added benefit through the individual account. Contracting out maintains free choice, and it may encourage private sector employers to provide pension plans.

This approach is called "a voluntary carve-out" in the United States. In Japan, contracting out has been provided on a fairly neutral basis with respect to incentive for participation, with the government neither subsidizing nor disfavoring it. The United Kingdom, by contrast, encourages contracting out by subsidizing it. This approach was proposed for the United States by President Bush in 2005 in his second inaugural address and subsequent State of the Union message.

A problem that may arise with contracting out, because of its voluntary nature, and a reason why full mandating is sometimes viewed as preferable, is adverse selection. With adverse selection, the workers who most benefit from contracting out leave the social security system, eroding its financial base. For example, in the United States, depending on the way the contracting out would be structured, and to the extent that the social security system redistributes income from upper-income to lower-income workers, upper-income workers may be more likely to contract out of the system than lower-income workers.

U.S. Social Security has a progressive benefit formula, providing a higher replacement rate for lower-income workers than for higher-income workers. This aspect of progressivity is offset by the higher mortality rates of low-income workers than high-income workers at older ages, which means that high-income workers receive their benefits for more years, on average.

Mandating. Increasing retirement income by mandating private pensions is an alternative to making Social Security more generous. While Social Security provides a uniform structure of benefits and contributions across the workforce, mandatory private pensions generally allow greater flexibility and diversity in the types of arrangements, including differences in early retirement age. The mandatory pension approach can either require employers to provide a pension plan for their workers or require workers to have an individual account plan with a third-party provider.

Australia and Switzerland mandate that employers provide pensions. Sweden mandates individual accounts managed by a government agency. The government collects the pension contributions and distributes them to the mutual funds chosen by workers, with the employer's only role being to transmit the workers' contributions to the government.

Mandatory pension systems that supplement a traditional social security system often do not cover all workers. They often exclude low-wage, part-time workers and short-tenure workers. Even with these exclusions, mandatory pension systems tend to have high coverage rates.

Relationship to Social Security

An alternative approach to the pathways approach to understanding the types of pension arrangements is to categorize pensions according to their relationship to social security. Pensions can either be add-ons to or carve-outs from social security. An add-on is a pension plan that supplements the social security benefit. The add-on does not affect social security benefit levels. A carve-out, by comparison, replaces part or all of the social security benefit. Though in reforms that completely replace an old system with a new one (such as in Sweden) this distinction can get blurred, in reforms such as the type being considered in the United States this is a major distinction.

Add-ons and carve-outs can be either voluntary or mandatory. This taxonomy results in four categories of pension plans: voluntary add-ons, mandatory add-ons, voluntary carve-outs, and mandatory carve-outs.

VOLUNTARY CARVE-OUT ACCOUNTS

With a voluntary carve-out, for example as proposed by President Bush, workers have a choice. They can remain in the Social Security system or withdraw from it, either partially or fully, depending on the structure of the voluntary carve-out. In exchange for a reduction in both current taxes and future social security benefits, the worker is obliged to contribute to an individual account. The employer's contributions to social security also may be transferred to the individual account.

The United Kingdom has such a system of "contracting out" of social security, known as the State Second Pension (S2P) Scheme (Blake 1995).[2] Rebates of social security contributions are paid into the individual accounts of people who give up their right to receive the State Second Pension or its forerunner, the State Earnings-Related Pension. Workers can invest these rebates in contracted-out company or personal pensions.

The United Kingdom was late in establishing an earnings-related social security program, which it did not do until the 1970s. At that time, a well-established private pension system was already in place. Voluntary carve-outs were permitted in the United Kingdom not to reduce a preexisting social security program but to protect a preexisting defined benefit private pension system. Later, for ideological reasons, workers were allowed to establish private accounts to reduce their participation in social security.

Generosity of the Trade-Off

The trade-off between contributions to an individual account and reductions in future social security benefits is the most important aspect of the structure of voluntary carve-outs, but it is difficult to calibrate the generosity of the trade-off. The smaller the reduction in the worker's future social security benefits that accompanies the reduction in the worker's social security payroll taxes, the more favorable to the worker is the voluntary carve-out—consequently, the more likely it is that the worker will choose it. However, another directly related trade-off exists: the more favorable the voluntary carve-out is to the worker, the more costly it is to the government. A generous voluntary carve-out may result in a substantial subsidy of individual accounts by the traditional social security system or by government general revenue.

The trade-off, or benefit offset, determines the voluntary carve-out's effect on social security's long-run solvency. If the worker is required to forgo a part of benefits actuarially equivalent to the benefits that would have been paid for by the reduction in his social security payroll taxes, social security's finances will not be affected over the long run. A transition effect occurs, however, as social security contributions are reduced years before the outflows are reduced. If the benefit offset deviates from actuarial equivalence, it will affect the desirability to workers of taking the carve-out, and will have a long-term effect on social security finances that could be either positive or negative.

The carve-out functions like a long-term loan to the worker from the social security system. The worker borrows from his future social security benefits, with the loan principal being the reduction in the worker's social security contributions. The worker receives the rate of return earned on his investment of his individual account, which would be an expected 3 percent real (but with interest rate risk) if he or she were to invest in U.S. Treasury bonds. The worker repays the loan through reduced receipt of social security benefits at the rate specified by the carve-out. If that rate were 2 percent real, workers would receive a government subsidy of 1 percent per year on the account balances in their individual accounts because they would be effectively borrowing from the government at 2 percent and receiving a rate of return on the investment of the loan at 3 percent.

The interest rate credited to workers' hypothetical accounts for determining the benefit offset is a risk-free interest rate since it is applied to the account with certainty. In contrast, the investment earnings rate workers receive on their accounts is a risky rate. Whether workers would take the voluntary carve-out would depend on three factors: 1) how risk-averse they are, 2) what other investments they have, and 3) what special tax incentives, if any, the government provides.

The Structure of the Trade-Off between Reduced Contributions and Reduced Benefits

For a voluntary carve-out account, the trade-off between reduced contributions to social security and reduced benefits from it can be structured other ways. For example, the reduction in social security benefits can be the same percentage as the reduction in the worker's social security contributions. The reduction in social security benefits with a carve-out can be set as an equal percentage reduction in social security benefits for all workers choosing to take the carve-out. For instance, if social security contributions by the worker are reduced by x percent, the future benefits accrued during that period are also reduced by x percent. This way is arguably the simplest administratively.

Age neutrality. An additional complexity in designing carve-outs is to make the reduction in social security benefits age neutral. With age neutrality, if a worker finds it optimal to take the voluntary carve-out at one age, the worker will find it optimal to continue opting out at older ages. This desirable, conceptually simple feature is difficult to achieve because of the difference in accrual patterns between traditional defined benefit social security plans and individual accounts.

For defined benefit plans and individual accounts with equal benefits at retirement, generally the individual account accrues benefits more rapidly for workers at young ages. In contrast, the defined benefit plan accrues benefits more rapidly for workers at older ages, because defined benefit plans tend to be backloaded in their benefit accruals. These different patterns of accrual create an incentive for workers to take the voluntary carve-out when young but not when older. The problem of the switching incentives this causes can be addressed by requiring that once a worker has chosen a carve-out, the decision is irrevocable. Such an arrangement raises issues of equity, however, if the terms of the trade-off are subsequently amended, which they almost certainly would be.

The United Kingdom's system demonstrates why these terms would likely be amended over time. Rather than having a single rebate rate for all workers, the United Kingdom has an array of rebate rates, depending on the worker's age. Younger workers receive lower rebates on their payroll taxes (known as National Insurance contributions) than older workers since individual accounts of equal lifetime generosity are more favorable than defined benefit plans for younger workers. In 2001–2002, a 20-year-old received a 4 percent rebate, while a 50-year-old received the maximum rebate of 9 percent. Age-related rebates designed to keep the contracting-out arrangements age neutral are complex, expensive to administer, and probably poorly understood by workers.

The rebate's size is not fixed for all time in a voluntary carve-out system, but can be expected to change over time. The UK rebate structure is reevaluated by the Government Actuary every five years to incorporate changes in life expectancy and interest rates. The rebates have been calculated based on the expense in the private sector of providing a replacement benefit, with an additional amount added to the rebate as an incentive to take it.

Gender neutrality. A further problem in designing voluntary carve-out individual accounts is to structure the trade-off so that it is gender neutral. Because women have a longer life expectancy than men, a gender-blind trade-off will not be gender neutral in effect. The trade-off in the United Kingdom is not gender neutral. Instead, it encourages men and women to take the voluntary carve-out at different ages. For example, in the late 1990s, 93 percent of eligible men in Britain aged 45–54 chose the individual account, compared to only 32 percent of eligible women in that age group (Whitehouse 1998).

For many years, Japan structured its voluntary carve-out with different rebates for men and women. With changed views of gender equity, that is no longer the case (Turner and Watanabe 1995). An additional issue relates to how changes in life expectancy affect benefits in a voluntary carve-out account and in social security.

In sum, the experience in the United Kingdom demonstrates that voluntary carve-out accounts are complex to structure and operate. It is difficult to set the relationship between the amount going into the carve-out account and the corresponding reduction in the worker's social security benefits.

PENSION PRIVATIZATION IN OECD COUNTRIES

While mandatory employer-provided pensions have long been favored by some people, they have not been at the top of the U.S. agenda for possible implementation for several decades. However, a number of countries have adopted them as they have sought to expand coverage from the lower coverage rates provided by a voluntary system.

Australia

Unlike in other countries in the Organisation for Economic Co-operation and Development (OECD), the basic social security benefit in Australia is an income-tested and asset-tested benefit, which about 70 percent of retirees receive. To qualify for this benefit, workers must prove that their income and assets fall below a set level. Australia is unique among developed countries in that it has never had an earnings-related social security program.

To supplement the income-tested benefit, Australia has introduced a privatized retirement income system, called the Superannuation Guarantee, less formally known as Super. That system involves requiring private sector employers to provide pensions that are primarily individual accounts. The contribution rate is 9 percent of salary. Since the government pension is unfunded, the change represents a move from an unfunded toward a funded system.

Because contributions are mandated by legislation and paid into funds administered and invested by the private sector, the government has introduced extensive safeguards to ensure that employees' pension entitlements are secure. This regulation has resulted in increased complexity and added costs. The safeguards place a heavy burden on trustee boards responsible for overseeing the funds' management.

Sweden

Sweden has instituted a mandatory individual account system that incorporates lessons learned from the experiences of Chile and other countries, particularly in ways to reduce administrative costs. This individual account system reflects a desire to increase the amount of prefunding in the Swedish retirement income system, and to move to a system with greater emphasis on the role of the capital market and individualism (Harrysson and O'Brien 2003).

Through measures that took effect in 1999 and 2000, Sweden replaced its traditional defined benefit social security program with a notional account plan supplemented by a mandatory, funded individual account. A notional account system is one where each worker has an account that is credited with contributions and interest earnings. However, the system is financed on a pay-as-you-go basis, so the individual accounts are not funded, and the account balances are bookkeeping entries. Out of a total contribution rate of 18.5 percent of earned income, 16.0 percent is for the notional account system and 2.5 percent is for individual accounts, called the Premium Pension. Starting in 2000, Swedish workers were allowed to choose from 460 pension funds to manage their pension investments, with the default fund being a government-run fund. By 2005, the number of funds had grown to more than 600.

The Premium Pension system is administered by a new government agency, the Premium Pension Authority (PPM, or Premipensions-myndigheten in Swedish). The PPM acts as a clearinghouse and record keeper for the funded individual account system. This new agency was needed because the individual account system includes a broad range of new activities that would have been difficult to undertake within the traditional functions of the National Insurance Board. In addition, a central agency is expected to help keep administrative costs low because of scale economies in administration (Palmer 2001).

United Kingdom

The United Kingdom has encouraged contracting out to individual account plans, but it is continuing to make changes in its retirement income system (Blake and Turner 2002). While every developed country has a social security system, the United Kingdom is unusual in giving every employer and every employee the option of contracting out part of social security. By comparison, contracting out in Japan is available only through employer-provided defined benefit plans.

Contracting out in the United Kingdom has developed into a highly complex system. In 1986, the United Kingdom passed an act designed to encourage contracting out from the State Earnings-Related Pension Scheme (SERPS), a defined benefit plan, using individual accounts. Previously, contracting out had only been possible with employer-provided defined benefit plans. That act enabled occupational plans to contract out by providing an individual account. It also enabled individuals to contract out of SERPS or out of their employer-provided contracted-out defined benefit plan using a personal pension called an Approved Personal Pension. Workers with personal pensions are permitted to recontract into social security if that later appears to be favorable, and many do so.

The United Kingdom replaced SERPS with a new pension program called the State Second Pension (S2P), which took effect in April 2002. Workers and employers are permitted to contract out of the State Second Pension. The S2P was initially earnings-related, but in April 2007 it became a flat rate benefit, even though contributions are earnings-related. While the State Second Pension is a flat rate pension, the rebates paid to workers opting out remain related to earnings. This arrangement provides greater incentive for lower-income earners to stay in the plan and for middle- and higher-income earners to opt out.

Employees who contract out of S2P receive a rebate on their social security contributions. The rebate is intended to reflect the savings to the government from not having to pay the pension to that participant. The rebate is paid directly into the employee's contracted-out pension fund.

CONCLUSION

This chapter presents an overview of mandating pension provision around the world. It discusses both contracting out and pension mandating, and it also discusses issues relating to mandatory individual accounts. The chapter describes the main features of mandated and privatized systems in several countries. Mandating has been far more common an approach than voluntary carve-outs.

While voluntary carve-outs may appeal because they expand the range of choice, the feasibility of managing such a system hinges in part on the complexities of structuring the rebate for the voluntary carve-out. The idea of offering the choice to participate in a funded individual account pension rather than in the social security program is appealing on ideological grounds to some people. However, it is difficult to structure voluntary carve-outs so that they are age and gender neutral and so that they are neutral in their effect on the financing of the social security program. These difficulties are among the reasons few countries have adopted voluntary carve-outs.

Notes

1. This chapter draws heavily from Turner (2006).
2. Prior to April 2002, it was called the State Earnings-Related Pension Scheme (SERPS).

3
Extending Pension Coverage

Roughly half of U.S. private sector workers are not covered by a pension. Policymakers have long struggled with the question of how pension coverage can be expanded within a voluntary pension system. The United States has instituted numerous pension policy innovations over the past several decades, including, notably, 401(k) plans. Raising pension coverage has been a policy goal over this period. Pension coverage, however, has remained stagnant at roughly 50 percent of private sector workers for full-time employees (BLS 2003). Frustration over the failure of pension policy to increase coverage has raised the question of what we can learn from countries with considerably higher pension coverage rates.

A worker is covered by a pension when the worker is eligible to participate in a plan offered by his or her employer. The term coverage traditionally has also been used to refer to pension participation because in defined benefit plans, but not defined contribution plans, the two are equivalent. Pension participation is the ultimate goal, and it occurs when the worker is accruing future benefits in the plan. While most of this book focuses on workers who are pension participants, this chapter examines reasons why roughly half of full-time workers are not pension participants.

Countries with well-developed pension systems use a considerable variety of policies to increase pension coverage rates. While the United States relies on voluntary provision by employers and uses tax incentives for motivation, that approach does not lead to high coverage rates. As a result, other countries, such as Australia and Switzerland, have mandated that employers provide occupational pensions, as discussed in the previous chapter. Still other countries, such as the Netherlands and Sweden, have widespread pension coverage because labor unions have a pervasive role in their labor markets. This chapter focuses on pension policy to extend coverage and participation within a voluntary pension system.

MEASURES OF COVERAGE

The goal of pension coverage is to provide income for families in retirement. The traditional measure of coverage is the percentage of workers participating in a pension plan at a particular point in time. Other measures, however, may better indicate the extent to which the goal is being met.

Family Rather Than Individual Coverage Rates

While pension coverage is traditionally measured as the percentage of workers eligible to participate in a pension, this approach is not consistent with the emphasis in public policy on the family or household as the economic unit. Coverage rates are higher for families or households than they are for individuals because the family would be considered as covered if one member had pension coverage. Over time, changes in family structure affect coverage rates. For example, when considering the coverage of women, the coverage rate is higher using a family measure than a worker measure. However, with increasing divorce rates and women increasingly living without a spouse, those changes reduce women's coverage rates over time (Even and Turner 1999).

Persistency of Coverage

Pension coverage only provides meaningful benefits if it persists over time. One study finds that contributors generally persisted in making contributions, but that the contribution rate tended to vary over time. Smith, Johnson, and Muller (2004) use the Survey of Income and Program Participation (SIPP) to look at the persistency of employee contributions to 401(k) plans for up to 12 years. Nineteen percent of contributors were intermittent (i.e., had breaks in their contributions).

Paul Smith (2001), using a sample of tax returns from 1987 to 1996, finds a high rate of drop-off in contributions to Individual Retirement Accounts (IRAs). Of those contributing in 1987, only 45 percent were still contributing in 1992, and 40 percent were contributing through 1996. Sarah Smith (2006), using the British Household Panel Survey, finds a link between pension contributions and changes in an individual's income needs, as measured by financial circumstances, health, having a baby, and moving to a new house.

Pension Coverage in Defined Contribution Plans

While coverage is synonymous with participation in defined benefit plans in the United States, in 401(k) plans covered workers generally must also contribute. Not all choose to do so.

To assess progress in improving pension participation, policy analysts need empirical measures of participation. Measures are needed that are consistent with the underlying goal of increasing the amount of retirement income provided through the private pension system. For comparability across plan types, the measure of pension participation for defined contribution plans should be consistent with the measure for defined benefit plans. Concepts that have been developed for defined benefit plans do not always transfer directly to defined contribution plans.

This section discusses the meaning of participation in a defined contribution plan. It presents a measure of active participation that requires that the worker be earning a benefit based on current contributions, made either by himself or by his employer. It compares that measure with a more traditional measure of participation (Turner, Muller, and Verma 2003).

Four definitions of participation in defined contribution plans have been used in empirical studies and reports. First, prior to 2007, an active participant in a defined contribution plan was defined by the Department of Labor in the Form 5500 statistics as a worker with a positive account balance in a defined contribution plan offered through his or her current employer. Total participants include beneficiaries and vested participants who have terminated employment with that employer. Thus, it is possible under this definition for workers and their employers to not be contributing to their defined contribution plan and still be counted as participating in the plan.

Second, as of 2007, the Department of Labor changed its definition of active participants to include any worker who is eligible to participate in a 401(k) plan, whether or not they do so. This definition of active participation is not an economically meaningful definition since it includes workers who are not participating and thus have zero account balances.

Third, in studies using data from the Current Population Survey (CPS), the Survey of Consumer Finances (SCF), and the Survey of Income and Program Participation (SIPP), workers generally are counted as participating if they respond that they are participating. Thus, the worker decides the definition of pension participation. It is not known what definition or definitions workers are implicitly using when responding that they are pension participants. In defined contribution plans, some workers may mean that they have a defined contribution plan with a positive account balance with their current employer, but others may be basing their response on the more restrictive definition of contributing to their plan.

Fourth, some analysts—for example, Kusko, Poterba, and Wilcox (1998) and Clark and Schieber (1998)—count only those employees contributing to the plan in a given year as participants that year. This definition does not include as participants employees who did not contribute but who had employers that contributed in their behalf. Thus, this definition does not apply to non-401(k)-type plans because employees do not contribute to those plans.

Active Pension Participation

Workers who are enrolled in a defined contribution plan or who have the option to be enrolled, but for whom no contributions are being made, are not participating in a meaningful economic sense. Workers who do not contribute during a year and for whom their employer does not contribute are not considered to be active participants in a defined contribution plan. That definition is consistent with the definition used for defined benefit plans, where workers are participants if they are accruing future benefits. This situation of no contribution being made for a worker who has a plan with an account balance with his or her current employer arises in profit sharing plans, because pension law does not require employers to contribute to those plans every year. It arises in 401(k) plans, where the employer's contribution typically depends on the employee having made a contribution. Also, if an employee makes a hardship withdrawal—for example, for a large medical expenditure—

the employer may temporarily suspend both employer and employee contributions.

One study suggests that nearly 30 percent of workers with 401(k) accounts may not be contributing to those accounts in a given year. The 1993 April CPS asked workers with 401(k) accounts whether they planned to contribute to their accounts, and only 68 percent responded that they did plan to contribute. However, others responded that they did not know whether they would contribute or refused to answer, and for some their employer may have contributed (Honig and Dushi 2003). A more recent study finds that possibly more than 20 percent of participants with a 401(k) account were not active participants because they did not contribute to the account, nor did their employer (Turner, Muller, and Verma 2003). These studies suggest a serious problem affecting the retirement account balances of a substantial number of workers participating in 401(k) plans.

POLICIES TO ENCOURAGE EMPLOYERS TO PROVIDE PENSION PLANS

The employer's willingness to provide pensions in a voluntary system is key. Aspects of pension policy affect the costs that employers face. For example, accounting and regulatory standards can limit employers' flexibility as to the timing of pension contributions, as discussed in the chapter on financing. Standards that limit the maximum amount of overfunding during economic boom periods may force plan sponsors to contribute more during economic slumps, when it is more difficult for them to contribute. Accounting and regulatory standards can limit their flexibility as to choice of portfolio composition. For instance, standards that discouraged plan investments in equity would cause a shift from equities to bonds, which could increase the cost of providing pensions.

With the voluntary approach, pension law does not require employers to provide pensions, and employees are not required to participate. If an employer chooses to provide pension coverage, however, nondiscrimination regulations may require that the employer offer coverage to most full-time workers. Part-time U.S. workers working less than 1,000 hours a year are excluded from the requirement. Nondiscrimination rules arguably have at least two effects. First, they cause some workers to be covered in firms offering pensions who might otherwise not be covered. Second, they cause some workers not to be covered in firms not offering pensions who might otherwise be covered if the firm could be more selective in its offering. Empirical research is needed to determine which effect predominates.

The voluntary approach to pension participation differs considerably between defined benefit and defined contribution pensions. With a defined benefit pension, if the employer provides a pension to a worker, the worker's participation is automatic. If an employer offers a defined contribution pension, participation by workers may be automatic—and some have proposed that it should be—but generally in 401(k) plans it depends on the worker choosing to contribute.

The economic costs and benefits of pension coverage, and thus the factors affecting whether it is provided by a firm, can be considered at three different locations in the firm's organizational structure.

- First, and the usual focus of analysis, are the tax and other incentives provided to employees to participate in a pension. The incentives provided by government policy create a demand by workers for pension coverage.

- Second, the compensation incentives provided through the pension plan to top management, who are the key decision makers in the firm, may be a factor in whether a firm offers a pension plan. These employees are the top-paid employees in the firm, so the focus is on the incentives provided for pension coverage to highly-paid workers. For example, some proposals would raise the limits on tax-deductible benefits highly compensated workers could receive.

- Third, there are costs and benefits to the firm and its shareholders in terms of how the profitability of the firm is affected by providing pension coverage. For example, firm profitability could be enhanced by its use of the pension to attract and retain talented employees. A firm's decision to offer a pension presumably is based on these three considerations.

Pension Coverage at Small Firms

Pension coverage at small firms is low relative to coverage at large firms, but has risen in recent years (Even and Macpherson 2008). Many small employers do not provide pension plans for their employees. This lack of pension provision may be because their employees place a higher priority on health insurance or on wages than on coverage by a pension plan. Coverage is low in part because workers at small firms tend to have low wages. It may also be low because pensions are more expensive to provide at small firms because of economies of scale.

IRAs

One factor shaping U.S. pension policy is the focus on individual responsibility. With this focus, all workers are covered by a pension plan—the Individual Retirement Account (IRA). They will receive a tax deduction (provided they are liable for taxes) if they contribute to the account.

IRA-Based Plans

One of the approaches that policymakers have taken to encourage employers to offer plans is to provide them with low-cost plan options. There are three IRA-based plan options: 1) the Payroll Deduction IRA, 2) the SEP (Simplified Employee Pension plan), and 3) the SIMPLE (Savings Incentive Match Plan for Employees) IRA. While the Payroll Deduction IRA and the SEP can be set up by any employer, the SIMPLE IRA can only be established by employers with 100 or fewer employees and no other type of pension plan. All three types of plans have no annual filing requirement for the employer. The Payroll Deduction IRA accepts employee contributions only, the SEP accepts employer contributions only, and the SIMPLE accepts both types of contributions. The three types of plans differ considerably in the maximum contributions allowed, which ranged in 2007 from $4,000 for a Payroll Deduction IRA to $45,000 for the SEP.

POLICIES TO ENCOURAGE WORKERS TO PARTICIPATE

With a progressive income tax system, under which marginal tax rates rise with worker income, low-income workers have less incentive to participate in a pension plan than do high-income workers. This approach targets incentives to higher-income workers because they have higher marginal tax rates. There is a trade-off between the cost to the government from the tax incentives offered and the amount by which pension participation is increased. Also, there may be a trade-off in a tax-based system between encouraging low-income workers to participate and providing too much in incentives to higher-wage workers, who are more likely to participate in any case.

U.S. employers and policymakers have used a number of approaches to encourage workers to participate in 401(k) plans. These approaches have included increasing the financial incentive for employees to participate, increasing the appeal of pensions through particular features, and making it easier for employees to participate.

First, employers can encourage workers to participate in 401(k) plans by offering a match for employee contributions. The match, for example, could be dollar-for-dollar up to a certain level of employee contributions, with a lower match rate, or no match, beyond that. A number of empirical studies find that employer matching contributions increase employee participation, but the marginal effect on employee contributions of a higher match rate is generally small (Clark and Schieber 1998; Munnell, Sundén, and Taylor 2000; Papke and Poterba 1995).

Second, with automatic enrollment, workers are automatically enrolled in 401(k) plans as the default option; however, workers may choose to not participate. The Internal Revenue Service (IRS) has issued rulings indicating that it is permissible for employers to automatically enroll participants in 401(k) plans provided that the employee is notified in advance and is permitted to leave the plan if he or she chooses to do so (Purcell 2004). With automatic enrollment, part of the participant's pay is contributed to a 401(k) plan and invested in a default investment option without any action required by the worker. Automatic enrollment has been adopted by a minority of plans, but the number is growing. As of 2004, only 11 percent of all 401(k) plans, and 31 percent of plans with more than 5,000 participants, had adopted automatic enrollment (Profit Sharing/401(k) Council of America 2005). Plans with automatic enrollment tend to be large plans.

Automatic enrollment has been shown to substantially increase pension coverage in studies of a few firms, but the wider applicability of the studies has not been demonstrated. For example, anecdotal evidence suggests that automatic enrollment may have little effect on pension participation during periods of dramatic decline in the stock market. Automatic enrollment is most effective when it makes it easier for people to do something they already wanted to do.

Automatic enrollment might lead to some employees having reduced benefits because they would have participated and contributed at a higher rate than the default rate, but with automatic enrollment they contribute at the default rate. Similarly, efforts to promote the automatic enrollment IRA could lead new or growing firms to choose auto-IRAs, which have no employer match and no ERISA protections for workers, rather than choosing a 401(k) plan.

A problem that may arise with automatic enrollment is lost pensioners. In firms where there is high job turnover, workers may quit without informing the firm, leaving behind small pension amounts in defined contribution plans. These small accounts are vested because of the requirement of immediate vesting of employee contributions, and they can be expensive for employers to maintain.

A British study interviewed employers at 14 firms that had considered implementing automatic enrollment but had rejected the idea (Horack and Wood 2005). It finds that employers were concerned about enrolling workers in plans without their prior knowledge or consent, especially when the workers were required to contribute. They were concerned that such a move would be disadvantageous to some employees. They also were concerned about their increased costs because of the need to make matching contributions for more workers, some of whom would not appreciate the expense to the employer.

Third, participation in 401(k) plans may be encouraged by requiring in a given time frame a decision on whether to enroll in the plan. For example, workers may be required to decide within the first couple of months of work on a new job (Choi, Laibson, and Madrian 2006;

Horack and Wood 2005). Active decisions are best used as the approach to enrolling workers when workers have differing needs and preferences and have a strong propensity to procrastinate. Under standard enrollment, which requires greater initiative by the employee, pension enrollment tends to increase with employee tenure. Active enrollment leads to workers enrolling more quickly and to higher enrollment levels. After three months with active enrollment, the percentage of workers enrolled equaled that which had been achieved previously after three years of standard enrollment. Even after 30 months, for the one firm in the study (Choi, Laibson, and Madrian 2006), participation for employees required to choose still exceeded that of those under the standard enrollment regime, by 83 percent to 69 percent.

Fourth, employers can encourage workers to participate by offering attractive features in their 401(k) plan. For example, offsetting the illiquidity of pension assets by offering loans from a 401(k) plan may encourage participation. In 1997, the General Accounting Office—now called the Government Accountability Office (GAO)—found that participation rates in plans that allowed loans were 6 percentage points higher than in plans that did not allow loans (GAO 1997). One study finds that allowing participant direction of investments increases worker participation (Papke 2004).

A plan design feature adversely affecting participation may be the complexity of the investment decision. One study finds a strong negative relationship between the number of investment options offered by a 401(k) plan and the participation rate. Increasing by 10 the number of funds offered led to a 1.5 to 2.0 percentage point decline in the average participation rate (Huberman, Iyengar, and Jiang 2003).

A UK study, however, finds that simplifying the application form had little effect. In some cases, all the worker had to do was to sign a form that contained information the employer already had obtained from payroll records (Horack and Wood 2005). This approach may have had little effect because workers still faced the problem of how to invest their pension money. Workers with no experience with investments may be reluctant to participate in a 401(k) plan, since they do not know what investments to choose.

Fifth, employers can encourage workers to participate by providing them with financial education about the need for adequate retirement savings (Bernheim and Garrett 2003; McCarthy and Turner 2000). Although it provides workers with additional information, financial education raises the costs of their plan, which workers may bear through added fees unless paid for directly by the employer.

A sixth possible option is to require married workers who do not participate in the individual account plan offered by their employer to get spousal consent to this decision. A related alternative would be that the spouse would be notified of the decision not to participate. These options, to our knowledge, are untried.

Seventh, an approach that has been discussed in Congress, but not enacted into law, links the pension coverage of executives with rank-and-file workers. It requires employers that provide a pension plan for executives to provide a defined benefit plan for rank-and-file workers.

The voluntary approach to pension participation maintains freedom of choice for individuals and employers. A weakness is that, practically without exception, countries that have used this approach have not raised pension coverage above 50 percent for private sector workers. With this approach, coverage rates tend to be relatively low among low-wage workers (Hinz and Turner 1998). Because tax incentives are provided by exempting contributions and investment earnings from income taxation, this approach offers greater incentives to higher-income workers than lower-income workers in a progressive income tax system because higher-income workers have higher marginal tax rates (Reagan and Turner 2000).

Within the voluntary approach, a relatively high degree of compulsion (incentive) would be achieved if employers offering a pension were required to cover all workers, if benefits were locked in until retirement, and if tax credits were offered. A relatively low degree of compulsion (incentive) would be achieved if the marginal tax rates workers faced were low, if the amounts that could be contributed were low, and if the tax treatment was relatively unfavorable—for example, by employee contributions not being tax-exempt.

Pension Coverage for Low-Wage Workers

In the United States and other countries with voluntary pension systems, the participation rate is considerably higher for high-income workers than for low-income workers. The participation rate in the United States was higher than 75 percent for groups with income higher than $80,000 a year in 1997, while it was only 22 percent for those workers with annual income under $20,000 (CBO 2003). Because, in a voluntary pension system, coverage rates tend to be lower for low-wage workers than for high-wage workers, this section focuses on efforts to raise the pension coverage rate for low-wage workers.

These efforts may be limited, without a subsidy, by concerns over reducing the already low wages of low-wage workers. Because of the pension-wage trade-off, providing pensions for low-wage workers would presumably result in a reduction in their wages. In any case, coverage is already available to all U.S. workers because they can contribute to an Individual Retirement Account (IRA), though few do.

Unions can play an important role in the coverage of low-wage workers. One study finds that while 34 percent of low-wage men were covered by a pension, 71 percent of low-wage men who were union members were covered by a pension (Ghilarducci and Lee 2005).

Within the basic voluntary framework of tax preferences for pensions, other policies can further encourage low-wage workers to participate. Small businesses can claim a tax credit for certain costs of starting a new plan for their employees. Low-wage workers work disproportionately at small businesses, and small businesses are more likely than large businesses to not provide pensions.

Tax preferences provide minimal incentives to the majority of American households—those who are in the 15 percent, 10 percent, or zero income tax brackets. The Saver's Credit, enacted in 2001, was designed to address this problem. Eligible moderate- and lower-income employees may be able to claim a tax credit for half of their pension contributions up to a maximum credit of $1,000 through the Saver's Credit for contributions to a retirement plan starting in 2002. As the only major pension tax incentive targeted specifically to the majority of American households, it was designed to level the playing field in terms of tax incentives received by upper- and lower-income taxpayers by giving taxpayers earning less than $50,000 a tax credit for contributions to 401(k) plans, IRAs, and similar retirement savings plans. The Pension Protection Act of 2006 made it permanent and indexed its income eligibility limits to inflation. Because the Saver's Credit is nonrefundable, it merely offsets a taxpayer's tax liability; it provides no saving incentive for about 50 million lower-income households that have no income tax liability.

Automatic enrollment is another policy to encourage low-wage workers to participate. Once they are automatically enrolled, inertia may keep them enrolled, though this effect has not been investigated over more than a few years. Furthermore, its effects may be undone at job change if workers withdraw their account balances. The positive effect on retirement savings may be short-lived, with workers cashing it out when they change jobs.

Coverage of Nonworking Spouses

Pension participation is generally limited to workers. However, workers are permitted to establish an Individual Retirement Account (IRA) for a nonworking spouse. This option is not available through 401(k) plans but would be a possible extension. In Sweden, the mandatory Premium Pension Plan permits a worker to contribute to the account of a spouse. Pension participation could be extended further to nonworkers by permitting anyone with income to establish a pension account, or even by permitting a pension account to be established for anyone—even for those without income. The account could be established, for example, by parents of nonworking or disabled children.

Participation in 401(k) Plans

One of the surprises of pension policy during the 1990s was that some workers do not contribute to a 401(k) plan even though their employer offers a matching contribution. It was thought that the matching contribution, on top of the tax incentive, would provide a powerful incentive. At least five reasons may explain noncontribution, and thus nonparticipation, by workers eligible to participate in a 401(k) plan (Turner and Verma 2007). The first is the traditional economic reason of lack of economic incentives to participate. In addition to that reason, four reasons apply to workers who do not fit the classic definition of being well-informed and rational:

1) high discount rates causing them to place little value on future consumption,

2) lack of information as to the economic benefits of participating in a pension plan,

3) lack of willpower to follow through on a decision, and

4) failure to make a decision because of passivity, ambivalence, or inertia.

Understanding the different reasons for nonparticipation by workers may aid in developing effective policies that would help workers achieve good pension outcomes.

The term "high discount rates" refers to the time discounting of future consumption by workers. If workers place a low value on future consumption relative to present consumption, they are less likely to save, including by participating in a pension plan. Some workers may not participate in a plan because they lack information about the plan, or perhaps they lack information about the need to save for retirement. Some workers may understand the need to save, but they are unable to discipline themselves when faced with the temptations of current consumption. Other workers may not register for coverage when coverage is not automatic because they have ambivalent feelings, because they mistrust financial institutions, or because they have a passive attitude toward this type of decision making.

Research in behavioral finance has provided lessons for plan design that may raise participation in 401(k) plans. Behavioral finance considers psychological issues affecting how workers make financial decisions. An insight from behavioral finance is the importance of defaults. Judicious choice of defaults by pension plan sponsors, so that coverage is the default option, may have the result that workers are more likely to have pension coverage.

Coverage Insights from Behavioral Economics and Behavioral Finance

An assumption underlying the system of voluntary employee participation in defined contribution plans is that individuals make good financial decisions that they are able to implement. The reality is that many individuals are passive, accepting the default, or make poor choices, resulting in retirement income that is insufficient to maintain their preretirement living standards. Behavioral finance theorists have used their insight into the roles that inertia and procrastination play in worker behavior to propose solutions that preserve worker choice while arguably achieving better long-run outcomes for many workers.

Behavioral finance and behavioral economics focus on psychological factors affecting individuals' decision making. These factors include how individuals deal with problems arising from the quantity and quality of information available to them. This approach expands on the methodology of traditional finance and economics, which focuses on the behavior of well-informed persons who are psychologically capable of implementing the decisions they make.

Encouraging Participation

The most commonly used arrangement for enrolling workers in 401(k) plans, called "standard enrollment," is that workers must sign up to participate. The default if the worker takes no action is nonparticipation. The worker who participates must choose how much to contribute, whether to change the contribution rate over time, and the asset allocation for his or her account.

Some workers whose employer offers a 401(k) plan may not participate in it because they are ineligible or because they do not choose to participate. Data from the Survey of Income and Program Participation (SIPP) for 2003 indicate that those who are eligible but do not participate constitute 22 percent of private sector workers eligible to participate in defined contribution plans (Turner and Verma 2005). Employees who work in firms that offer 401(k) plans but who do not participate in any plan offered by their employer tend to be younger than participants, to be female, and to have lower education, earnings, and tenure (Hinz and Turner 1998; Turner and Verma 2005).

Economic studies of pension participation (Hinz, Turner, and Fernandez 1994) indicate characteristics of workers who do not participate when offered a pension plan. They generally do not examine the workers' reasons for why they do not participate. For example, it is unclear whether workers' nonparticipation reflects an affirmative choice made by them or reflects inertia which has caused them not to make an active choice. Furthermore, inertia could be caused by different factors—indecisiveness, lack of interest, or inability to act on a decision.

The Survey of Income and Program Participation (SIPP) for 2003 asked nonparticipating workers who were offered a pension why they did not participate (Table 3.1). More than 40 percent of nonparticipating men and nearly 40 percent of women replied that they could not afford to contribute. Roughly 20 percent of nonparticipating men and nearly 30 percent of women indicated that they did not want to tie up the money. The next most common reason given by both men and women (more than 14 percent of each not participating) was that they hadn't thought about it. Other responses included that the worker did not need the plan, or that the worker or spouse had other pension coverage. With this set of questions, most participants gave economic, rather than behavioral, reasons for not participating—they couldn't afford to, they didn't want to tie up their money, or they didn't need the coverage.

These responses can be compared to those from an earlier study of federal government workers who did not choose to participate in the Thrift Savings Plan (Hinz and Turner 1998). The Thrift Savings Plan

Table 3.1 Reasons Why Workers Who Are Eligible to Participate in a Pension Plan Do Not Participate (%)

Reasons for not contributing	Men	Women
Cannot afford to contribute	43.6	39.7
Do not want to tie up money	21.6	28.8
Haven't thought about it	14.4	14.5
Do not plan to be on job long enough	7.2	4.6
Have an IRA or other pension coverage	4.6	4.6
Spouse has a pension plan	4.2	1.4
Employer doesn't contribute or doesn't contribute enough	3.7	4.2
Do not need it	3.6	3.5
Started job too close to retirement	2.3	1.2
Some other reason	23.2	25.6

NOTE: Figures represent percentage of noncontributing eligible workers. Percentages sum to more than 100 because workers can provide multiple answers.
SOURCE: 2003 SIPP data set (Turner and Verma 2005).

Table 3.2 Reasons for Not Contributing to the Federal Thrift Savings Plan (%)

Reasons for not contributing	Men	Women
Can't spare the money	28.7	34.2
Prefer other investments	24.2	19.7
Too close to retirement	16.7	13.1
Don't understand the Thrift Savings Plan	13.7	16.0
Don't want money tied up	14.2	14.2
Don't have enough information	12.0	14.5
No confidence in the plan	10.3	5.8
Haven't considered the Thrift Savings Plan	10.1	9.6
Never got around to it	7.3	13.7
May not stay in federal government	3.9	3.8

NOTE: Figures represent percentage of noncontributing eligible workers; multiple responses were possible.
SOURCE: Hinz and Turner (1998); computations from 1990 Federal Retirement Thrift Investment Board data.

was designed to be similar to 401(k) plans. The most common answer, given by more than a fourth of men (29 percent) and a third of women (34 percent), was that they could not afford to contribute (Table 3.2). However, factors other than income were clearly among the determinants of the response that the worker could not afford to contribute. Most (81 percent) of the workers in the lowest income quartile did not give that response, while a few (7 percent) of the workers in the highest quartile did give that response.

The SIPP data give two possible responses for not contributing that may relate to noneconomic reasons ("Haven't thought about it" and "Some other reason"). In contrast, the data used in the Hinz and Turner (1998) study provide a number of noneconomic reasons as options. Nearly one in six men and women (16 percent of each) did not contribute to the Thrift Savings Plan because, they reported, they did not understand the plan, and nearly as many (12 percent of men and 15 percent of women) did not contribute because, they reported, they did not have enough information. A tenth of the noncontributors (10 percent each of men and women) did not contribute because they had not considered whether to do so. More than one-eighth of women (14 percent), but fewer men (7 percent), did not contribute because, as they reported, they had not bothered to sign up to do so.

Information problems. How much workers and their spouses should save for retirement is a complex problem. The answer depends on factors such as the age at which they started saving for retirement, their expected age at retirement and what their life expectancy is at that age, the expected rate of return and risk associated with their investments, whether they have employer-provided retiree health insurance, and whether they own their home and expect to have paid off the mortgage by retirement. Some workers may not participate in a pension plan because they do not understand how much they need to save for retirement or the consequences of saving inadequately. Some may not participate because they find pensions too complex to feel comfortable making that decision, especially since it involves substantial sums of money.

Undersaving for retirement may occur because some workers underestimate their life expectancy. They may do so because they are unaware of how quickly life expectancy is improving, basing their own life expectancy on that of their older relatives. Thus, "demographic literacy" as well as "financial literacy" may be a source of problems in individuals' planning for retirement.

A study by the Society of Actuaries (2004) finds that a majority (67 percent of preretirees) of the male respondents underestimated the life expectancy of the average 65-year-old man. Of that group, 42 percent underestimated average life expectancy by five years or more. Roughly half (54 percent) of preretiree females underestimated the life expectancy of the average 65-year-old woman. A British study finds that on average people over a range of ages underestimated their life expectancy by 4.6 years for males and 6.0 years for females. Males ages 30 to 39, an age range where they may be considering seeking employment that provides pension coverage, underestimated their life expectancy by 6.3 years, while females in that age range underestimated their life expectancy by 6.5 years (O'Brien, Fenn, and Diacon 2005). These findings suggest that a substantial part of the population may considerably underestimate its life expectancy, which could be a cause of undersaving for retirement.

Choice of defaults. If all workers actively made wise decisions concerning their pension participation, defaults in designing 401(k) plans would be irrelevant. However, some workers do not make a choice and are automatically placed in the status determined by the default. Defaults may have a socially desirable function when they can be structured so that workers end up in a situation that increases their retirement savings.

Evidence from U.S. studies suggests that automatic enrollment may be a more successful way to increase pension coverage than employer matching contributions. For example, Madrian and Shea (2001) find that automatic enrollment led to substantially higher enrollment among new employees in one firm than a system that relied solely on offering a match. Choi, Laibson, and Madrian (2004), using data for three firms, find that automatic enrollment had its largest effect on participation at short job tenure, but after three years of tenure, the participation rate among employees hired under automatic enrollment was still 30 percentage points higher than among employees hired under standard enrollment with the same tenure.

For workers who are uncertain about how to invest, automatic enrollment has the advantage that the investment choice is made by default. A British study suggests that automatic enrollment is successful in part because some workers who do not choose to participate are intimidated by the choice of investments (Horack and Wood 2005).

These studies have been based on a small number of large firms that have been innovators in how they provide benefits. The experience in these firms may not be typical of that across the U.S. labor market, especially in smaller firms and in firms with predominantly low-wage workforces. The extent to which the results can be generalized to the entire private sector workforce has not been assessed.

Some changes have been made in federal law to encourage automatic enrollment. The Pension Protection Act of 2006 clarified that federal law in this area preempts state law. In addition, federal law could be changed so that employees who were automatically enrolled but accumulated only small amounts and wished to withdraw the funds from their accounts could do so without penalty. To increase the incentive for firms to offer automatic enrollment, Congress could limit the current safe harbor rules concerning antidiscrimination to only those plans that offer automatic enrollment and automatic increases in contributions, so as to assure that workers taking the default are contributing a sufficient amount (Gale, Iwry, and Orszag 2005).

Other factors affect workers' decisions to participate. For example, several studies find that workers covered by a defined benefit plan provided by their employer are less likely to participate in a 401(k) plan the employer provides than workers who are not covered by a defined benefit plan (Andrews 1992, Bernheim and Garrett 2003). Since the early 1980s, roughly 15 percent of the private sector wage and salaried workforce has been covered by both a defined benefit and a defined contribution plan (USDOL 2005a).

CONCLUSION

Several 401(k) policy options could encourage workers to participate. Many of the ideas discussed here have resulted from developments in behavioral finance and relate to the choice of defaults. Studies suggest that the choice of defaults can have a large effect on workers' behavior, and that the judicious choice of defaults may ultimately lead to workers' having larger 401(k) plan account balances at retirement. However, these studies have been done for only a few large firms and may not be generalizable to small firms. The findings also may not be generalizable to periods when the stock market is falling. Further, its effect appears to dissipate over time, and may be undone at job change by workers' withdrawing money from their accounts.

Traditionally, the default for workers unable to decide whether to participate in a 401(k) plan has been nonparticipation. However, some plan sponsors have established defaults that preserve freedom of choice for workers wishing to make a choice but that result in good decisions for workers who are uncertain as to what to do. These defaults start with automatic enrollment in the plan unless workers affirmatively decide to not participate.

Automatic enrollment creates problems of inadequate buildup of assets if the default contribution rate is low and the default investment is highly conservative. Thus, some firms have established a default contribution rate that starts low but gradually increases over a period of years. Some firms have made the default investment a life-cycle fund, where the default investment is more heavily weighted to stocks for younger workers but gradually shifts towards bonds as workers' expected retirement approaches. If workers change jobs, the default in some 401(k) plans is that the plan assets are rolled over into an IRA.

While defaults may not be optimal for all workers, such as short-tenure workers, in a 401(k) plan they help assure that more workers will accumulate assets that are available to finance retirement consumption. The effects of the defaults on women, minorities, and low-wage workers, in particular, deserve further attention.

4

Labor Market Policy

Portability and Retirement

Pension plans contain labor market incentives and disincentives that may affect important life decisions of workers. These incentives may affect whether workers change jobs and the age at which they retire. The incentives, and the resulting decisions, may affect the efficiency of the matching of workers to jobs in labor markets, impeding or encouraging attachment of workers to particular jobs.

PORTABILITY

Pension portability is an issue primarily for workers in defined benefit plans. It is the ability of workers to change jobs without losing future pension benefits. The extent to which this feature is part of a pension system depends on the particular design of the pension plans in the system, which may be affected by government regulations establishing minimum standards.

Two factors have made pension portability an important policy issue. First, U.S. workers have a relatively high level of job change. Second, Social Security benefits are relatively modest, which has led U.S. workers to rely more on employer-provided pensions than workers in most other countries.

Job tenure has decreased for older male workers. While average job tenure has increased when one considers workers of all ages, that has occurred because of the aging of the workforce, since older workers have higher average job tenure than younger workers. For male workers ages 45–54, their median job tenure declined from 12.8 years to 8.1 years, a decline of 37 percent, from 1983 to 2006 (Valletta 2007). Median job tenure increased for women, but because it is lower than

55

for men the influx of women into the labor market lowered average job tenure.

Portability losses vary by type of plan. Workers in defined contribution plans suffer negligible portability losses because their vested benefits continue to be invested the same as if no job change had occurred. Workers in multiemployer plans have no portability losses to the extent that they change employers within the plan. However, workers with single-employer, final-average-pay plans can suffer sizable portability losses (Turner 1993).

Workers who change jobs and are covered by defined benefit plans often suffer pension losses that result in reduced retirement income. Facing such a loss, a worker may decide not to make a job change that would otherwise be desirable, raising concerns for labor market efficiency. Because of penalties for workers who leave a job before retirement, defined benefit plans can inhibit workers from making job changes that would otherwise be desirable for them and for the efficient functioning of the labor market.

As well as affecting job changers, defined benefit plans can penalize workers who are laid off, suggesting the possible need for policy to protect those workers when healthy firms reorganize. Defined benefit plans may also penalize people who must quit jobs because of family responsibilities, which is particularly a problem for women.

This section describes ways that pension portability for U.S. job changers has been achieved. It describes both the minimum standards mandated by law and the arrangements that some employers have made that exceed those requirements. While it indicates the most commonly used methods to achieve portability, it discusses other, less commonly used methods because they are possible models for extending portability to more workers.

Portability losses are only one aspect of the risks facing workers who participate in pensions. While portability is achieved more readily in defined contribution plans than in defined benefit plans, risks also occur in defined contribution plans with respect to investment in financial markets and converting account balances to annuities that do not occur in defined benefit plans.

Pension portability has traditionally been considered to be the ability of a worker to carry a pension from one pension plan to another.

More recently, policy analysts have expanded its meaning to include the ability of workers to preserve the value of pension benefits at job change.

Defined Benefit versus Defined Contribution Plans

Pension portability largely presents a problem only for traditional single-employer defined benefit plans. For defined contribution plans, such as 401(k) plans, portability is not a serious problem. Workers generally do not suffer portability losses in defined contribution plans once they have vested. "Vested" means that the worker has an irrevocable right to a future benefit.

The most common type of U.S. defined benefit plan is the single employer plan. Typically, workers who participate in that type of plan and who leave a job before they are eligible for retirement benefits suffer a loss in future benefits. There are two important exceptions, however—cash balance plans and multiemployer plans.

Cash balance plans are hybrids incorporating features of both defined benefit and defined contribution plans. Under U.S. pension law, all plans must be categorized as either defined benefit or defined contribution plans. It would be desirable to amend U.S. pension law to recognize hybrid plans, such as cash balance plans, as a separate category with its own regulatory framework. Cash balance plans are categorized as defined benefit plans because the employer must provide a promised level of benefits. They accrue benefits in a pattern similar to defined contribution plans, which is more favorable to short-term workers than the accrual pattern in traditional defined benefit plans. With a cash balance plan, each worker has an individual account to which contributions are credited, and interest is credited on the account balance. However, the individual account is purely an accounting entry, and thus is considered "notional." No assets are assigned specifically to the account, and the crediting interest rate is not related to the return received on assets held by the plan. The plan differs from a defined contribution plan in that the interest crediting is fixed in advance or is tied to an index rather than being tied to the investment earnings on the assets held by the plan.

Multiemployer defined benefit plans are typically provided when one union has contracts with a number of employers. Multiemployer plans are more common in some European countries than they are in the United States; they play an important role in the pension systems in Denmark, France, the Netherlands, and Sweden.

Causes of Pension Loss for Job Changers

When workers change jobs or are laid off, they suffer a loss of benefits in single-employer defined benefit plans. Portability losses can be grouped into two categories: 1) loss of real value of benefits the worker has accrued to date, and 2) the worker's loss of the right to an increase in benefit generosity with increased job tenure. Some types of pension plans reward workers with long tenure, and loss of that aspect of benefit generosity causes many workers who change jobs to have lower pension benefits at retirement than those who stay with a single employer.

Loss of benefits accrued to date. Portability loss for job changers includes the loss of pension assets because of lack of full vesting. This loss occurs in both defined benefit and defined contribution plans. When workers start participating in a pension plan, they begin accruing benefits, but they do not have full ownership rights to those benefits until they have vested. The loss of benefits due to a worker failing to vest is generally relatively small in defined benefit plans because workers accrue relatively little in the way of pension benefits in their first few years of work. That occurs in part because their wages are relatively low and in part because of back-loading, which, when calculating pension benefits, places relatively little value on earnings received early in life. However, as the worker approaches the point of vesting in a plan that requires five years of covered work for vesting, the size of the portability loss grows. For young workers, the loss in benefits that would have been received at retirement from the failure to vest a small account balance in a defined contribution plan can be substantial because of the growth in investment earnings over many years.

Portability loss also includes a loss in the real value of pension benefits accrued in a defined benefit plan at the point of job change compared to the value of accrued benefits at job change if the worker were to remain in the job until retirement age. In defined benefit plans, when a worker changes jobs or is laid off, his pension benefit is based on his nominal earnings at the point of job termination. U.S. defined benefit plans do not index for inflation between the time of job change and the time the worker starts receiving pension benefits. Thus, inflation may seriously erode the pension's real value. Portability loss tends to be highest for long-term workers who change jobs or are laid off a few years before they are eligible for retirement benefits (Turner 1993). These workers have accumulated significant benefits, but they still have a number of years over which inflation erodes the real value of their accumulated benefits.

UK pension law requires defined benefit plans to index the benefits of vested terminated workers for inflation up to a maximum of five percent per year (Blake and Turner 2002). A similar requirement exists in Ireland. These requirements greatly reduce portability loss, both for job changers and for people who are laid off.

A simplified view of pension benefit loss for job changers may focus only on two factors. The first is the loss due to lack of vesting. The second is the loss in defined benefit plans due to the lack of inflation indexing between the point of job change and the point of commencement of benefit receipt of wages used to calculate the benefits of job leavers. Of these two factors, the lack of inflation indexing is far more significant as a source of portability loss. Ending that source of loss of pension benefits by requiring employers to price-index wages used in benefit calculations would go a long ways toward eliminating portability losses in defined benefit plans, but also would be expensive for employers. In a voluntary pension system, policy changes that place added cost on employers may induce some to stop providing a pension plan.

A third aspect of portability loss not discussed in previous analyses is the problem of lost pensions and lost pensioners. When workers change jobs or leave the labor market and leave a pension benefit with a former employer, they ultimately may be unable to find that employer to claim a benefit at retirement age. This problem occurs in both defined benefit and defined contribution plans, but is more prevalent in defined benefit plans because they are less likely to provide portability (Bruce, Turner, and Lee 2005). The employer may have changed location, changed names, been bought out by another firm, merged with another firm, gone bankrupt, or simply gone out of business. Because of these changes, workers may encounter difficulties finding their pension plans to claim benefits. Similarly, an employer attempting to find a former employee who has moved may be unable to do so.

The lost pension problem has been largely solved for Australian and British job changers. Both countries have national pension registries. The registries, however, do not solve the problem for workers who do not realize they are eligible to receive a pension. Pension portability helps to resolve the problem to the extent that workers are able to maintain a single pension plan with their current employer, or to maintain an IRA. Employees can readily claim their benefits from these plans.

Loss of the option to receive future tenure-based accruals. A more complete view of portability considers several other aspects of pension benefit loss. These aspects include features that cause benefits to accrue more rapidly for long-tenure workers or for workers near retirement than for short-tenure workers.

First, portability loss includes the job changer's loss of the right to generous future pension accruals when pension accrual rates increase with job tenure. This feature can occur in either defined benefit or defined contribution plans, but is much more common in defined benefit plans.

Second, job changers may suffer a benefit loss in a defined benefit plan because of the difference in generosity between normal and early retirement benefits. Job changers' benefits usually are calculated based on retirement at normal retirement age, rather than at early retirement age. Benefits at early retirement age often are more generous in terms of the lifetime value of benefits than those received at normal retirement age. Employers may structure benefit formulas this way to encourage workers to work until the early retirement age and then take early retirement. For example, a plan may specify that benefits are reduced by 6 percent per year before the normal retirement age if the worker leaves before the early retirement age, but only by 3 percent per year from the benefit receivable at the normal retirement age if the worker leaves at the early retirement age (Gustman and Steinmeier 1995).

The Accrual and Transferability of Pension Benefit Rights

The following sections discuss portability issues for job changers relating to the accrual and transferability of benefit rights. The issues occur with both defined contribution and defined benefit plans.

Vesting. The benefit protection workers receive by vesting differs greatly between defined benefit and defined contribution plans. With vesting, workers in a defined benefit plan acquire a right to a nominal benefit (not indexed for inflation) that workers retain if they change jobs. In a defined contribution plan, workers acquire a right to their account balance. Since account balances in defined contribution plans continue to benefit from investment experience, they generally continue to grow in real value after a worker leaves a pension plan. The reverse happens for defined benefit plans, where inflation erodes the real value of the nominal earnings used to calculate benefits.

Vesting standards for private sector pension plans, set by U.S. pension law, establish the maximum period allowed before vesting occurs. Firms can choose to provide vesting earlier. U.S. pension law gives employers some flexibility in choosing how rapidly to provide full vesting. Under the standard many employers choose, workers must vest in their pension benefits within five years of participation in the plan. This vesting rule is called cliff vesting because the employer can provide zero vesting up to the time when the employee has five years of participation, followed by 100 percent vesting at five years. Under graded vesting, the employer must provide 20 percent vesting after three years of participation, following which the percentage of vesting increases by 20 percent a year, so that the employee reaches 100 percent vesting after seven years of participation. In either case, if a pension plan terminates, all employees fully vest immediately.

Some policy analysts have argued for shorter vesting requirements, such as are in place in some European countries, which permit short vesting periods. Vesting occurs after nine months in Denmark, one year in Belgium, and two years in Ireland and the United Kingdom (Commission of the European Communities 2002).

Employees accruing creditable service for vesting must work a minimum number of hours in a year. That minimum is set in pension law at no greater than 1,000 hours, which is approximately half-time work for a year. With this minimum, a worker could work a substantial amount of time for many years and never be covered by the plan provided by his or her employer. Some participants' advocates have argued for lowering the exclusion level to 750 hours per year.

Employee contributions (both voluntary and mandatory) to their pension plans vest immediately. If employees change jobs, they can receive refunds of those contributions plus the earnings on those contributions. Employee contributions are common in defined contribution plans but rare in U.S. private sector defined benefit plans because employee contributions to defined contribution plans are exempt from taxable income but contributions made to private sector defined benefit plans are not. Most public sector defined benefit plans require employee contributions, and those contributions are tax deductible for state and local government employees. Tax deductible employee contributions are common in pension plans in Canada, the Netherlands, and the United Kingdom.

Employers often make matching contributions in 401(k) defined contribution plans. These contributions match contributions made by employees where, for example, the employer contributes up to three percent of pay when the employee contributes an equal amount. Employer matching contributions must vest within three years for cliff vesting, or with graded vesting must be 20 percent vested after two years, increasing in 20-percentage-point increments up to full vesting after six years.

Defined contribution plans often provide vesting after shorter periods than required by law, while defined benefit plans generally do not. Thus, defined contribution plans tend to provide quicker vesting than defined benefit plans. The reason for this difference may be that employers tend not to use defined contribution plans as a personnel tool to encourage worker attachment to their firms, while they may view defined benefit plans as serving that purpose. An alternative explanation may relate to the need to encourage the participation of low-wage workers in order to meet nondiscrimination rules.

Transferability of benefit rights—rollovers. One advantage to workers of pension portability is convenience: it is simpler for workers to keep all their pension assets in a single plan rather than in multiple plans, including plans from former employers. It is also more efficient for workers to have one larger pension account rather than several smaller ones, because of economies of scale in the cost of managing accounts. This results in lower total fees.

A pension rollover occurs when a worker transfers pension assets from one plan to another plan. The transfer of assets from one pension plan or individual account to another occurs without current income tax liability to the pension participant. It allows job changers to consolidate their pension plans. Rollovers occur more commonly from defined contribution plans than from defined benefit plans because not all defined benefit plans permit them. They almost always are made to defined contribution plans.

Rollovers generally are voluntary. Workers voluntarily make them. Firms voluntarily offer them as an option to departing workers. Plans voluntarily accept them from new workers.

Portability across persons. The concept of portability usually refers to portability across plans for a given worker, but it can be extended to include the transfer of pension benefits between people. The Economic Growth and Tax Relief Reconciliation Act (EGTRRA) of 2001 expanded the types of pension plans that are eligible for rollovers from survivors. A surviving spouse now has the same rollover opportunities as the participant would have enjoyed. For example, surviving spouses can roll their deceased spouse's pension plan benefits into their own defined contribution plan if the surviving spouse's employer's plan permits it. Portability between persons could be expanded further by allowing it between same-sex partners, between parents and children, or between any two persons.

Permitting rollovers from defined benefit plans to defined contribution plans may eliminate benefits for surviving spouses. In a U.S. defined benefit plan, a joint and survivors' annuity must be an option. Furthermore, the worker must choose that option unless the worker's spouse signs a notarized statement waiving his or her right to that option. When the funds are transferred to a defined contribution plan, however, survivors' benefits are not provided. However, defined benefit plans do not typically provide benefits for surviving children, although the remaining account balance can be inherited by the surviving children of a single parent.

Back-loading of Benefits

Portability broadly means that both short-tenure and long-tenure workers receive pension benefits of roughly equal generosity relative to their compensation. Generosity of benefits received by short-tenure workers depends on the extent to which benefits are front-loaded or back-loaded. Front-loaded benefits accrue relatively more rapidly for workers beginning their careers, while back-loaded benefits accrue relatively more rapidly later in one's career. To protect the benefit rights of short-tenure workers, pension law limits the extent of back-loading.

In defined benefit plans, the extent of back-loading of accruals depends on the benefit formula. The law specifies that plans must satisfy one of three tests. One of the tests is that the accrual rate in any future year of service may not be more than one-third higher than the accrual rate for the current year. Benefits amounts under this test may be expressed as dollar amounts or as a specified percentage of compensation. This rule must be used for all defined benefit plans having a career average formula.

Plans based on final average earnings are back-loaded and may be of little benefit to employees who change jobs several times during their careers. These plans are back-loaded because the benefits accumulate at a more rapid rate relative to compensation later in a worker's career. As a worker gains more experience, one larger amount—the worker's pay, which generally grows over his or her career—is multiplied by another rising amount, years worked. The multiplication in the benefit formula of two factors that are both growing with tenure yields benefit accrual rates that increase with tenure.

Cash balance plans provide workers greater portability than traditional defined benefit plans. Workers have a readily determinable balance in their accounts, and the value of the balance is not affected by job change. With cash balance plans, benefits generally accrue more rapidly for short tenure than is typically the case in traditional defined benefit plans. The extent to which these plans favor short-tenure workers compared to other defined benefit plans, however, depends on the plans' parameters. With cash balance plans, for a given level of generosity over a full career, the greater the contribution rate and the lower the crediting rate, the more favorable is the plan to short-service workers. For a given level of generosity, the higher the crediting rate, the more back-loaded the plan. Also, however, most cash balance plans provide pay credits that increase based on the participant's age or service, which adds an element of back-loading. A survey of cash balance plans provided by Fortune 1000 companies found that only 35 percent paid level pay credits for all participants, meaning that all workers received the same crediting rate relative to their compensation. For example, one plan provides annual pay credits of 3 percent for participants having four years of service or less, with incremental increases up to 9 percent for participants with 25 or more years of service (GAO 2000).

Portability in Defined Contribution Plans

The growing importance of defined contribution plans is improving the portability provided by the U.S. pension system. Once a worker has vested in a defined contribution plan, that worker may change jobs with no loss of accrued benefits.

Many workers, particularly those with short tenure and small account balances, when they change jobs, take the money out of their pension plans. Pension law has changed the default so that when a worker leaves a job with a small amount in his pension account—between $1,000 and $5,000—the employer rolls it over into an Individual Retirement Account (IRA) rather than the worker cashing it out. This policy is designed to discourage workers from cashing out their 401(k) accounts and to encourage them to keep their accumulated pension assets in the retirement income system. When a worker leaves a job with a larger amount, it might be desirable for pension plan sponsors to make automatic rollover into an IRA the default to discourage workers from taking the account balance as a lump sum.

Pooling assets across employers is easily achievable for defined contribution plans. Because generally no portability losses are associated with vested assets in defined contribution plans, pooling of assets is mainly a convenience so that workers do not maintain account balances in different plans. Pooling across employers is achieved for most university professors through the Teachers Insurance and Annuity Association and the related College Retirement Equities Fund (TIAA-CREF), which both offer defined contribution plans. TIAA-CREF covers 12,000 nonprofit institutions, including government and private universities, other educational institutions, nonprofit research organizations, and some museums. In this network, U.S. university professors can change jobs among most colleges, universities, and nonprofit research institutions and maintain their defined contribution pension account with TIAA-CREF.

Individual Retirement Accounts (IRAs) are not tied to a particular employer. When a worker changes jobs and receives a preretirement distribution from his or her pension plan, that distribution can be deposited into the worker's IRA without tax consequences, as long as it is done within a certain number of days after receiving the distribution or it is sent to the IRA directly by the plan of the former employer. A large part of the assets in IRAs are due to these deposits. If a worker declares bankruptcy, IRAs are not protected from the worker's creditors, while other pension plans are protected. Thus, a worker loses bankruptcy protection by rolling over an employer-sponsored pension into an IRA.

Portability in Defined Benefit Plans

Portability in defined benefit plans can be achieved three ways: 1) preserving the real value of benefits or assets within a single employer plan, 2) pooling pension assets across employers in a multiemployer plan, and 3) transferring pension assets or credited service between plans.

Preserving the real value of benefits or pension assets in a single employer plan. For most U.S. single-employer defined benefit plans that are not cash balance plans, workers suffer a portability loss when they change jobs. This loss occurs in part because the benefits accrued to date but received later at retirement are based on the worker's nominal earnings at the point of job change, which are not indexed for inflation between that time and the date at which the worker reaches retirement age and is eligible to collect those benefits. In a cash balance plan, by contrast, the worker has an account to which interest continues to be credited after he changes jobs.

Pooling assets across employers in a multiemployer plan. Multiemployer plans offer a number of positive features for workers. Pooling assets across employers occurs when multiple employers establish a multiemployer pension plan in which their employees may participate. Pooling pension assets across employers may help employers reduce administrative costs because of economies of scale. This type of pooling arrangement allows workers to change jobs among employers participating in the plan without changing plans and without a portability loss. U.S. multiemployer pension plans are predominantly defined benefit plans. They provide portability of service in that workers can change employers within the plan and their service with the different employers counts without penalty towards the accrual of retirement benefits.

U.S. multiemployer plans generally are established as a result of a collective bargaining agreement between a union and a number of employers. They cover many occupations in one industry, or one occupation in many industries. They tend to encompass a limited geographic area, such as the metropolitan area associated with a large city. In recent years, some multiemployer plans have merged; combining in this way provides enhanced portability across jobs because more jobs are covered within a single plan. This trend may have been facilitated by developments in computer technology that have simplified the administration of plans with many employers.

Multiemployer plans tend to develop in industries with many small firms. The workers in the industry generally are skilled, and all of them belong to the same labor union. The industry tends to have both a high turnover of firms and a high turnover of workers across firms. In the construction industry, for example, carpenters and plumbers typically work on one project until it is completed, then work on another project with a different employer. The decline of unionism has reduced the importance of multiemployer plans.

An example of a geographically based multiemployer plan is the Unified Food and Commercial Workers Fund in Northern California. The International Ladies' Garment Workers' Union and the Amalgamated Clothing and Textile Workers Union merged in 1995 to form the Union of Needletrades, Industrial and Textile Employees (UNITE), which covers production workers in the needle trades. By contrast, unions for the sheet metal workers, bricklayers, carpenters, and other building trades have funds that cover particular trades in many industries (Ghilarducci 2001).

Years worked for different employers participating in the same multiemployer plan all count toward vesting. Once vested, workers continue to be vested if they work for other employers within the plan. A further advantage of such pooling arrangements is that there may be economies of scale in plan administration and investment management, particularly compared to each participating employer's having a separate plan. Pooling is also an advantage to small firms because it overcomes the problem of providing pension benefits that arises after the short lifespan of many small firms.

Firms must cooperate with one another to coordinate the establishment of a multiemployer plan. Because of the difficulty of doing this among firms competing against each other in the same industry, most multiemployer plans are coordinated by a union or are in a nonprofit setting. Another disadvantage is that the arrangements are voluntary. When one firm sees itself as subsidizing other firms, it has an incentive to leave the plan (Ghilarducci 2001).

An example of portability having a different structure from that provided by most multiemployer plans is the arrangement for musicians. Many professional musicians belong to the American Federation of Musicians, a labor union affiliated with the AFL-CIO. Musicians often work part time. They may work for a number of employers in a year, doing short-term jobs, some not lasting more than a few hours, and receiving pension contributions paid by their employers to the union. Thus, this pension plan provides portability for highly transient workers. In this situation, the portability feature is part of the contract provided to employers hiring musicians for union-related jobs. The monthly benefit at retirement is based on a crediting rate, which varies by age at retirement. The crediting rate is applied to the total of contributions made to the plan on behalf of the worker. This type of benefit formula is unusual, but it provides an alternative approach for achieving portability.

Transfers of Service or Assets across Plans

Transfers across plans for job-changing workers, depending on the two plans, can include transfers of service and transfers of assets. The transfer of assets directly to another plan, instead of to the worker in the form of a lump sum distribution, is rare in defined benefit plans, affecting less than one percent of employees in private sector plans (BLS 2000).

Transfer of service. In a defined benefit plan, benefits are generally based on the worker's years of service and earnings. Therefore, one way portability can be achieved is through the transfer of service credits from one plan to the next. With transfer of service, participants are allowed to count their years of service with a previous employer when determining benefits from a subsequent employer. For example, one plan, either a defined benefit or a defined contribution plan, may recognize that a worker achieved vesting in another plan and automatically vest the worker in the new employer's plan. The employee ultimately receives benefits from both plans.

Reciprocity agreements. Reciprocity agreements are transfer arrangements for workers changing jobs among two or more plans. Those agreements allow the transfer of benefits, service, or assets among plans when the employee changes jobs (Harris 1998). In some cases, each plan counts the service in both plans when determining vested status or benefits. In other cases, plans transfer the full credit and the funds for that credit. In this way, the final employer is responsible for the full benefit. Reciprocity agreements are common among multiemployer plans covering members of local unions within the same international union, where the plans agree to give pension credit for service under any of the plans. The agreements benefit both employers and employees in the construction industry, allowing employees to move from areas where construction work is scarce to areas where it is booming.

Both transfer of service and reciprocity agreements are rare. They are discussed here not because of their prevalence but because of the possible model they provide. Nonetheless, they are difficult to arrange because of differences between defined benefit plans that complicate the calculations of equivalence.

Purchase of service credits in defined benefit plans. A defined benefit plan may establish the rule that it recognizes the service in another plan only if the worker buys service in the new plan. If both plans are defined benefit plans and the new plan is more generous than the old one, transferring assets directly from one plan to the other would buy less service than the worker had accumulated in the old plan, but comparable benefits.

Workers' ability to purchase service credits in a defined benefit plan using accumulated retirement savings in a defined contribution plan is one way to make benefits portable between the two types of plans. Similarly, a government plan participant who terminated employment without sufficient tenure to vest, but was later rehired, may repay any contributions or investment earnings that were refunded earlier because of having terminated employment. Workers typically would receive a refund of their own contributions, possibly with interest, if they terminated employment before vesting. Payment may be made to that plan or another plan maintained by a state or local government employer within the same state.

Transfer of assets out of a defined benefit plan. Portability may involve the transfer of assets out of a defined benefit plan, generally as a lump sum distribution or as a rollover, into a defined contribution plan.

When an employer calculates a lump sum payment or transfer from a defined benefit plan, U.S. pension law requires that its value be at least the present value of the annuity if it had been taken at normal retirement age. The plan, at its discretion, can base the lump sum on a subsidized early retirement benefit, which would provide workers a larger lump sum benefit. To protect participants from plans using unfavorable assumptions that would reduce the value of their benefits, ERISA specifies discount rate and life table valuation factors in discounting retirement benefits. In calculating the value of a lump sum benefit, U.S. pension law requires that the plans use the same mortality rates for both males and females, even though the actual mortality rates for females are lower. The present value of the annuity computed using this interest rate and mortality table is the minimum that the plan can pay a participant. Using unisex mortality rates in this case is advantageous to men, since those rates produce a higher present value of benefits than would male mortality rates.

In calculating the amount of assets to be transferred, defined benefit plans are not required to take into account future cost-of-living adjustments unless those are written into the plan, which is rare but does occur in some plans. A plan may have an unwritten policy of making ad hoc cost-of-living adjustments depending on the extent of inflation. It would not be required to take this practice into account in calculating the value of benefits for someone changing jobs.

When assets are transferred out of a defined benefit plan for a worker who has terminated his employment, though the minimum value allowable is regulated by law, the question sometimes arises as to the appropriate calculation of the lump sum amount that the worker has accrued. A study in 2002 by the Inspector General of the U.S. Department of Labor found that 22 percent of companies studied that had converted defined benefit plans to cash balance plans had given workers who had changed jobs too little in pension benefits as a result of errors in calculating how much in benefits workers were owed from their cash balance plans (USDOL 2002). The errors occurred at least in part, however, because of complexities of cash balance plans that do not apply to other types of plans. The study found that for the traditional defined benefit plans maintained by companies in the sample, there were no problems in calculating the benefit amount to be transferred. However, it did find that in two plans the present value calculation was based on constant value annuities, although the plans specified that the benefit would increase with inflation.

Portability network or clearinghouse. A portability network or clearinghouse can facilitate the transfer of assets between plans. It holds pension funds and combined benefits from multiple plans. Some networks, such as the National Automobile Dealers Association, were started by employer associations. These networks cover a single industry's workers and permit service portability for workers transferring between employers in the network. Portability clearinghouses are widely used in the Netherlands to transfer deferred vested benefits in defined benefit plans.

Portability Policy Options

With a voluntary pension system, government is limited in what costs it can impose on employers by the employers' willingness to continue offering pension plans. Thus, while it may be considered desirable from the public policy perspective to mandate a feature that would increase the portability of pensions, if doing so causes employers to stop offering pension plans, the indirect consequences of the policy would outweigh the direct beneficial consequences. This consideration needs to be borne in mind in when considering the following policy options:

- Encourage development of industry-based multiemployer plans. Industry-based pensions allow workers to change jobs within their industry without changing pension plans. The usefulness of this policy, however, is limited by the extent that the workforce is unionized, because these plans generally are sponsored by unions.

- Encourage development of cash balance plans. Among defined benefit plans, cash balance plans provide better portability than single-employer defined benefit plans. A policy encouraging the development of cash balance plans would need to protect the benefit rights and future benefit accruals of older workers when a traditional defined benefit plan is converted to a cash balance plan.

- For workers who are laid off by financially healthy employers, require price indexing of benefits in defined benefit plans for inflation up to the participant's early retirement age. This change would protect laid-off workers from portability loss for a job change that they had not initiated.

Summary

This section discusses ways that pension portability has been achieved by describing relevant aspects of U.S. pension law and surveying the existing portability arrangements that pension plans provide. Pension portability is achieved most easily through defined contribution plans. It is generally difficult to achieve with traditional single-employer defined benefit plans. Cash balance plans, however, provide better portability than do other single-employer defined benefit plans. Multiemployer defined benefit plans allow workers to change jobs among participating firms and suffer no portability loss. Portability for single employer defined benefit plans could be improved by requiring price or wage indexing of wages used in calculating pension benefits at retirement, but that would be expensive for employers and probably would cause some employers to stop offering defined benefit plans.

Portability losses are only one aspect of the risks facing workers who participate in pensions. While portability is achieved more readily in defined contribution plans than in defined benefit plans, risks also occur in defined contribution plans that do not occur in defined benefit plans with respect to investment in financial markets and converting account balances to annuities.

RETIREMENT

This section considers ways that pensions affect older workers' decisions to reduce their hours of work or to retire.

Phased Retirement

Phased retirement allows workers to gradually transition into retirement (Latulippe and Turner 2000). Some older workers may suffer poor health or develop a physical disability that limits their ability to work. Other people may have to provide caregiving services to family members. These concerns may be eased by employment and pension arrangements that allow workers flexibility to gradually retire by phasing out of work over time.

Phased retirement also may help workers who need to work past their desired retirement age to supplement their retirement benefits. Others may wish to work to enhance their standard of living or for nonfinancial reasons, such as for the social interactions that work provides. For these purposes, many people would prefer not to work full time.

Surveys corroborate that some people prefer retiring from work gradually rather than abruptly. For example, according to the 2001 Retirement Risk Survey, sponsored by the Society of Actuaries, two-thirds of preretirees (66 percent) and almost half of retirees (47 percent) said they were or would have been very or somewhat interested in being able to gradually cut back on the hours they worked at their current job, rather than stopping work all at once. Moreover, almost two in ten retirees (19 percent) described their retirement process as closest to "gradually reduced the number of hours you worked before stopping completely" (Society of Actuaries 2004).

Phased retirement may provide benefits to workers and society. For many workers, a gradual transition is better than one that is abrupt. For society, such an arrangement could offset the expected labor force shortage with the retirement of the baby boom generation. It also helps contain the cost of pensions. And from a business perspective, it may be important to retain and use long-service employees to mentor and train younger workers.

Despite their positive effects, formal phased retirement arrangements are rare. That is at least in part because of barriers to their implementation. An employer wishing to offer flexible employment faces numerous hurdles arising from tax law, as found in the Internal Revenue Code; pension law, as found in the Employee Retirement Income Security Act (ERISA); and age discrimination law, as found in the Age Discrimination in Employment Act (ADEA) [Chen and Scott 2003; Penner, Perun, and Steuerle 2007].

The Pension Protection Act of 2006 permits distributions from defined benefit plans to workers still working for the employer sponsoring the pension, starting at age 62. This change in law was designed to make phased retirement feasible, with receipt of a pension and continued work, but the implementing regulation largely vitiated the effect. Because it is often difficult for workers to collect a pension while phasing out work, people may retire earlier than they really want to, doing so to access their pension.

Though in principle hardly anyone opposes phased retirement, it seems workers do not find employers' offers for phased retirement attractive (Hutchens and Chen 2007). Among the legal issues associated with some options for phased retirement are issues concerning extending health insurance to phased retirees, when that is not part of a formal program but is done in special circumstances where employers especially want a full-time worker to stay on working part time. An example of "special circumstances" might be a worker who moves from full-time to part-time employment after attaining a minimum of, say, 10 years of job tenure. Since the main barrier to this proposal is the nondiscrimination rules promulgated by the IRS, the issue is about whether this enhanced health insurance for phased retirees favors high-wage workers.

Employers apparently prefer to provide phased retirement through ad hoc arrangements rather than through formal programs. Ad hoc arrangements may provide employers greater flexibility as to who is eligible for phased retirement.

While taking phased retirement has some advantages for workers, they may find that it is disadvantageous in two respects. First, if they are covered by a defined benefit plan based on the highest years of salary, the extra work at a relatively low annual salary because of the reduced hours may not affect their defined benefit plan benefits.

Second, if they have already worked 35 years under Social Security, they may find that the extra work also does not affect their Social Security benefits, even though they continue paying Social Security taxes. If the wages from their part-time work are less than their indexed covered earnings in their previous years of work and they already have 35 years of covered work, the extra work, and extra Social Security payroll taxes paid, will not affect their Social Security benefits. Thus, workers taking phased retirement could pay thousands of dollars in Social Security taxes without raising their benefits.

Benefit Receipt While Working

Benefit receipt while working permits workers to take partial retirement, receiving income both from part-time work and from a pension. Allowing partial retirement, with part-time work and receipt of a pension, permits workers to gradually reduce their work hours and adjust their lifestyle as they approach full retirement. Arrangements for partial retirement can be provided more easily in a defined contribution system than in a traditional defined benefit system because partially annuitized benefits can be provided more easily in a defined contribution system. Partial receipt of benefits from a defined benefit system would require complex actuarial calculations.

Phased retirement is facilitated in defined contribution plans by the possibility of receiving in-service distributions from a defined contribution plan at age 59 ½. In-service distributions cannot be received from a defined benefit plan until age 62. As an aspect of leveling the playing field between the two types of pensions, the ages should be equalized. With phased retirement options, it is not known whether, on balance, workers reduce their hours of work earlier than they otherwise would, whether they continue working longer than otherwise, or whether some workers may be affected one way and other workers affected the other way.

In most pension plans, older workers can retire and receive pension benefits from a former employer while working for a different employer. However, in collectively bargained plans, the worker's benefit can be suspended if he or she works for any employer in the same industry, even if it is a nonunion job. This policy is an example of disparate treatment of workers in similar circumstances, and thus consideration should be given to changing it.

In Sweden, Chile, and the United Kingdom, workers can continue working while receiving benefits. The Swedish workers can claim full or partial (one-quarter, one-half, or three-quarters) benefits from the mandatory individual account system starting at age 61. They can continue working while they draw benefits, in which case they would continue contributing.

Chilean workers need not stop working to collect benefits if they meet minimum requirements. This feature allows workers to take partial retirement or phased retirement, combining either full-time or part-time work and the receipt of pension benefits. As a tax incentive to continue working, workers receiving benefits from the individual accounts system do not need to continue contributing to the system. Since 1988, workers could receive benefits but continue working once their replacement rate reached 50 percent of their own wage and 110 percent of the minimum benefit guarantee. In 2004, these limits were raised to 70 percent of their wage and 150 percent of the minimum benefit guarantee to encourage workers to accrue higher benefit levels. A high proportion of workers have met these conditions in their early 50s (James, Martinez, and Iglesias 2006).

British workers can continue working while receiving benefits. The United Kingdom permits the phased purchase over time of annuities. Workers can draw down the rest of the pension fund gradually after retirement.

Because women are more likely to work part time than men, receipt of benefits while working may be an option that is particularly valuable for women.

Defined Benefit Plans and Phased Retirement

This section considers how defined benefit plans hinder or facilitate phased retirement. Early retirement in physically demanding occupations can be facilitated by defined benefit pensions. Discussions of retirement age policy often focus on people with physically demanding jobs where postponed retirement would be difficult (Turner and Guenther 2005).

Early retirement age. Social security systems establish a minimum age (62 in the United States) at which benefits can first be received. Without such a minimum age, some shortsighted people would take their benefits at an earlier age, which they would later regret because they would have insufficient money to finance their long retirement period. A policy trade-off exists, however, between raising the retirement income of people who might take benefits too early versus giving people the ability to allocate their lifetime consumption as they see fit (Liebman 2002).

With continued increases in life expectancy at older ages, the annual benefit that a given account balance can finance decreases for successive cohorts. The level of payments is reduced to take into account increasing life expectancy at retirement. With increased life expectancy, for a given account balance the level of annual benefits for future cohorts will fall. Eventually, benefits will fall so much that the replacement rate that they provide relative to preretirement income will fall below the level deemed acceptable by policymakers and retirees. At that point, policy options include increasing the age at which benefits could be received, or imposing the attainment of a minimum benefit level as a qualifying condition for benefit receipt.

Because picking the appropriate early retirement age is a complex problem, many countries follow a rule of thumb for their social security programs. The rule of thumb most countries used originally to pick an age was that the age be divisible by five—55, 60, 65, and, in the earlier years of the last century, 70 (Turner 2006). Since establishing their original retirement ages, the systems have been incrementally modified, and the prevalence of ages divisible by five has decreased.

Retirement Age

Defined benefit plans often provide subsidized early retirement benefits. In addition, some plans favor retirement at a particular age by structuring the benefit formula so that increased years of work are penalized by relatively little increase in annual pension benefits and a decrease in the lifetime value of benefits. Thus, these plans reward workers who have long careers and retire at the early retirement date. For that reason, these plans tend to favor high-wage males over low-wage workers and females. High-wage workers who have other job opportunities are more likely to retire at the early retirement age and change jobs, doing similar work for another employer. Workers whose alternative job opportunities are not as favorable relative to their current job are more likely to continue working past the early retirement age and not to benefit from the early retirement subsidy. Thus, these plans can have adverse incentives from the perspective of the employer, encouraging the best employees to retire and the less productive retirees to continue working. These plans are also adverse to women, who are less likely than men to have a long career that continues through to the early retirement age.

Some employers interested in downsizing, such as General Motors and Chrysler, have used defined benefit plans to encourage early retirement. They have offered generous lump sum benefits through the pension plan to encourage eligible workers to retire. Because these benefits are offered through the pension plan, workers are able to take the lump sum and roll it over into an IRA, thus avoiding having to pay taxes at that point on the amount. By contrast, if the company had paid them the lump sum from outside the pension plan, the workers would have had an immediate tax liability, at a relatively high marginal tax rate.

While it is often assumed that defined contribution plans do not affect retirement decisions, empirical evidence suggests otherwise. Workers postpone retirement during economic downturns because of the decline in their account balances, possibly destabilizing labor markets by increasing labor supply at a time when demand is reduced (Hermes and Ghilarducci 2007). From the perspective of workers, however, this behavior offsets the capital market risk they face because of reduced account balances in their pension plans.

Maximum age for first receipt. Some countries set a maximum age by which workers must receive benefits. They do so to assure that retirees use benefits to finance retirement consumption rather than to bequeath wealth to survivors.

The issue of wealthy participants accumulating bequeathable pension wealth does not arise in the Swedish system because workers cannot bequeath their account balances to their survivors. Chilean workers, by contrast, are allowed to bequeath their account balances. A maximum age for first receipt is a feature that generally only affects upper income workers, and for this reason is more likely to affect men than women.

Countries That Have Raised the Earliest Age at Which Employer-Provided Pension Benefits Can Be Received

Some countries have raised the earliest age at which benefits from employer-provided pensions can be received. This survey indicates international experience with respect to the earliest retirement age in occupational pension plans.

Australia. In June 1992, the Australian government announced that it would increase the retirement age for the mandatory employer-provided pensions, called the superannuation benefit, from 55 to 60. The new rules took effect on July 1, 1999. The minimum retirement age is 55 for both men and women born before July 1, 1960. For those born after that date but before July 1, 1961, the minimum age is 56. In similar fashion, the minimum age rises by one year for every subsequent annual birth cohort until it reaches age 60 for persons born after June 30, 1964 (Kehl 2002).

Belgium. In 2003, a pension law was passed in Belgium stipulating that occupational pension benefits cannot be paid before age 60. Previously benefits could be received at age 58 or earlier. For all existing plans, current rules are applicable until January 1, 2010 (Watson Wyatt Worldwide 2003).

Switzerland. In 2005, Switzerland raised the early retirement age for employer-provided pension plans to 58.

United Kingdom. The United Kingdom has raised the minimum age at which occupational pensions can be received from 50 to 55.

U.S. Defined Benefit Plan Responses to Increased Worker Longevity

With increasing life expectancy raising pension costs, it might be expected that defined benefit plan sponsors would adjust by raising the plans' early and normal retirement ages. The "early" and "normal" retirement ages do not refer to the ages at which workers retire or start collecting benefits, but rather to ages specified in pension plan documents. Employers could argue that employees are healthier and more able to work at older ages than in the past, and that work is less physically demanding for many workers, which are factors that make it feasible for workers generally to retire at older ages.

Other factors, however, have also changed. The large increases in life expectancy that workers have experienced at older ages have been accompanied by, and probably are in part due to, large increases in per capita wealth. Thus, the resulting positive wealth effect on the demand for leisure might translate into pressure to maintain current pension plan retirement ages to ensure a longer retirement period for workers.

While large increases in life expectancy have occurred, U.S. pension law has not raised the minimum age at which benefits can be received, and has not raised the maximum normal retirement age, which is age 65. U.S. pension plans have generally not raised their early retirement ages, though they could do so. Several hypotheses may explain that result.

Employers have a number of cost-cutting options to respond to the increased pension costs caused by increased life expectancy. They cannot reduce benefits that workers have already earned, defined in terms of annual benefits at the normal retirement age, but prospectively they can reduce benefits received at normal retirement or cut early retirement benefits.

While the move by employers from traditional defined benefit plans to cash balance plans may be done primarily for other reasons, it eliminates the impact of increased worker life expectancy on the plans' liabilities because benefits are accrued in the form of an account balance. In addition, most conversions to cash balance plans involved ending subsidized early retirement, which was a feature of the defined benefit plans that were being replaced.

Employers could raise the early retirement age, but making this change is administratively complex when done for current employees. It could be done more easily for new employees. Such an approach would be legal under pension law, and might be viewed by employees as fair, since it would become part of their labor agreement at time of hire. Alternatively, employers could reduce the generosity of benefits for new hires. Some companies have done this a couple of times over the past decade.

CONCLUSION

Workers who participate in defined benefit plans and who change jobs or are laid off by their employers suffer benefit losses. They suffer benefit losses because their benefits are frozen in nominal terms at the point of job termination, and the real value of those benefits is eroded by inflation between that point and the point at which they qualify for retirement benefits. Plans can make these workers wait until age 65 to receive benefits. For laid-off workers, the loss of pension benefits can be more serious than the loss of wages, while providing an actuarial bonus to employers. This suggests that, at least for healthy employers, it would be desirable to require price indexing of benefits up to retirement, as is done in the United Kingdom for workers leaving before being eligible to receive benefits.

As life expectancy at older ages has increased, a number of countries have raised the earliest age at which pension benefits can be received. Doing so has been part of a policy to encourage workers to retire at older ages.

5
Tax Policy

Influencing Coverage and the Structure of Pensions

Tax policy concerning pensions has come under increasing scrutiny. That scrutiny is due to the high cost of pensions in terms of lost tax revenue. It is also due to the fact that tax policy provides larger incentives for higher-income workers than for lower-income workers because higher-income workers have higher marginal tax rates. Thus, the tax system provides the largest incentives to workers who are most likely to save and provides the smallest incentives to workers who are least likely to save.

While governments in a number of countries are using increasingly aggressive policies to encourage or mandate private pensions, tax policy is the engine of pension policy for the U.S. pension system. It encourages the growth of the private pension system by providing favorable tax treatment of private pension assets relative to other assets. All countries with well-developed voluntary pension systems provide tax preferences for saving through pensions, and no country lacking a tax preference for pensions has a robust pension system.

Tax policy, along with regulations, also provides brakes on the pension system. It sets limits as to the types of pension plans that receive preferential tax treatment. Some tax provisions, such as those relating to early distributions, are not designed to raise government tax revenue but rather are designed to regulate pension plans by influencing the behavior of pension plan sponsors or participants.

While the broad goals of pension tax policy are similar across developed countries, specific policies and practices vary considerably. This chapter examines pension tax policy across countries. Differing policies and practices demonstrate the range of options available to policymakers.

OVERVIEW

Pensions function by means of three transactions: 1) contributions, 2) investment earnings, and 3) benefit payments. The most common approach to taxing pensions in countries providing preferential treatment combines tax deduction of contributions, tax exemption of investment earnings, and taxation of benefits under the personal income tax. This is the U.S. approach. For workers facing the same marginal income tax rates while working and in retirement, they earn the preincome tax rate of return on their pension savings because the investment earnings on pension funds are not taxed under the personal income tax. This approach is called "exempt, exempt, taxed," or EET, for the tax treatment of the three stages of the worker's participation in the pension plan.

This tax arrangement is referred to as an expenditure or consumption tax because savings are not taxed. The personal tax only is levied when the benefit is received and presumably spent. Under a consumption tax, retirees generally pay higher taxes than under a personal income tax that raises equal revenue. A consumption tax avoids the double taxation of savings that occurs when 1) income is taxed when received and 2) the income on investments is also taxed. This avoidance of double taxation is a desirable aspect of a tax system, given the concern over inadequate savings, but its effect on total savings may be diminished by workers' reducing savings in other forms.

Under this approach, U.S. pension holdings in equities are not exempt from the corporate income tax paid by the corporations for which the pension fund holds shares. The United Kingdom provides relief to pension funds for the corporate income tax paid on the shares they hold.

Defined benefit pensions hold a tax advantage over 401(k) plans. No Social Security payroll tax is paid on pension contributions to defined benefit plans because defined benefit plans are financed almost entirely by employer contributions. By contrast, the Social Security (FICA) payroll tax is levied on workers' contributions to 401(k) plans. This tax treatment of employee contributions to 401(k) plans limits the erosion of the Social Security payroll tax base and is done to bolster Social Security financing.

A fundamental assumption of retirement income policy is that people will not save adequately for retirement on their own. That assumption justifies preferential tax treatment for pensions, compared to the taxation of most other forms of savings, because it encourages retirement savings. Without a tax subsidy, families arguably would save even less for retirement. Explanations for families saving insufficiently include that they are myopic, not adequately anticipating future needs, or that they lack discipline to save for the future needs that they recognize. However, workers contributing to a pension give up liquidity in that they often cannot access the money until retirement, or can access it only after paying a penalty. A tax incentive is needed to overcome this disincentive to participating in a pension.

By encouraging pensions through favorable tax treatment, governments incur a cost in lost tax revenue. Revenue is lost compared to what the government would have received if the pensions had been taxed in the same way as taxable savings accounts. The lost revenue is called a "tax expenditure" because it is equivalent in some respects to a government expenditure to finance pension benefits.

Some policy analysts are concerned about the distributional aspects of the tax expenditure. Because of the pattern of pension coverage, the tax expenditure disproportionately favors middle- and upper-income workers. Arguably, however, distributional issues should be considered within the larger framework of retirement income policy, including Social Security.

These tax subsidies, which take the form of income tax deductions or exclusions, deliver tax savings in proportion to the worker's marginal tax rate. This arrangement is "upside down," because it provides minimal incentives to the majority of American households—those who are in the 15 percent, 10 percent, or zero income tax brackets and who most need to save more to provide for basic needs in retirement—while reserving the largest incentives for the highest-income households.

Moreover, as a strategy for promoting national saving, these subsidies are poorly targeted. Higher-income taxpayers are likely to respond by shifting existing assets from taxable to tax-preferred accounts (Gale, Iwry, and Walters 2007). For these reasons, a tax credit, which would provide an incentive per dollar contributed to a pension for all participants paying taxes, arguably would be more efficient in encouraging savings than the current system which provides higher subsidies per dollar contributed to a pension for people in higher tax brackets. Higher-income participants would still have an advantage because of the tax exemption of investment earnings on pension accounts.

Tax law plays a major regulatory function. To be "tax-qualified," a plan must meet minimum standards concerning participation, vesting, and fair treatment of lower-paid employees (nondiscrimination rules). When plans do not meet these requirements, the employer's contribution to the plan must be included in the employee's taxable income to be tax deductible for the employer, a situation that employees do not want.

PENSION TAX POLICY IN OECD COUNTRIES

Most high-income countries in the Organisation for Economic Co-operation and Development (OECD) use the EET approach to the tax treatment of pensions.[1] Ten countries—Austria, Canada, Finland, Greece, Iceland, the Netherlands, Norway, Poland, Switzerland, and the United States—come close to the pure EET approach in which pension benefits are subject to the same progressive income tax rates as other retirement income. Another twelve countries—Belgium, France, Germany, Ireland, Japan, Korea, Mexico, Portugal, the Slovak Republic, Spain, Turkey, and the United Kingdom—also use the EET approach, but withdrawals are generally taxed more leniently than in the first group of countries, or contributions are granted a tax credit rather than a deduction (Yoo and de Serres 2005). For instance, the United Kingdom, Ireland, Spain, France, Mexico, and Turkey allow a partial tax-free withdrawal of benefits in the form of a lump sum, while France, Germany, and Turkey allow a similar tax privilege to annuity pension income. In Mexico, Turkey, and the Slovak Republic, pension income up to a specified limit is tax free, while income above the limit is taxed at a relatively low rate.

While social security programs sometimes provide more generous benefits to larger families through benefits that are linked to family structure, employer-provided pensions and individual account plans rarely have such a feature. In Germany, however, contributions to the individual account pensions called Riester pensions receive a subsidy that is larger the greater the number of children in the family. This tax treatment of pension contributions is consistent with a general German tax policy of encouraging families to have children.

The practice in other OECD countries differs from the EET approach because contributions or investment income are taxed. In Italy, Denmark, and Sweden, the tax treatment of private pensions is closer to the model of exempt (E), taxed (T), and taxed (T) concerning the treatment of contributions, investment earnings, and benefit payments. While these three countries allow for the deferral of taxation on contributions, they tax accrued income from fund investment—albeit at preferential rates—and pension benefits at withdrawal. In Sweden, for example, all capital income is taxed at a preferential flat rate of 15 percent on the theory that because capital is more mobile than labor, Sweden cannot tax capital at the same rate that it taxes labor income. This tax treatment of capital income is carried over to the taxation of the investment earnings of pension funds at a flat rate of 15 percent.

Australia, New Zealand, the Czech Republic, Hungary, and Luxembourg tax contributions to private pension schemes. In the latter three countries, either employees' or employers' contributions are exempt from taxation, but not both. In the United States, employee contributions to 401(k) plans are tax exempt, but employee contributions to private sector defined benefit plans are not.

TAX POLICY ANALYSIS

This chapter now discusses in greater detail effects of the tax treatment of pension contributions, investment earnings, and benefit payments. Tax systems can be analyzed in terms of whether they affect the choices made by workers and employers by causing them to take actions they would not have done in the absence of the taxes. Pension taxation can affect decisions concerning wages, deferred wages, other employee benefits (such as health insurance), defined benefit versus defined contribution pension plans, employee contributions versus employer contributions, self-employment versus employee status, lump sum benefits versus annuities, and equity versus bond investments in pension portfolios.

Contributions

Contributions can be made both by employers and employees, and the tax treatment differs in the United States.

Employer contributions. The United States, Canada, the United Kingdom, and most other countries with well-developed pension systems allow a tax deduction for employer contributions to pensions. In this way, employer contributions for wages and pension contributions receive equal tax treatment under the corporate income tax.

U.S. employer contributions to a pension plan are not taxed as income to the employee, avoiding both personal income taxes and Social Security taxes. The exemption from Social Security taxes reduces the current tax burden on workers, but it also reduces their future Social Security pension benefits in the United States, where future benefits are tied to Social Security–covered compensation.

Employee contributions. In the United Kingdom, Canada, and most other OECD countries, employee contributions are also tax deductible to both defined benefit and defined contribution plans. This treatment creates equality of tax treatment between the two types of plans. In the United States, however, employee contributions are not tax deductible to defined benefit plans in the private sector. The tax treatment differs between the public and private sectors. Employee contributions are tax deductible for state and local government employees. Thus, the nondeductibility of employee contributions to U.S. private sector defined benefit plans is an oddity in the pension world.

Employee contributions are tax deductible for certain types of defined contribution plans, such as 401(k) plans, but not others, such as money purchase plans. Perhaps because of this feature, 401(k) plans are by far the most popular type of defined contribution plan. Employee contributions to those plans are tax deductible under the personal income tax but still are taxed under the Social Security payroll tax so as to not erode the tax basis for Social Security. In pension parlance, employee tax deductible contributions are equivalent to a salary reduction contribution. If an employee contribution reduces the employee's taxable salary, it is equivalent to a tax deductible contribution.

Providing the option of tax deductible employee contributions to defined benefit plans might make defined benefit plans more attractive to employers. Employee contributions could provide an assured steady source of funding for those plans. Presumably, when employees are required to contribute to their pension plans, wages adjust upwards in comparison to what they would be in a similar job where the employer was responsible entirely for the funding of the defined benefit plan. This assumption of economists, based on the theory of compensating differentials, is not accepted by many pension practitioners, but it is clearly visible in the setting of collective bargaining.

If a U.S. employee does not fully make use of his or her tax deduction to the pension plan for the plan year by making the maximum allowable contribution, the missed contribution cannot be made up in the future. By contrast, the system in Canada allows workers greater flexibility as to the timing of their contributions. An individual's unused contribution in a year is carried forward indefinitely for use in subsequent years, subject to certain dollar limits. Similarly, contributions not deductible in the year they are paid because they exceed the allowable amount may be deducted in subsequent years.

This flexibility in Canada for contributions to defined contribution plans was introduced to achieve equal footing with the flexibility available to employers for contributions to defined benefit plans. In most countries, employers with well-funded plans have flexibility as to the timing of their contributions, so long as their plans are not overfunded to the extent that further contributions are not allowed or underfunded to the extent that large contributions are required.

The tax preferences provide weak incentives to the majority of American households—those who are in the 15 percent, 10 percent, or zero income tax brackets. The Saver's Credit, enacted in 2001, was designed to address this problem. As the only major pension tax incentive targeted specifically at the majority of American households, it was designed to level the playing field by giving taxpayers earning less than $50,000 a year a tax credit for contributions to 401(k) plans, IRAs, and similar retirement savings plans. Although it was originally proposed as a permanent tax credit, Congress sought to save revenue for other purposes by enacting the Saver's Credit with a 2006 sunset date. The Pension Protection Act of 2006 has made the Saver's' Credit permanent and indexed its income eligibility limits to inflation (Gale, Iwry, and Walters 2007). Because the Saver's Credit is nonrefundable, it offsets a taxpayer's tax liability; it provides no saving incentive for lower-income households that have no income tax liability.

Employee nondeductible contributions. Three reasons explain why employees may make nondeductible contributions to pension plans. First, employee contributions to defined benefit plans are not deductible. While it is unusual in the private sector, a few defined benefit plans require employee contributions, which are nondeductible. Second, some employees make nondeductible contributions to Individual Retirement Accounts because they wish to contribute to those accounts and they are not eligible to make deductible contributions. Third, some employees make nondeductible contributions to 401(k) plans because they wish to contribute more than the allowable limits on deductible contributions.

When employees claim benefits, they are not taxed on that part of the benefits that equals the nominal value of the nondeductible contributions they made. Contributions made 20 years earlier or more, however, could easily have lost half their value as a deduction because of inflation. Thus, this treatment of nondeductible contributions, which does not recognize the eroding effect of inflation on the value of past nominal contributions, results in unfavorable tax treatment because of the limited deduction for those contributions when benefits are received.

Table 5.1 summarizes the tax treatment of employee contributions and highlights the lack of deductibility for contributions to private sector defined benefit plans. Contributions are tax deductible for contributions to 401(k)-type plans in both the private and public sectors. Employee contributions are tax deductible for defined benefit plans for state and local government employees but not federal government employees. The major exception to the tax deductibility of employee pension contributions in the United States, and indeed around the world, is for U.S. private sector defined benefit plans.

Table 5.1 Tax Treatment of Employee Pension Contributions

	Defined benefit	401(k)-type plans
Private sector	Not tax deductible	Tax deductible
State and local government	Tax deductible	Tax deductible

NOTE: Employee contributions to defined benefit plans are not tax deductible for federal government employees. Employee contributions to non-401(k)-type defined contribution plans are not tax deductible.
SOURCE: Author's calculations.

Contribution limits. Countries generally set a maximum on allowable tax deductible contributions that can be made by, or on behalf of, a worker. The maximum is expressed both as an absolute amount and as a percentage of the worker's pay, with the lower maximum being effective. Maximums are set to limit the government's loss of tax revenue. Also, as a matter of fairness to low-income taxpayers, the maximums limit benefit amounts and tax preferences received by high-income workers.

The tax treatment of pensions in Canada is based on the principle that all workers should have equal access to a tax-preferenced pension, whether or not their employer provides a pension plan. This principle is viewed as an important policy aspect of interpersonal equity, and it is not an aspect of the U.S. pension system. To achieve it, each worker's maximum allowable contribution to a Registered Retirement Savings Plan (RRSP) is reduced by a pension adjustment to reflect the worker's accruals in an employer-provided defined benefit or defined contribution plan. RRSPs are the Canadian equivalent of Individual Retirement Accounts (IRAs) in that they are individual plans established by workers without the involvement of employers. Integrating contribution limits for employer-provided plans with individual plans assures that all workers may set aside a roughly equivalent amount in tax-preferenced pension plans. This policy differs considerably from the tax treatment of U.S. pensions, where employer-provided plans are heavily favored relative to individual plans in terms of allowable contributions.

The maximum allowable tax deductible contribution for UK personal pension plans increases with the worker's age. It rises from 17.5 percent of earnings for those under age 36 to 40 percent for those ages 61 to 74. The idea behind this policy is that older workers are more aware of their retirement income needs and may be more motivated to save for retirement. The United States has adopted a simplified variant of this approach; it allows higher tax deductible contributions, called "catch up" contributions, for workers age 50 and older than for younger workers. That policy could be extended by allowing even higher catch-up contributions for workers age 60 and older.

Perhaps because the aging of populations has raised the level of total tax deductions for pensions in many countries, a trend has occurred toward reducing the maximum amount that a worker can deduct (relative to wages). This reduction has occurred in Australia, Canada, the United Kingdom, and the United States, where maximum contributions are considerably lower in real terms than they were in the past.

Investment Earnings

In Canada, the United States, and the majority of countries with well-developed private pension systems, the investment earnings on pension funds accumulate tax free, which is the second E in the EET tax system for pensions. This is not the case, however, in Australia, Belgium, and Sweden.

Defined benefit plans in the UK offer employers the chance for a windfall tax shelter for surplus pension funds. Because an employer withdrawing surplus funds will have received the benefit of tax preferences, employers have an incentive to contribute more to their pension plans than is required to assure adequate funding. British employers are allowed to withdraw surplus funds without terminating a plan, whereas the only way a U.S. employer can withdraw surplus funds is to terminate the plan, and then the surplus funds are subject to extra taxes. These taxes have basically ended that strategy. By denying tax deductibility to contributions when funding reaches a certain level, the UK's Inland Revenue (the tax collection authority) has limited contributions to plans with surpluses.

Some U.S. policy analysts have discussed the possibility of encouraging greater funding by creating "sidecar trusts," also called solvency trusts. The money employers contribute to these trusts could be used to fund a defined benefit pension if needed or could be used to finance other employee benefits, such as retiree health, if the associated defined benefit pension fund had surplus assets.

Assets

Pension assets are not taxed in most countries. However, as they grow in size in conjunction with an aging population and the maturing of pension systems, the political pressure to tap this potential source of revenue may grow. Pension assets are taxed, for example, in Japan, Australia, and Belgium.

Disbursements

The tax system can be used to favor particular forms of benefit receipt. For example, taxation can be used to favor or discourage workers' taking lump sum benefits as compared to annuitized benefits. The progressive taxation of benefits can cause income redistribution toward lower-income taxpayers. Sweden, Chile, and the United Kingdom tax benefits the same as wages. Progressive taxation of pension benefits tends to favor women because they generally have lower incomes than men.

Taxing pension benefits as ordinary income received by retirees is the most common way for pension disbursements to be taxed. Any payment from a Canadian or U.S. pension plan, whether at death, retirement, or end of service, is taxable income, except for payments that are essentially repayments of contributions that were taxable, which is called "basis" in U.S. tax terminology.

While it is commonly assumed that contributing more to a tax-favored pension plan is financially advantageous, that may not always be the case, for three reasons. First, taxable withdrawals in retirement can put the participant in a higher tax bracket in retirement. Second, withdrawals can cause the participant's Social Security benefits to be taxed. Third, the tax rates could be higher in retirement than while working (ESPlanner 2005).

An important aspect of pension benefit policy is whether the money contributed to a pension plan is "locked in" until retirement. In the United States, pension payments received before retirement are subject to a penalty tax, while in Canada pension payments cannot be made until retirement age.

Pension policy analysts generally favor annuities over lump sum distributions. Annuities provide insurance against retirees outliving their pension benefits. Some countries provide special tax treatment for annuities. In Japan, pension annuities are subject to preferential income tax treatment. They are tax free up to a certain amount per year, with a deduction that declines in percentage terms in increments for benefits exceeding a certain level. In 2006, Spain reduced the generosity of the tax treatment of lump sum benefits to encourage workers to purchase annuities (Social Security Administration 2007).

Tax Treatment of High Earners

One of the policy debates is over the extent to which high earners should benefit from the tax preferences afforded pensions. One argument, based on a particular concept of fairness, favors limiting the maximum benefits and maximum contributions to a lower level to limit the tax preferences going to higher earners. The opposite argument, based on a supposed incentive effect, favors higher limits for benefits and contributions to encourage national savings and because high earners may be more likely to support providing pensions for lower-income workers. Sometimes trade-offs are suggested, such as allowing for higher maximum benefits and contributions for high earners if the company covers all of its employees.

Plan Terminations

If a U.S. plan sponsor terminates an overfunded defined benefit plan and reverts the excess assets to the employer, the sponsor must pay a 50 percent tax on the reversion. This tax is in addition to a 35 percent corporate income tax and state income taxes. Together, the taxes rise nearly to 100 percent, with the purpose of the excise tax being to discourage plan terminations with reversions. Not surprisingly, no tax revenue is raised by this tax because no reversions are taken (Pang and Warshawsky 2009).

Pension Taxation versus Social Security Taxation

An issue in judging the tax treatment of pensions is whether it ought to be, and is, equivalent to the tax treatment of Social Security benefits. The issue is complicated by the different tax treatment of defined benefit plans and 401(k) plans, and by different treatment of low and high earners. U.S. Social Security benefits are tax free for people earning below a fixed level of income, making the tax treatment of Social Security benefits more favorable for many people than the tax treatment of pensions, where the benefits are taxed as regular income for most people. Lower-income retirees are not taxed on their Social Security benefits, while higher-income retirees must include 50 percent of their benefits in taxable income, a figure that rises to 85 percent at even higher income levels. The effective income tax rate on the employee's share of Social Security contributions and the part of the benefits that the employee must include as taxable income depend on the employee's income tax rate, which varies across people and in some cases is zero.

Social Security receives equal contributions from workers and employers. Workers contribute from after-tax income (they cannot deduct the contributions from their taxable income), while employers' contributions are from before-tax income (they can deduct them from their taxable income, and the contributions are not treated as taxable income to workers).

Implicit Taxes

An implicit tax may effectively reduce pension benefits received by some U.S. retirees by taxing them at a high marginal rate. As just mentioned, Social Security benefits are taxable under the personal income tax when a retiree's income exceeds a certain level. For some workers, this causes double taxation of pension benefits in the sense that the marginal tax rate jumps because of the taxation of Social Security benefits. Double taxation occurs when pension benefits raise the retiree's total income to a level where Social Security benefits are taxable. Each extra dollar of pension benefits raises the retiree's tax payments by the tax on the pension benefit plus the tax on the Social Security benefit.

In Canada, the income-tested component of the social security system discourages low-income workers from participating in pension plans. For each dollar of retirement income exceeding a certain amount, social security Guaranteed Income Supplement benefits are reduced by 50 cents. The net result is that Canadian retirees with low lifetime earnings face a 50 percent tax rate on private pension income on top of any personal income tax liability. A similar effect can occur in the United States if pension benefits cause a reduction in eligibility for food stamps for low-income recipients.

Tax Expenditures

The federal government, as well as state and local governments, loses tax revenue because of the preferential tax treatment of pensions. This revenue loss is called a tax expenditure. The Office of Management and Budget (OMB) and Congress's Joint Committee on Taxation (JCT) define tax expenditures as losses in revenues resulting from deviations from the "normal" individual and corporate income tax bases. The tax expenditure is the cost side of the tax preferences–provided pensions. It is measured relative to the tax treatment of standard, nontax-preferred savings vehicles. One study has measured it as 27 cents per dollar contributed to a pension plan in the United States, with a comparable figure of 13 cents for the Netherlands and 31 cents for Canada (Table 5.2).

Table 5.2 Net Tax Cost per Dollar Contributed to a Pension, Different Countries, 2006

Country	Net tax cost (%) per dollar contributed to a pension
Canada	30.6
Japan	23.8
Netherlands	13.2
United Kingdom	29.9
United States	26.8
OECD average	21.5

NOTE: The net cost is the reduction in taxes per dollar contributed.
SOURCE: Yoo and de Serres (2005).

The measurement of tax expenditures is controversial. Policy analysts have no commonly agreed-upon tax baseline against which to measure departures. In spite of this, most economists believe that measuring tax expenditures is useful because tax benefits can have the same effect on beneficiaries as direct spending programs, and they impose similar opportunity costs in terms of higher taxes, reduced federal spending, and higher deficits (Burman, Toder, and Geissler 2008).

Workers' wages, their marginal tax rates, and their probability of participating in the pension system tend to rise with age, which would raise the annual tax expenditure per person as pension participants age. However, a factor that generally more than offsets this pattern is that for a given wage level, the tax expenditure is higher for younger workers because they have more years over which they benefit from the tax free buildup in their pension plans.

Two assumptions used in the tax expenditure calculations can have a particularly important effect on the results. Those assumptions are 1) the choice of a discount rate in the present value discounting and 2) the assumed tax rates on future withdrawals, which depend on assumptions as to tax rates in the future.

Three approaches are commonly used in estimating tax expenditures (Yoo and de Serres 2005). First, the revenue-foregone method measures the amount by which tax revenues are reduced by a particular tax concession, usually assuming unchanged behavior by workers and firms. Second, the outlay-equivalent method measures the cost of providing the same monetary benefit through direct spending, assuming also that behavior is unchanged as a result of the tax concession. Contrasting with those two approaches, the revenue-gain method considers potential behavioral responses and provides an ex ante measure of the expected increase in revenues if the concessions were repealed.

Within these methods, at least two approaches can be used—the present value approach and the cash flow approach. The present value approach, used in the United States, considers the future flows of revenues foregone on accrued income and of revenues collected on withdrawals corresponding to contributions made in a given year. In this respect, it is not influenced by the history of past contributions or by demographic changes. Given that the present-value method directly incorporates the intertemporal shift in tax revenues, it may provide a more accurate picture of the underlying budgetary cost associated with participation in tax-favored schemes, in particular during the first few years after a plan has been introduced.

The more commonly used cash flow method differs from the present value method in that it does not consider future offsetting flows. Its budgetary cost in a given year is measured as the net amount of revenues foregone on contributions, revenues foregone on accrued investment income, and revenues collected on withdrawals, which are all realized during that same year. In such a case, the revenues foregone on accrued investment and the revenues collected on withdrawals correspond to contributions made in previous years. The latter approach is better suited to capture the influence of demographic changes on the profile of net fiscal revenues from tax-favored retirement plans at different points in time. The approach has been used in recent studies to estimate the current and future profile of tax costs and benefits related to tax-favored pension regimes in OECD countries (Boskin 2003; CBO 2003).

CONCLUSION

In the private sector, employee contributions to 401(k) plans are tax deductible. In the public sector for state and local government employees, employee contributions to both defined benefit and defined contribution plans are tax deductible. The only major group of participants in the U.S. pension system who are denied tax deductibility of contributions are participants in private sector defined benefit plans. Extending tax deductibility to those participants would level the playing field between defined benefit plans and 401(k) plans. Tax deductibility of employee contributions is provided in most countries with sizable pension systems.

Tax changes could be made to encourage annuitization through 401(k) plans. Such changes could include providing less favorable tax treatment to lump sum payments through 401(k) plans.

The tax system could be used to encourage broader coverage through defined benefit plans. For example, the allowable maximum income considered for determining defined benefit plan benefits could be raised in plans that provided 100 percent coverage to all full-time workers. Switching to a tax credit instead of a tax deduction would provide greater incentive for participation to low-income workers.

Note

1. This survey summarizes the study done for the OECD by Yoo and de Serres (2005).

6
Managing Pension Risk

Risk is a fundamental aspect of pension systems. Because pension plans promise to pay benefits at a future date, risk is inherent.[1] Some party must bear the economic and demographic risks associated with providing retirement benefits—employers, employees, insurance companies, other financial service providers, or the government. The risks include the financial market risk associated with the investments of the plans, the portability risk experienced by job changers and workers who are laid off, the interest rate risk associated with converting investments into an annuity, the longevity risk associated with the length of life after retirement, and the inflation risk for the accrual of pension benefits and pension benefits in payment.

The rules that determine benefit amounts and contributions determine who bears the risk. An employer's first decision when considering the amount of pension risk to bear, and how much to shift onto workers, is whether to provide a defined benefit plan, a defined contribution plan, or a hybrid plan. The risks plan sponsors bear may affect their willingness to offer pension plans and the types of plans they offer.

In comparing the merits of defined benefit and defined contribution plans, we should bear in mind that the choice isn't mutually exclusive. The positive features of both can be achieved simply by an employer providing both. In 2003, an estimated 14 percent of the U.S. private sector workforce participated in both an employer-provided defined benefit and an employer-provided defined contribution plan (Buessing and Soto 2006). Alternatively, hybrid plans, discussed more in Chapter 7, combine features of both defined benefit and defined contribution plans.

This chapter investigates a broad range of risks facing pension participants and plan sponsors. It considers policy options for dealing with those risks. The chapter first discusses risks arising for workers in both defined benefit and defined contribution plans. It then discusses the two types of plans separately. Finally, it discusses the Pension Benefit Guaranty Corporation, the federal government agency that insures private sector defined benefit plan benefits.

RISK IN PENSION PLANS

Inflation Risk

Inflation can be a risk for workers, as it affects the real value of their benefit accruals in some types of plans. It also affects the portability loss of job changers and workers who are laid off. However, for workers participating in defined benefit plans and for workers who annuitize their defined contribution plans, it is primarily a risk retirees face. Having a fixed annuity increases a person's exposure to inflation risk. Even a low rate of inflation considerably erodes the real value of benefits over the retirement period if benefits are not adjusted for inflation. It is unusual for U.S. defined benefit plans to provide automatic indexation for inflation, though a few do. The plans that do provide this generally provide indexation up to an annual cap, such as 3 percent per year.

Pension policy could require defined benefit plans to provide inflation-indexed benefits to protect retirees against inflation eroding the value of their benefits. While that would provide protection to long-lived retirees, particularly women, it would be expensive. In the UK, pension plans are required to do so. They were formerly required to provide indexation up to 5 percent per year; now that has been reduced to 2.5 percent per year. The reduction was made because of the costs imposed on defined benefit plans by this requirement. If this requirement were placed on pension plans and they were not permitted to adjust the generosity of the initial benefits they provided, it would considerably increase their pension costs, which in a voluntary pension system could lead to erosion in the willingness of employers to provide defined benefit plans. In the United Kingdom, it is estimated that imposing mandatory inflation indexation plus mandatory survivors' benefits raised the liabilities of final-salary defined benefit plans by 40 percent (House of Lords 2003).

A major difference between social security programs and employer-provided pensions is the protection they provide against inflation. While the social security systems in most high-income countries provide inflation protection, pension systems generally do not provide inflation-indexed benefits. They do not do so because few countries have well-developed markets for inflation-indexed securities that could be used to provide the financial backing for inflation-indexed annuities. When inflation protection is provided on a cost-neutral basis, initial benefits are lower than they would be without such protection, while benefits received at older ages are higher because of the indexing of benefits. Chile is unusual in that it has a well-developed market for price-indexed bonds, allowing pensioners to receive benefits from price-indexed annuities.

Inflation indexing of annuities is particularly valuable for people with long life expectancy. For this reason, inflation indexing is particularly valuable for women.

Replacement Rate Risk

Replacement rate risk is the risk that workers will have a lower income replacement rate provided by their pension than expected. The income replacement rate can be measured in different ways, but in broad concept it is the percent of preretirement earnings that are replaced by retirement income. Replacement rate risk is influenced both by financial market risk, which affects the level of benefits in defined contribution plans, and by risk in the worker's preretirement earnings, which is a factor for both defined contribution and defined benefit plans.

Litigation Risk

The United States is a litigious society. Increasingly, plan sponsors face litigation risk. Plan sponsors in both defined benefit and defined contribution plans face the risk that they will be sued. In 401(k) plans, a number of lawsuits have been related to the fees that plans charge participants. Participants have also brought lawsuits regarding the investment options provided to participants and the participants' investments in employer securities in companies that eventually have gone bankrupt.

Litigation risk is tied to the fiduciary liability that employers incur based on the pension decisions they make. Litigation risk may be particularly large in the United States, given the litigious nature of U.S. society. A 2007 proposal of the ERISA Industry Committee (ERIC 2007) has signaled that employers are willing to give up control of the investment decisions in defined benefit plans if they can also shield themselves from fiduciary risk relating to investment decisions.

RISK IN 401(k) PLANS

Workers with 401(k) plans face an array of risks, and those plans do little to protect workers from risks. Workers face capital market risks on their investments. When they do not annuitize, workers face risks as to their ability to monitor their consumption during retirement so as to not spend too quickly, and they face risks as to their own life expectancy. If they have the good fortune of living longer than they expected, they need to have annuitized income or to have saved adequate assets to cover their living expenses for the longer period. The opposite risk is that they will be overly conservative in avoiding this risk and spend less than they could. However, empirical studies indicate that few people fall in the latter category (Butrica and Mermin 2006).

Investment Risk

Workers bear investment or rate-of-return risk from their 401(k) investments in financial markets. This risk is particularly great for workers who are near retirement because they have relatively little time to wait for the stock market to recover following a downturn. This risk can be reduced at the expense of reducing expected rates of return by investing in low-risk assets such as government bonds or by purchasing an insurance company product. When workers with defined contribution plans seek to minimize this risk by investing overly conservatively, they increase their replacement rate risk that they will not have adequate assets in retirement.

If workers were to maintain a constant portfolio mix over their working lives, the risk of a large loss would increase as retirement approached because the workers' account balances would be larger. Workers can offset this risk by gradually moving into bonds, but because of inertia, it appears that many workers do not make that change. For this reason, life-cycle mutual funds have been developed that automatically make that adjustment. With life-cycle funds, the fund is diversified with a mix of stocks and bonds that shifts toward bonds as the worker approaches his planned retirement date.

The financial market meltdown of 2008 has highlighted the financial market risk borne by older workers. Perhaps the best way of dealing with this type of risk prospectively is to invest in life-cycle funds, where the fund's portfolio switches increasingly into bonds as the worker's retirement date approaches. As with any good idea having to do with 401(k) plan investment management, recognizing the poor job that many participants do of managing their accounts, this approach could be voluntary, it could be the default, or it could be mandatory.

Investment risk is borne by the plan sponsor in defined benefit plans. The risk may be partially shifted to workers in some plans when the extent of price indexing of retirement benefits is affected by the investment rate of return received by the plan.

Because of the long time horizon of pension plans, with their long-dated liabilities, it can be argued that investment risk is different for them than for some other types of investments. For example, if a plan were to purchase long-dated bonds that it planned to hold to maturity, the fluctuations in the value of those bonds would be irrelevant to the plan. A mark to market approach, which would force a contemporaneous recognition of the fluctuation in their value, would impose a false element of volatility.

Investment risk is borne in different ways by participants in hybrid plans. In cash balance plans, the participants may bear some investment risk to the extent that the crediting rate varies with the rate of return in capital markets. In the collective defined contribution plans in the Netherlands, employers contribute a fixed amount, and all investment and demographic risk is borne by workers collectively. However, because benefits are based on a benefit formula, the risk is not borne through changes in benefits but through changes in the contributions made by workers. Thus, workers nearing retirement and retirees receiving benefits bear relatively little risk. This pattern of risk-bearing is superior to that in 401(k) plans, where workers nearing retirement and retirees are most affected by investment risk.

Individual Management Risk

Individual management risk arises from individual errors in managing pension investments. Evidence has accumulated that many individuals systematically make errors in managing pension investments, and that these errors affect their retirement income. Life-cycle funds have been developed to help individuals manage the investments of their 401(k) plans. Individual management risk is discussed more thoroughly in Chapter 8.

Individual management risk does not arise in traditional defined benefit plans, which generally are managed by financial professionals. However, financial professionals also may make investment management mistakes, whether by following what other professionals are doing ("herding"), by trading too aggressively, or by engaging in short-term strategies. The risk associated with bad financial management is borne by the plan sponsor of defined benefit plans.

Agency Risk

Defined contribution pension participants are subject to risks arising from the improper or self-serving financial management of the agents they entrust to handle their investments. Agency risk arises because the pension participant's investments are handled by agents rather than directly by the participant. These agents include mutual fund managers and the corporations in which the investments are made. The risk is limited to a small extent by workers' being able to choose their investments. An example of agency risk is when the CEO of a company in which the worker has invested receives a high salary while mismanaging the company. This risk is borne by the plan sponsor in defined benefit plans but by the individual worker in defined contribution plans.

Longevity Risk

Longevity risk for workers has two components. First, longevity risk arises because of changing mortality rates up to the point of retirement. This aspect of longevity risk affects the annuity value if the individual decides to annuitize the account balance, or it affects the amount the individual can withdraw through phased withdrawals if he chooses not to annuitize. Second, individuals who do not annuitize their account balances face the risk of living longer than expected and not having sufficient funds. Both aspects of longevity risk are borne by the plan sponsor in defined benefit plans but are borne by the worker in defined contribution plans.

Risks Associated with Annuities

While annuities provide insurance against outliving one's income, they also pose risks to the purchaser. Annuity providers have developed options that deal with many of the risks workers face in an attempt to make annuities a more appealing financial and insurance product for pension participants.

Prepurchase market risk. Workers face financial market risk concerning the value of an annuity. The value of the assets in their account may be relatively low because of a downturn in financial markets shortly before the date at which they plan to retire and purchase an annuity. This risk to some extent can be dealt with by phased or delayed purchase of annuities.

Mortality risk. Retirees who annuitize face the risk of dying unexpectedly early, in which case they would have been better off not annuitizing their account. This risk can be dealt with by purchasing an annuity that guarantees a death benefit to the purchaser's beneficiary or that guarantees payment for a minimum number of years whether the purchaser is alive or not. Another way for workers to deal with this risk is simply to annuitize a smaller part of the account balance.

Default. A further risk is that the annuity provider will default. Insurance companies provide annuities. These companies face the risk of bankruptcy if, for example, they misprice their products or if people live substantially longer than the insurance company expected. This risk is addressed to some degree through state guarantee funds and can be further mitigated through reinsurance. Reinsurance is an agreement whereby an insurance company transfers risk of loss under insurance policies it writes by means of a separate contract with another insurance company.

The Chilean government guarantees the annuities of retirees in its mandatory pension system. The government provides this guarantee without charge to the participants or the insurance companies. The guarantee is for 75 percent of the annuity, subject to a maximum amount. To prevent the need for this insurance being used, the Chilean government sets stringent regulations on insurance companies. Thus far, for the 25 years the Chilean system has operated, no claims have been made against the insurance (James, Martinez, and Iglesias 2006). Issues related to annuities are discussed further in Chapter 10.

Interest rate risk at purchase. When a worker purchases an annuity, the worker's account balance is converted to an annuity based on an interest rate, which varies with the long-term interest rates available in capital markets. When interest rates are relatively high, the annual value of the benefits provided by an annuity are higher than when interest rates are low. Thus workers face the risk that interest rates will be relatively low when they convert their account balance to an annuity.

Variations in interest rates used to convert account balances to annuities can have a large effect on the level of annual pension benefits received. For a 65-year-old U.S. male, a 4 percent interest rate generates annual payments of $686 per $10,000 annuitized. This amount rises to $830 at 6 percent and $982 at 8 percent (Ameriks 2002). Higher interest rates produce higher annual payments because the interest income produced by the account balance invested at those interest rates will be greater. The higher payments do not necessarily imply higher lifetime benefits because higher interest rates tend to be associated with higher inflation rates. This interest rate risk can be largely eliminated by investing individual accounts in the period leading up to annuitization in long-term bonds.

Interest rate risk may be offset to some extent by offsetting changes in asset prices. That occurs if interest rates are low, producing a low annuitized benefit for a given account balance when stock prices are relatively high.

Under a guaranteed annuity conversion option, a pension plan guarantees to convert a worker's account balance to a life annuity at a fixed interest rate. Alternatively, the interest rate can be guaranteed to be no lower than a fixed minimum. If the annuity rates provided under the guarantee are more beneficial to the participant than the prevailing rates in the market, the plan, employer, or some other entity must make up the difference in the purchase price of the annuity.

Fixed rate guarantees are vulnerable to prolonged falls in interest rates (Turner and Rajnes 2006). Alternative approaches can be used to limit the interest rate risk associated with annuity conversions. One approach is to allow workers to partially annuitize in steps, spread over time. This approach reduces the interest rate risk associated with completely annuitizing at a single point in time. Another approach is to allow workers to initially take phased withdrawals and later take an annuity, thus giving workers greater flexibility in picking the date at which they annuitize.

Sweden provides an interest rate guarantee for annuity conversions. The government, as the provider of annuities in the Swedish mandatory Notional Defined Contribution system, limits interest rate risk for workers by providing the guarantee. The interest rate used to determine the annuity varies based on market interest rates but is guaranteed to be no lower than 3 percent (Engström and Westerberg 2003).

RISK IN DEFINED BENEFIT PLANS

For many workers, particularly those with long careers working for a single employer, defined benefit plans provide retirement benefits with substantially less risk than 401(k) plans. Defined benefit plans, however, can be risky for workers who change jobs or are laid off, particularly at older ages. They also pose greater risks for workers than do defined contribution plans in the case of the bankruptcy of the sponsoring employer or plan termination for any reason. Because the earnings used to calculate defined benefit plan benefits are not indexed in the United States (but are in the United Kingdom), these events can cause a substantial loss of benefits, compared to what would have been accrued for those years of work if the person had continued working at the job until normal retirement age. Portability risk to participants due to changing jobs or layoffs is discussed in Chapter 4.

Risk That Benefits Will Be Cut

U.S. pension law prevents a cut in accrued vested benefits. However, employers can modify their pension plans to reduce future accruals of benefits. Thus, a person who was hired with the expectation that the pension plan at hire would be the one providing benefits at retirement may have his expectations disappointed. The benefits he expected to receive can be cut.

In bankruptcy, workers may experience a cut in benefits because of limitations on the benefits that the PBGC insures. In addition, workers generally will experience a cut in the benefits that they expected to receive, when those expectations were based on a long career and the continued existence of the plan.

Risk Sharing in Career Average Defined Benefit Plans

Career average defined benefit plans provide a form of risk sharing between the plan sponsor and workers that does not occur in final average pay plans. Career average plans base benefits on the nominal average of wages over a career. Because of inflation, the nominal average of wages does not keep pace with the current standard of living. Thus, these plans periodically have benefit enhancements. However, risk sharing occurs in that the benefit enhancements typically depend on how well the plan is doing concerning its investments and its experience with increased worker life expectancy.

Risks to Plan Sponsors in Defined Benefit Plans

Investment risk. In the early 2000s, several changes occurred that may have made defined benefit plans appear to employers to be riskier than they previously had thought. These changes may have contributed to a declining support for defined benefit plans among employers. In what some commentators called a perfect storm, both the stock market and interest rates declined. The decline in the stock market lowered the value of assets, while the decline in interest rates raised the value of liabilities. In addition, the increase in worker life expectancy at older ages may have been greater than anticipated by plan sponsors.

These changes, however, also affected defined contribution plans. The decline in the stock market would make defined benefit plans relatively less desirable to employers, but it would also make defined contribution plans relatively less desirable to employees. Unexpectedly long life expectancy would similarly make defined benefit plans less desirable to employers but more desirable to employees, with the reverse pattern holding true for defined contribution plans. A reduction in interest rates increases the cost of annuitizing in both defined benefit plans and defined contribution plans.

Investment mismatch risk. Plan sponsors bear the risk that their assets and liabilities are mismatched, so that their liabilities may grow faster than their assets. Their assets and liabilities may react differently to changes in interest rates.

The effects of uncertainty in improvements in life expectancy. Uncertainty as to future changes in life expectancy may affect employers' pension decisions. For example, the increasing obesity in the population may cause life expectancy to increase less than projected, while a revolution in medical science may cause the improvements to be greater than projected. Experts disagree as to the likely future increases in life expectancy. The Social Security actuaries have projected an increase of 6 years between 2000 and 2080 for life expectancy at birth; but the 2003 Technical Panel on Assumptions and Methods (2003), which examined the basis for that projection, recommended projecting an even greater increase in life expectancy—about 7.5 years. Most of this increase will occur at older ages because mortality is already low at younger ages.

Pension plan sponsors may have poorly anticipated improvements in life expectancy. Many defined benefit plans were established during the 1940s and 1950s, a time when life expectancy at older ages had increased relatively little during the preceding decades of the twentieth century. Life expectancy at age 65 rose from 11.7 years in 1900 to 21.2 years in 2000, an 81 percent increase. However, 75 percent of this increase occurred after 1950, and thus may not have been anticipated by the sponsors of defined benefit plans at the time that many plans were started. The improvements in life expectancy at older ages generally accelerated over the century, thanks especially to an unprecedented reduction in mortality from cardiovascular disease beginning in the late 1960s (Technical Panel on Assumptions and Methods 2003).

Markets can pool idiosyncratic longevity risk, which is the risk that a particular individual will live longer than expected. However, pension providers also take on systematic longevity risk, which is the risk that an entire cohort will live longer than expected.

Longevity bonds are a financial instrument that would protect defined benefit plan sponsors from the risk that an entire cohort lives longer on average than expected. Longevity bonds have a payout that is structured so that the larger the percentage of a particular age cohort that survives during the postretirement years, the larger the payout. These bonds have been offered, but a market has not been developed for them.

When an employer provides annuities through a defined benefit plan, the employer takes on idiosyncratic and systematic longevity risk. That risk can be reduced in larger plans by the diversification across plan participants. By the same token, the risk is larger in small plans than in large plans because small plans have a smaller pool of retirees across which they can diversify the risk.

Systematic longevity risk is expensive for a plan sponsor to bear because it is positively correlated across workers. However, it is relatively inexpensive, compared to idiosyncratic risk, for individual workers to bear because for each worker the increase in life expectancy is relatively small, and the worker benefits from that increase through the associated longer life. It is efficient for plan sponsors, rather than individual workers, to bear the idiosyncratic risk because plan sponsors of large plans can diversify it away. It may be efficient for workers to bear the systematic risk because they are also the beneficiaries of the longer life expectancy.

Systematic risk can be transferred to workers by raising the plan's normal retirement age in connection with improvements in life expectancy. An increase in the normal retirement age means that benefits are reduced at all calendar ages younger than the new normal retirement age, including at the plan's earliest retirement age. The reduction in benefits is designed to maintain a constant lifetime expected value of benefits in the face of increased life expectancy. U.S. plans are not permitted to have a normal retirement age higher than age 65, an aspect of pension law that has not been adjusted to reflect increasing longevity.

The increase in the plan's normal retirement age can be done in several ways. Similar to the increase for Social Security benefits, the increase can be determined in advance according to a fixed schedule. This approach eliminates any risk as to the timing and amount of the changes. Alternatively, the increase can be linked to increases in life expectancy. That approach would entail some risk as to the timing and amount of reductions in annual benefits, but would assure that for the pension population as a whole the expected lifetime value of benefits would be maintained. The increase could occur for all workers, or it could be limited to new hires.

Pension participants as a group have longer life expectancies than the general population because they are healthy enough to work. Also, they have higher average income than the population average, which is associated with longer life expectancy. The life expectancy of pension participants may change at a different rate from that of the general population, which should be taken into account in indexing increases in a plan's normal retirement age.

Regulatory risk. Regulatory risk is the risk that pension commitments will be made more expensive for plan sponsors because of regulatory changes. For example, a change that required all plans to provide cost-of-living adjustments for retirees, or that required plans to index benefits during the preretirement period for workers the plan sponsors lay off, would raise plan costs.

Pension Insurance for Defined Benefit Plans: The PBGC

In a dynamic economy, new companies are being created at the same time that older companies are shutting down.[2] The bankruptcy of firms, though distressing for owners and employees, is part of the normal functioning of a competitive, efficient economy. If government wants to further that competitive economy, it will avoid subsidizing firms in declining industries.

The bankruptcy of firms generally hurts pension participants in defined benefit plans. In an employer-provided defined benefit system, workers may lose their retirement benefits if their employer declares bankruptcy at a time when its defined benefit pension is underfunded. When employers are under financial stress, contributing to a pension plan may take a low priority. In the absence of regulations preventing employers from forgoing contributions, typically such an employer seeks to place the minimum amount into the pension plan, leading to underfunding.

The PBGC protects the pensions of U.S. workers in private defined benefit plans. The PBGC's operations are financed by insurance premiums set by Congress and paid by sponsors of defined benefit plans; they are also financed by investment income, assets from underfunded pension plans the PBGC has taken over, and recoveries from companies formerly responsible for the plans. The PBGC maintains separate insurance programs for single-employer defined benefit plans and for multiemployer defined benefit plans because of the difference in risk of termination between the two types of plans. The PBGC charges a premium that is based in part on the number of participants in the plan and in part on the extent of underfunding. However, the premium is not risk-related in that it is not larger for sponsors that are more likely to go bankrupt. Thus, weak companies having plans with a significant degree of underfunding are not charged the full premium that would be charged using insurance principles.

Table 6.1 indicates that the net assets of the PBGC single-employer trust fund declined by an astounding $33 billion between 2000 and 2004. This experience demonstrates that the PBGC is somewhat like a casualty insurance company that insures catastrophic events. The financial status of the pension benefit insurer can change dramatically in a short period of time.

Causes of the deficits. These deficits reflect in part the effects of a three-year downturn in the stock market, starting in 2000, plus the decline in interest rates over the period. At the beginning of 2000, the PBGC had a surplus of $9.7 billion rather than a deficit.

Claims on the PBGC's insurance are sensitive to changes in interest rates and stock returns, overall economic conditions, the development of underfunding in some large plans, the economic performance of particular industries, and the bankruptcy of a few large companies.

Table 6.1 PBGC Single-Employer Trust Fund Financial Status, 2000–2007

Year	Overfunding (deficit)
2000	$9.7 billion
2001	$7.7 billion
2002	($3.6 billion)
2003	($11.2 billion)
2004	($23.3 billion)
2005	($22.8 billion)
2006	($18.1 billion)
2007	($13.1 billion)

SOURCE: Annual Reports of the PBGC.

Defined benefit pensions face long-term challenges due to the earlier retirements and increasing life expectancies of their participants. In 2003, an average male worker would expect to spend 18.1 years in retirement, compared to 11.5 years in 1950 (PBGC 2003). The additional seven years of retirement must be funded.

Since pension plans with unfunded benefits are more likely to be sponsored by weak companies, the variable premium the PBGC charges is a step toward a risk-related premium that a commercial insurer would assess. The next step would be to increase the 0.9 percent to reflect the probability of the employer becoming bankrupt.[3] However, that gets difficult, for the following five reasons: 1) the correct premium could be huge for employers that are about to go bankrupt; 2) not all companies are rated; 3) ratings can be incorrect (e.g., Enron), so the PBGC might need to audit employers; 4) the large premium could be enough to bankrupt a weak employer; and 5) the premiums would go to the PBGC, whereas the best place for the money would be to put it into the plan.

Since it could be difficult to get payment of this large risk-related premium from a bankrupt employer, the PBGC could put a cap on it. Another idea is to restrict benefits. For example, when a weak employer is funded at less than 60 percent, U.S. pension law restricts the employer from improving benefits. These rules could go further in four ways: by 1) setting a higher threshold than 60 percent; 2) restricting improvements targeted at employers with a below-investment-grade credit rating;

3) further restricting benefits, such as by freezing all accruals[4] and disallowing lump sums and early retirement subsidies; and 4) avoiding the guarantee of poison pill provisions or shutdown benefits unless they were funded. It should be noted that advocates for workers oppose the 60 percent rule, arguing that workers should not be penalized for the poor funding, which is the responsibility of employers. These benefit restrictions have been discussed in response to plan funding ratios plummeting because of payments of subsidized lump sums to people who get all their money out before plan termination by lump sum. Because of the way that the PBGC guarantees benefits,[5] the participants remaining in these plans will get less from the PBGC.

Principles for Evaluating the PBGC

This section discusses basic principles for evaluating the PBGC. A fundamental issue in establishing a pension insurer is the extent to which it should act as a profit-making insurer would, providing market-based insurance, versus the extent to which it should provide social insurance, where social goals are met through the transfer of resources across firms.

Adequate pension funding. The PBGC would not be needed if government regulation could assure that pension plans were always adequately funded. However, with the volatility of equity and bond markets and the desire of employers to gradually pay for new or larger benefits, it is difficult to require that pension plans always be adequately funded.

Because pension contributions are tax deductible under the corporate income tax and the earnings on contributions are generally not taxed, profitable tax-paying firms have an incentive to prefund pension plans. For firms in financial distress that are not paying taxes, the incentive is the opposite: these firms try to minimize contributions.

When a firm promises a defined benefit pension to its workers, economic theory posits that those workers accept a lower amount in wages, depending on the risk associated with the promise of benefits and the value that workers place on future compensation versus current compensation. As a matter of public policy, many people believe that the trade-off of lower wages for future pension benefits should not be a gamble that depends on the fortunes of the employer.

Requiring adequate funding for pension plans, rather than placing too much burden on using risk-based premiums, limits the premium costs for employers. Ensuring adequate funding through funding regulations is the best way to keep down the level of the required levy and to assure employers that the cost of the levy will not become burdensome.

Funding issues can be divided into two groups: those that occur during periods of economic strength and those that occur during periods of economic weakness. During periods of economic strength, funding rules need to assure that an adequate cushion of extra assets is built up in pension funds to cover the difficult economic periods. The funding during periods of strength is important, since funding during those times is less burdensome on firms because they tend to have adequate resources in those times.

During periods of economic weakness, the PBGC is more at risk of claims. Adequate safeguards in funding rules can be used to avoid underfunding. Funding rules need to assure that employers are required to contribute to underfunded plans.

Because of concerns about lost tax revenue due to pension funding, the amount of overfunding allowed in pension plans during periods of strong capital markets generally is restricted. During periods of strong financial markets, plans need to develop an adequate cushion of overfunding.

Concern may be raised about excess pension funding making a firm an attractive target for a corporate takeover. That issue was dealt with in the United States by a steep tax on asset reversions when a corporation terminates an overfunded plan and reverts assets to the corporation (or to a corporation that has taken over the original corporation). The reversion tax is 50 percent, on top of a federal corporate income tax of 35 percent. With state income taxes, the total tax can exceed 90 percent of the reversion. If the employer uses surplus assets to improve benefits or start a replacement plan, the excise tax is lowered to 20 percent. Even with this lower excise tax, the total tax would exceed 50 percent. Thus, U.S. employers rarely terminate pensions to get a reversion. The funds are more valuable in the plan. However, the reversion tax may reduce funding levels. In good years, when an employer could contribute more to a pension plan, they don't, because if the pension assets do well they may exceed the value of all future benefits, and the employer won't be able to access them without paying the steep excise tax. Thus, the employer may never get the advantages of the good returns.

The funding situation in pension plans, however, can change dramatically over a short time period, due to falling equity values and rising liabilities. In addition, if an employer goes bankrupt it needs to replace its pension promises with annuities, which generally are determined using bond rates of return. These annuities are more expensive than the present value of the pension promises, using expected long-term rates of return.

A major source of funding problems has been flat benefit plans. Periodically unions renegotiate the pension benefit formula, which leaves these plans perpetually underfunded. This problem could be dealt with by prohibiting increases in benefit generosity in plans that are underfunded and prohibiting increases in benefit generosity that cause underfunding beyond set limits.

Moral hazard. Moral hazard arises because people may take less care to avoid an undesirable outcome if they are covered by insurance and thus compensated if that event occurs. This problem is considerably more significant for pension benefit insurance than for life insurance or fire insurance because with moral hazard, financially weak firms have an incentive to take actions that increase the liabilities of the PBGC.

Another factor making moral hazard particularly a problem for government-provided pension benefit insurance is that weak firms, through the political process, may seek to influence the pension benefit insurance legislation to subsidize them. This is particularly likely to happen when an industry is struggling, such as the airline industry is, and when various firms are able to work together to mobilize political support.

For financially stable firms, pension benefit insurance may suffer less from adverse incentives due to moral hazard, because these firms have countervailing motivations. A firm that expects to continue to be in existence will want to maintain its reputation as a trustworthy employer and as a responsible institution in society.

These countervailing motivations do not limit the incentives of moral hazard for financially stressed firms with little in the way of future prospects. Because of the likelihood of their eventual bankruptcy, those firms may attempt to increase their claim on the PBGC so that their limited resources can be used for providing compensation for their senior management. Also, a firm in financial trouble may engage in measures to preserve the firm that would be described as desperate. It is presumably more likely to engage in financial activities that a financially sound firm would not do, including skipping required pension contributions to pay wages, or increasing future pension benefits instead of current wages.

The existence of the PBGC diminishes the influence of concern for reputation as a restraining force on the problem of moral hazard for weak firms. This occurs because firms that are concerned about the welfare of their employees, and for that reason would take steps to fund their pension benefits, now can rely on the PBGC to provide those benefits. For example, immediately after PBGC was created in 1974, unless a large employer was in very bad financial condition, it generally did not enter bankruptcy (and all the difficulties that entailed) just to get help with its pension plan. However, that has changed. Employers realized that bankruptcy could help them in other areas (such as allowing them to break labor agreements). A few large employers used Chapter 11 bankruptcy rules (reorganization, not liquidation) in the 1980s to eliminate debts and reorganize, relying on the PBGC to pay their pension debts (with their competitor's premiums). These companies set a precedent, and an increasing number of large employers are using Chapter 11 bankruptcy rules for just these purposes. For this reason, Congress amended U.S. pension laws to make it more difficult in Chapter 11 reorganization for the employer to dump the pension plan on the PBGC. The bankruptcy judge must find that the company cannot continue unless the pension plan is terminated.

Without pension benefit insurance, employees have a strong financial interest in the extent to which their pension plans are funded. They express these concerns explicitly in labor negotiations and implicitly in the labor markets, where workers choose among various employers with competing offers (CBO 1993). Even with this incentive, however, workers may be able to do little to influence the funding of an underfunded pension plan. Nonetheless, pension benefit insurance means that employees have weaker incentives to assure that their pension plans are adequately funded.

Policy to Deal with Moral Hazard

Monitoring. Monitoring the status of firms at risk can allow the PBGC to take steps to limit its exposure. Monitoring can occur through mandatory advance reporting of activities of firms, such as change in corporate ownership, or it can occur through indicators, such as a decline in bond rating. When the PBGC learns that a strong company is selling a subsidiary to a weak buyer, it may require that the pension plan be well funded, or that the strong seller back its funding requirements for five years.

Coinsurance. Coinsurance, in which employees are not fully insured against pension benefit losses, is one way to preserve incentives for employees to pressure their firms for better pension funding. With top executives, coinsurance may have some influence on their decisions because they would lose pension benefits if the plan terminated with insufficient funding. This idea has not been as successful in the United States as originally hoped, however, because employees, except those at the very top, have little effect on an employer's funding of the pension plan, especially if the firm is weak. In addition, the employees at the very top may be insulated from this concern by having their separate (and much larger) contractual pension benefits vest when the company is in difficulty. Congress is considering ways to prohibit this vesting and tie the interests of the top employees to the prospects of the company's pension plan.

Coinsurance can also occur with other creditors of firms in financial distress. The PBGC is a creditor of the bankrupt defined benefit plan sponsor. The more money the PBGC receives from the bankrupt firm, the less the other creditors receive. Consequently, other unsecured creditors are also coinsurers of pension insurance. They would want the pension plan funded better (and wages not increased as much). Through the decisions to provide loans (and loan covenants that can call in the loan) they may be able to affect the plan sponsor's behavior.

Policy concerning top executives. In some U.S. firms making claims on the PBGC, high executives have retired shortly before the firm filed a claim, taking their entire pension benefits as a lump sum or in accelerated payments. This strategy has enabled them to receive their full pension benefit amount, rather than the reduced amount they would receive if they had taken an annuity, which would have been subject to the maximum insurable benefit. It also in some cases has considerably reduced the assets in the plan and decreased the plan's funding ratio. This type of practice has since been prevented by not allowing lump sum benefit payments when a pension is underfunded below a certain level.

Top executives in failing firms may have an incentive to pay themselves high compensation rather than funding their pension plans. This incentive may be a reason for the PBGC to monitor executive compensation in firms with low funding ratios and even to limit maximum compensation in that situation.

Protections Against Political Risk

The political forces affecting the PBGC may result in it being structured in a way that leads to it having insufficient financing. Political risk has two major aspects. First, financially weak firms will exert pressure so that they will be subsidized by financially strong firms through the PBGC. Second, the government, in order to reduce the loss of tax revenue occurring due to the tax deductibility of pension contributions, will set too low a ceiling on the allowable level of pension overfunding.

Special interest group politics work against the financial soundness of pension benefit insurance. The companies most likely to make a claim on the pension benefit insurer tend to be in the same industry, which facilitates their efforts to influence the government in ways opposed to the interests of other taxpayers.

Economic downturns are a difficult time in which to require greater pension funding. In the past, bills have been introduced in the U.S. Congress that would permit underfunded plans to reduce their contributions because of hard economic times. Thus, political pressure could worsen the PBGC's financial situation, unless it helps some companies stay afloat long enough to maintain their plan and fund it better in the long run. Unfortunately, the PBGC has experience with companies that got funding breaks only to eventually come back later and dump their plan on the PBGC, but this time with larger underfunding.

CONCLUSION

Life expectancy risk can be divided into the idiosyncratic risk that a particular individual will live longer than expected and the cohort risk that an entire cohort on average will live longer than expected. Annuity providers are able to deal with idiosyncratic risk by pooling it across large numbers of people, effectively diversifying it away. However, no pooling mechanism exists for dealing with cohort risk. Longevity bonds would provide a hedge, but a market for them has not developed. Longevity bonds have a higher payout when the percentage of a cohort that is surviving is higher. Life expectancy indexing of benefits is one way of dealing with this risk. The idiosyncratic risk is borne by the annuity provider, who can diversify it away. The cohort risk is borne by workers, who are the beneficiaries of the improved life expectancy.

The PBGC insures pension benefits but itself is subject to risks arising from political pressures. The financial problems of the PBGC have not been resolved, even though it has been in existence for some 35 years.

Inflation risk remains a problem in the U.S. pension system. Few workers have benefits that are protected against inflation. While annuities protect workers against outliving their resources and are particularly valuable for women because of their longer life expectancies, the real value of annuity benefits can be greatly eroded in old age for long-lived retirees. An issue in dealing with this problem is that the trade-off of reduced benefits at retirement in exchange for higher benefits a decade or two later does not seem to be appealing to most retirees.

Notes

1. The reader is reminded that the term "pension plans" refers in this book to both defined benefit and defined contribution plans, and that 401(k) plans, because of their dominance, are generally discussed when discussing defined contribution plans.
2. This section draws heavily on Gebhardtsbauer and Turner (2004).
3. In addition, the risk premium could reflect two things—1) the risk levels of the pension plan's assets and 2) whether the plan is too large for the employer to afford—by comparing the plan's cost and liabilities to items on an employer's balance sheet and the balance sheet's earnings or cash flow. However, not only would this be complex, but it could entail the PBGC involving itself in the employer's business in an unprecedented way.
4. Not just disallowing benefit improvements, which really only hurts hourly plans that don't base benefits on final pay averages.
5. The PBGC may pay larger benefits in plans that are better funded.

7
Hybrid Plans

The Best of Both Worlds?

Hybrid pension plans combine features of both defined benefit and defined contribution plans. A factor motivating their development appears to be the desire by employers to shift the risk they bear in defined benefit plans to plan participants. In traditional defined benefit plans, the employer bears the investment risk and the risk relating to the longevity of participants. In hybrids, one or both of these risks is shifted to participants. Hybrid defined benefit plans preserve aspects of defined benefit plans for workers, such as collective management of investments, while reducing the risks that employers face, such as mortality risk.

This chapter discusses risk-sharing approaches through the use of hybrid pension plans. It first discusses the types of hybrid plans in existence. It then discusses possible types of hybrid plans that have been proposed.

TYPES OF HYBRID PLANS

The four main types of hybrid plans in the U.S. private sector are 1) cash balance plans, 2) pension equity plans, 3) floor offset plans, and 4) multiemployer plans. This section also discusses sequential hybrids, which are offered in the United Kingdom, and the huge ABP plan in the Netherlands. Features of the types of hybrid plans are summarized in Table 7.1.

The plans are described and their handling of risks analyzed based on the actual functioning of each type of plan. For example, while cash balance plans offer annuities, the usual practice is that workers take their benefits as lump sums. Thus, the analysis of the distribution of risk concerns the distribution of risk as the plans actually function, not as they possibly or ideally could function.

Table 7.1 Types of Hybrid Pension Plans

Plan name	Employee (EE) or employer (ER) contributes	Defined benefit or defined contribution accrual	Account balance or benefit formula	Risk borne by:			
				Investment risk	Interest rate risk for annuitization	Mortality	Post-retirement inflation
Defined benefit–based							
Cash balance plan	ER	DC	A	ER and EE	EE	EE	EE
Pension equity plan	ER	DB	A	ER	EE	EE	EE
ABP plan (Netherlands)	ER and EE	DB	B	ER and EE	ER	ER	EE
DB(k)	ER and EE	DC	A	ER	EE	EE	EE
Plain Old Pension Plan	ER	DB	B	ER and EE	ER	ER	EE
Life expectancy–indexed defined benefit plan	ER	DB	B	ER	ER	EE and ER	EE
Combination of defined benefit plan and defined contribution plan							
Floor offset plan	ER, with EE in some plans	Greater of DB or DC	Greater of A or B	ER and EE	ER	ER	EE
Sequential hybrid (UK)	ER and EE	DB and DC	A and B	ER and EE	ER and EE	ER and EE	EE

NOTE: A = account balance, B = benefit formula, DB = defined benefit plan, DC = defined contribution plan, EE = employee, ER = employer.
SOURCE: Author's compilation.

Cash balance plans. Cash balance plans appear to workers to be a defined contribution plan. About a quarter of active participants in U.S. defined benefit plans are in cash balance plans (USDOL 2008). These plans provide each worker with an account to which contributions and interest are credited. Cash balance plans are communicated to workers in terms of a balance in an individual account, they are readily portable at job change, and their benefits are based on earnings over the worker's entire period of participation in the plan. In a cash balance plan, each participant's account is periodically credited with a dollar amount by the sponsoring employer, usually based on a percentage of the individual's salary. Unlike a traditional defined benefit plan, a cash balance plan provides workers with hypothetical or notional individual accounts.

Cash balance plans are required to offer annuities because the Department of Labor regulates them as defined benefit plans. Typically, however, workers withdraw their benefits in the form of a lump sum payment, which, in the United States, is a defined contribution plan characteristic. Workers may bear some investment risk because the interest rate used to credit accounts may vary with rates of return in capital markets. Like traditional defined benefit plans, workers are automatically enrolled in cash balance plans.

Although a cash balance plan portrays benefits to employees in the form of an individual account, the account balance does not depend on the performance of plan assets. Contributions and investment earnings are not allocated to individual accounts; instead, contributions are made to a common trust fund for all participants, and benefits are paid directly from the fund.

From the perspective of employers, cash balance plans have many features of defined benefit plans (Turner 2003a). Pension law treats them as defined benefit plans because they specify a monthly benefit at retirement. They are funded by employers as defined benefit plans, with a single, collectively managed fund. Also like traditional defined benefit plans, cash balance plan benefits are insured by the Pension Benefit Guaranty Corporation (PBGC).

The cash balance pension formula determines benefits as a function of wages, pay credit rates, and interest credit rates. Contributions credited to the employee's account by the employer (pay credit) are generally quoted as a given percentage of the employee's pay. Interest credits equal to the product of the employee's credited account balance times an interest credit rate are also accrued in the account. An interest credit rate is either a fixed rate or a variable rate tied to an index, such as the 30-year Treasury bond rate, or the rate on one-year Treasury bills reset every six months.

In a cash balance plan, the employer bears the investment risk of the underlying assets in which the plan is invested. Employees, however, may bear some investment risk because of fluctuations in the rate of return on the asset that determines the crediting rate. Employees bear interest rate risk if they choose to convert their account balances to annuities. They bear longevity risk if they do not convert to annuities, which is the usual practice. Reasons why employees do not choose annuities are discussed in Chapter 10.

Pension equity plan (PEP). A pension equity plan (PEP), called by the more descriptive name of final salary lump sum plan in the United Kingdom, allows for the accrual each year of a certain percentage of final average pay. That percentage can rise with tenure so as to reward long-tenure workers. At retirement, the total percentages accrued over the employee's entire career are summed, and then that percentage is applied to the final average pay to determine the final account balance. The benefit payable is then determined from that balance (McGill et al. 1996). PEPs are classified under pension law as defined benefit plans and are insured by the PBGC.

In a PEP, the employer bears the investment risk on the assets in which the plan is invested. The employee bears no investment risk. As in cash balance plans, employees bear interest rate risk if they choose to convert their account balances to annuities, and they bear longevity risk up to the point of retirement if they annuitize, and beyond retirement if they do not annuitize.

This type of plan is similar to a cash balance plan in that workers have individual accounts that are credited each year. While cash balance plans have accrual patterns similar to defined contribution plans, PEPs have accrual patterns similar to defined benefit plans.

Floor offset plans. Floor offset plans, also called floor plans, and called underpin plans in the United Kingdom, combine two separate plans: a defined benefit plan and a defined contribution plan. The defined benefit plan provides a guaranteed minimum benefit and is insured in the United States by the PBGC. Thus, employees do not bear the downside risk of financial market investment, but to the extent that the defined contribution plan accumulations produce a larger benefit than that payable from a defined benefit plan, employees can gain from that upside potential. To limit the financial market risk to the employer, the plan may limit the investment options from which the employee may choose in the defined contribution plan. The defined contribution plan must be converted into an annuity, but the participant generally must bear the longevity and interest rate risk of the conversion.

Multiemployer plans. Multiemployer plans are collectively bargained plans that cover more than one employer, and in most cases they cover a number of employers. Multiemployer plans are defined benefit plans from the perspective of workers, with benefit formulas that determine the value of benefits. From the perspective of employers, they operate like defined contribution plans, at least for the period of a bargaining cycle. Over a bargaining cycle, which is typically two or three years, the contributions of the sponsoring employers are fixed. In these plans, however, the future benefit accruals of workers are more likely to be affected by the level of plan funding than is the case in single employer plans.

Sequential hybrids. A sequential hybrid is two distinct plans, rather than a single plan with hybrid features. With a sequential hybrid, provided by some employers in the United Kingdom, typically the employer offers a new employee membership in a defined contribution plan at hire. After a fixed period that the employee remains with the employer, such as five years, the employer enrolls the employee in a defined benefit plan. This type of arrangement provides the positive features of defined contribution plans for short-tenure employees and the positive features of defined benefit plans for long-tenure employees (Wesbroom and Reay 2005).

The ABP plan. In the Netherlands, the ABP plan, which is the largest pension plan in Europe in terms of assets, is for Dutch government employees (de Jong and Turner 2001). This plan bases benefits on a benefit formula, as is done in defined benefit plans. However, the plan is financed by contributions by employees and employers, and the contribution rate varies annually based on the investment performance of the pension fund. The calculation of the contribution rates uses a procedure that smoothes the fluctuations in the rates so that the annual variation is small.

Dutch collective defined contribution plans. In the early 2000s, Dutch employers started using a new hybrid plan called a collective defined contribution plan. This type of plan shifts both investment risk and longevity risk to plan participants. A collective defined contribution plan has a benefit formula similar to a defined benefit plan. However, in these plans all the investment risk is shifted to employees as a group. In a traditional defined contribution plan, by contrast, the investment risks are borne by employees individually, and for that reason can be particularly problematic for older workers.

In a collective defined contribution plan, employees accrue benefits based on a career average benefit formula. The level of benefits accrued in a year depends on the salary the worker earns that year. These plans provide benefits in the form of a price-indexed annuity. Employers contribute a fixed percentage of wages to these plans and have no additional liability if the investments of the plans perform poorly.

If a collective defined contribution plan suffers investment losses and becomes underfunded, the plan's governing body, which includes representatives of both employers and employees, decides how the adjustment is to be made. It can be made by an increase in contributions of employees (but not employers) or a reduction in benefit indexing and in the accrual of benefits. If the plan's investments perform well and the plan becomes overfunded, the workers rather than the employer benefit. Some Dutch companies have added the feature that if the plan becomes overfunded, they can reduce their contribution, but such plans do not qualify as a collective defined contribution plan.

These plans appeal to employers because the employer bears less risk than with a traditional defined benefit plan. They can be appealing to employees because the employee bears less risk than with a traditional defined contribution plan.

Hybrid Plan Proposals

Several types of hybrid plans have been proposed by pension analysts.

DB(k). DB(k) plans are defined benefit plans with 401(k) features (American Academy of Actuaries 2001). This type of plan was enabled by the Pension Protection Act of 2006, but the effective date for its implementation is 2010. This plan option will be available to employers with 500 or fewer participants. This type of pension plan would look like a combined defined benefit plan and 401(k) plan to workers. The defined benefit component is either a benefit formula of 1 percent of final average pay for up to 20 years of service, or a cash balance formula that increases with the participant's age. The 401(k) component would include an automatic enrollment feature (using 4 percent as the automatic enrollment contribution rate), and would provide for a fully vested employer matching contribution of 50 percent on the first 4 percent contributed by workers. Each worker would have an account, to which would be credited the worker's contributions and the matching contributions of employers. The account would be credited with a rate of return that would be determined in advance, or it would pay investment returns based on bond rates.

DB(k) plans differ from cash balance plans in that the contributions credited to the worker's account are not determined in advance by a formula in the plan document but are determined by the amount that the employee decides to contribute. Also, employees would have a choice among accounts in which to place their contributions.

Employees would bear interest rate risk if they chose to convert their account balances to annuities. They bear longevity risk if they do not convert to annuities.

Plain Old Pension Plan. The Plain Old Pension Plan (POPP) is a variation on the traditional defined benefit plan (Conversation on Coverage 2007). It would provide a modest guaranteed benefit accrual that employers could boost for a year and then reduce back to the basic benefit in future years. In these plans, the employer bears the financial market risk, but that risk is shifted back to the employee to the extent that employers reduce the level of benefit accrual when financial markets are performing poorly. The employer bears the interest rate and longevity risk.

Life-indexed DB plan. Life expectancy risk can be divided into two parts: the idiosyncratic risk that workers face concerning the uncertainty of their individual life expectancy, and the systematic risk that annuity providers face concerning the life expectancy of a birth cohort. Workers are concerned about the idiosyncratic risk, while pension providers are concerned about the systematic risk. With large numbers of participants, the idiosyncratic risks of workers are diminished in aggregate for the plan provider through the pooling of risks.

A hybrid plan option that would shift the systematic life expectancy risk to workers but would protect them from the idiosyncratic risk is the life-indexed DB (LI-DB) plan (Muir and Turner 2007). With this type of plan, the benefit formula in a traditional defined benefit plan would be modified so that for each new retirement cohort, the generosity of the plan would be slightly reduced to offset the effect of the long-term trend of increased life expectancy on the present value of future benefits. This plan has the advantage for employers that they do not have to deal with the uncertainty of future improvements in life expectancy.

ANALYSIS OF RISK-BEARING IN HYBRID PLANS

This section groups the hybrid plans considered according to how they deal with financial market risk, longevity risk, and interest rate risk.

Financial Market Risk

Financial market risk is shifted to workers in a number of the hybrid plans. Workers can bear financial market risk either through variations in their future benefit levels or variations in their contributions in defined benefit plans that require worker contributions. Plans in which the risk is borne through variation in future benefit levels can affect benefit levels at least three ways: 1) through the effect on the worker's notional account balance in plans that mimic defined contribution plans, 2) through benefit level in plans that retain the traditional defined benefit formula as the method for determining future benefits, or 3) through actual defined contribution account balances in plans that combine a defined contribution plan with a defined benefit plan.

Effect on a notional account balance. In cash balance plans, workers bear financial market risk through variations in future benefits to the extent that the crediting rate on their accounts varies with financial markets. In DB(k) plans, workers would bear financial market risk through variability in future benefits due to variations in the crediting rate on their account balance.

Effect on an actual defined contribution plan account balance. In floor offset plans, workers bear financial market risk through future benefit variability to the extent that they receive their benefits from the defined contribution part of the plan. In sequential plans, workers also bear financial market risk on the defined contribution part of their pension arrangement.

Effect on the value of traditionally calculated defined benefit plan benefits. In the Plain Old Pension Plan, the accrual of benefits varies depending on the investment performance of the plan.

Effect on contributions to a defined benefit plan. In the ABP plan, workers bear financial market risk through the level of their contributions.

Life Expectancy Risk

Life expectancy risk that relates to the life expectancy of the individual can be transferred to workers by paying benefits as a lump sum, rather than as an annuity. Life expectancy risk that relates to changes in the life expectancy of an age cohort can be transferred to workers by life expectancy indexing of benefits at retirement.

Individual life expectancy risk. Individual life expectancy risk is transferred to workers by paying lump sum benefits in cash balance plans, in DB(k) plans, and in the defined contribution part of floor offset and sequential plans.

Cohort life expectancy risk. Cohort life expectancy risk is transferred to workers in life-expectancy-indexed defined benefit plans.

Interest Rate Risk

Interest rate risk arises when workers desiring annuitized benefits must convert lump sum benefits. This risk occurs in the same plans that shift individual life expectancy risk to workers by generally paying lump sum benefits: cash balance plans, DB(k) plans, and the defined contribution part of floor offset and sequential plans.

CONCLUSION

Pension risks can be shared by workers, employers, and insurance companies in many ways. In a traditional defined benefit plan, the investment risk, the interest rate risk associated with annuitization, and the risk related to workers' longevity are all borne by employers. In a traditional defined contribution plan, these risks are all borne by workers. This chapter discusses hybrid defined benefit plans where the investment risk, interest rate risk, or longevity risk is shifted to workers.

Defined benefit plans have declined considerably in terms of the percentage of the workforce covered by them in the United States and the United Kingdom, and less dramatically in Canada. Hybrid plans are of particular interest because they may provide an option that is more attractive to employers than traditional defined benefit plans, while preserving for workers some of the risk protections of traditional defined benefit plans.

This chapter analyzes hybrid employer-provided defined benefit plans currently in existence: cash balance plans, pension equity plans, floor offset plans, the Dutch ABP plan, and sequential plans in the United Kingdom. It also analyzes types of hybrid plans that have been proposed.

One of the proposals for hybrid plans is the life-indexed defined benefit plan. This plan, similar to notional defined contribution plans, would adjust the benefit received at the point of retirement for improvements in life expectancy. That adjustment would result in a small downward correction in benefits for each successive birth cohort. This plan shifts cohort life expectancy risk to workers through the downward adjustment of benefits. However, it shields them from individual life expectancy risk because it provides benefits as an annuity.

8

Financing Pensions for Adequacy and Security

This chapter begins by considering some fundamental issues in pension financing: who ultimately bears the cost, and how to deal with inherent conflicts of interest. It considers issues common to both defined benefit and defined contribution plans, as well as issues affecting them separately. It addresses a central issue in pension policy—the choice between defined benefit plans and defined contribution plans.

FINANCING ISSUES COMMON TO DEFINED CONTRIBUTION AND DEFINED BENEFIT PLANS

Who Bears the Costs of Pensions?

Economic theory holds that it does not matter whether pension contributions are made by the employer or the employee. In either case, competition in labor markets causes wages to adjust so that the net compensation of the employee, including the accrual of future benefits, is the same regardless of whether the employer provides a pension, and this net compensation is tied to the employee's productivity. Thus, if the employee receives a pension, the employee's wage is reduced by the value of the pension. Noneconomists tend to view this theory's stated result with skepticism, and behavioral economics may eventually decide that who makes the contribution matters because of an effect resulting from the visibility of the contribution to workers. It may be also that the theory holds true in some circumstances and not others.

The argument that employees bear the costs of pensions is particularly strong, however, in the case of collective bargaining. It is clear that employees trade off higher benefits in return for higher wages when negotiating agreements.

On the other hand, the argument that employees bear the costs of pensions is particularly weak when considering the defined benefit pension costs of unanticipated improvements in life expectancy. Unanticipated improvements in life expectancy raise the pension accruals associated with past service. The economic theory of compensating differentials arguably only applies to the effect of current nonwage compensation costs on current wages. Thus, while improvements in life expectancy raise the costs of providing benefits equally through a defined benefit plan, and workers may bear the costs to the extent that the improvements are anticipated at the time the worker is accruing benefits, the costs associated with unexpected improvements in life expectancy may be borne by employers. Consequently, unexpected increases in life expectancy may be a reason why employers want to switch to defined contribution plans.

Conflicts of Interest

U.S. pension law requires plan sponsors to act solely in the interest of plan participants. However, plan sponsors face a conflict of interest because they also have a duty to act in the interest of their corporate shareholders. For example, this conflict of interest may occur in defined contribution plans, where, because of the need for diversification, it is generally not in the interest of participants to be heavily invested in the stock of their employer. However, it may be in the employer's interest in the case of takeover attempts to have employees holding a large block of company stock. Also, employees may more closely ally their interests with those of the company when they own company stock.

Conflicts of interest are inherent in economic relations. They occur when one party is acting as an agent for another party; this is called the agency problem. The conflict of interest concerning the plan sponsor's duty to its shareholders could be resolved by requiring plans to be managed by independent third parties, as is done in Japan. However, this arrangement simply substitutes another conflict of interest for the existing one: a for-profit entity managing a pension fund has a duty to its shareholders that conflicts with the interest of the pension participants. In this case, the conflict can be dealt with by requiring clear disclosure of fees paid so that participants, or the plan sponsor, can make an informed choice between competing pension fund managers.

Joint Trustees for Plan Management

Joint trustees are one way of dealing with conflicts of interest and the agency problem for pension plan management. With joint trustees, the board of trustees is composed of both employer and employee representatives. The United States is one of the few countries that have single-employer defined benefit plans where those plans are managed entirely by the employer. U.S. multiemployer plans are jointly trusteed. In the United Kingdom, Australia, and elsewhere, single-employer defined benefit plans are managed by a joint board of workers and employer representatives. In Australia, the trustee boards are made up of equal numbers of employee and employer representatives. The trustees must meet minimum standards of fitness established by regulation, and are licensed by the Australian government.

In theory, joint trusteeship better protects the interests of the employees than does relying on the good intentions of employers. Which approach yields better outcomes for pension participants is an empirical question that has not been investigated.

The Choice of Defined Benefit Plans versus Defined Contribution Plans

Perhaps the most significant aspect of pension financing, with major consequences for participants, is whether pensions are provided through defined benefit plans or defined contribution plans. Both types of plans provide employees with the opportunity to earn tax-favored returns on their retirement savings, to benefit from economies of scale in investment transactions, and to have a commitment mechanism for saving, which is beneficial to people who lack the self-control to save independently (Aaronson and Coronado 2005).

Employers have shifted pension coverage dramatically from defined benefit to defined contribution plans, not only in the United States but also in the United Kingdom. The shift has been less dramatic in Canada and Ireland, and little shift has occurred in Japan (Turner and Hughes 2008). The shift in the United States has been primarily to 401(k) plans, and a shift among other types of defined contribution plans to 401(k) plans has also occurred. Possible causes of this shift can broadly be fit into two categories: 1) changes in the economy that affect the demand for defined benefit pensions, and 2) changes in regulation that affect the supply or cost of providing defined benefit pensions.

A third, noneconomic factor that affects the demand for defined benefit pensions is changes in ideology. Conservative ideology tends to favor individually managed defined contribution plans. Defined contribution plans are preferred for ideological reasons by some people. It is felt that they are superior in terms of enhancing individual choice and individual responsibility for retirement. In addition, financial service providers may prefer defined contribution plans as providing greater fee income than defined benefit plans.

Changes in the economy include the decline in unionism and the decline in manufacturing. Unions favor defined benefit plans, and defined benefit plans tend to be offered in manufacturing industries. Changes in the economy also include a workforce that is increasingly mobile, and defined contribution plans are more favorable to a mobile workforce than defined benefit plans. Changes in government regulation include regulations favoring 401(k) plans, such as allowing tax deductibility of employee contributions; this deduction is not allowed for private sector defined benefit plans.

Defined contribution plans face less restrictive regulations than defined benefit plans in the United States. Defined benefit plans are required to offer annuities as an option, and require mandatory spousal consent if other options are chosen, while 401(k) plans do not face that requirement. Defined benefit plans allow workers to receive benefits while still working for the sponsoring employer starting at age 62, while the corresponding age for 401(k) plans is 59 ½. Employers sponsoring defined benefit plans are required to provide benefits for a larger fraction of their workforce than is the case for 401(k) plans. Employee contributions to 401(k) plans are tax deductible, but employer contributions are not tax deductible when made to defined benefit plans.

The shift from defined benefit to defined contribution plans has spurred a policy reaction: the attempt to "DB-ify" defined contribution plans. Examples of such proposals include automatic enrollment in defined contribution plans, having professional management of defined contribution plan investments, having phased purchase of annuities in defined contribution plans, and making annuities the default form of benefit receipt.

DEFINED CONTRIBUTION FINANCING ISSUES

While pension financing decisions for single-employer defined benefit plans are made by employers in the United States, such decisions for defined contribution plans are made primarily by employees.

Financial Literacy

A major weakness of the U.S. pension system's being largely based on 401(k) plans is that for it to function well it requires everyone to be an expert on financial market issues. With the move from defined benefit plans to 401(k) plans, increasingly workers must make financial decisions that affect the amount of resources they will have during retirement. Because few workers annuitize their 401(k) account balances at retirement, financial decisions must be made during retirement concerning the management of their accounts.

Many participants do not understand the basic mathematics of finance, do not know basic facts about different financial instruments and their levels of risk, and do not understand basic financial principles, such as risk diversification. For example, few Americans understand the relationship between a change in interest rates and the resulting change in the value of bonds (which is an inverse relationship). Surveys from other countries indicate that financial illiteracy is also a problem there (Lusardi 2007).

Financial literacy cannot be achieved by having a worker attend a couple of seminars. Some financial issues are complex. The economic literature on the effects of financial education indicates mixed success in affecting participant behavior by providing pension participants with more information about their investments. Clark et al. (2004) examine the effect of worker participation in financial education seminars on their retirement savings decisions. Individuals reported that they planned to change their retirement saving behavior based on knowledge gained at the seminar. Women were much more likely to alter their retirement goals and saving behavior than men. Lusardi (2004) also finds a positive effect of financial seminars on participants' decision-making, with the effect being particularly large for participants with less education.

Employee Contributions

Employee contributions to defined contribution plans exceed employer contributions by about 50 percent (USDOL 2008). Employee contributions are generally voluntary in 401(k) plans, but if the employee does not contribute, the employer also does not contribute. Some plans have established automatic enrollment, generally only for new employees, as a way of encouraging greater participation and greater employee contributions. However, some evidence suggests that when automatic enrollment is used, the default employee contribution rate is lower than if automatic enrollment had not been used.

Employee contributions to private sector defined benefit plans are rare because they are not tax deductible. Employee contributions to 401(k) plans, however, are tax deductible, and are a key source of financing. Once a worker has decided to participate in a 401(k) plan, the factor that has the largest effect on the amount of assets accumulated at retirement is how much has been contributed to the plan (Choi, Laibson, and Madrian 2004).

Workers and their families may have a difficult time determining their retirement income needs and how those needs translate into required pension contributions. Workers who underestimate their life expectancy will save insufficiently even if they are saving adequately for their perceived life expectancy. Even for workers with accurate estimates of their life expectancy, there is no simple answer to the question, "How much do I need to save for retirement?" Further, some workers may not contribute to 401(k) plans because they distrust financial institutions (Agnew et al. 2007).

Persistence of Contributions

Many employees do not consistently contribute to their defined contribution plans. While a number of studies have examined determinants of pension contributions in the United States and in the United Kingdom, far fewer have examined the persistency of workers' contributions. One study found that contributors generally persisted in making contributions, but that the contribution rate tended to vary over time. Smith, Johnson, and Muller (2004) use the Survey of Income and Program Participation (SIPP) to look at the persistency of employee contributions to 401(k) plans for up to 12 years. Nineteen percent of contributors were intermittent (i.e., had breaks in their contributions), 24 percent were rising contributors (increasing their contribution rate over time), 8 percent were falling contributors, and 23 percent were fluctuating contributors. Only 27 percent of individuals were steady contributors (i.e., made persistent contributions at a stable contribution rate). While the study finds that workers raise their contribution rates after reaching significant life course milestones, such as the birth of a child, it did not find changes in contributions associated with negative income shocks or changing consumption needs.

Paul Smith (2001), using a sample of tax returns from 1987 to 1996, finds a high rate of initial drop-off in pension contributions to Individual Retirement Accounts (IRAs). Of those contributing in 1987, only 45 percent were still contributing in 1992, and 40 percent contributed through 1996. Sarah Smith (2006) uses the British Household Panel Survey to examine the persistency of contributions to individual account defined contribution plans. Her results suggest a link between pension contributions and changes in an individual's income needs, as measured by financial circumstances, health, having a baby, and moving to a new house. Data from Canada indicate that between 1991 and 1993, about half of participants in Registered Retirement Savings Plans (RRSPs, similar in some respects to IRAs) contributed in only one or two of the three years (Maser 1995).

Policy Options

Several strategies may help in encouraging workers to contribute to their 401(k) plans.

Match. Offering an employer match for employee contributions increases participant contributions. One study finds that a 1 percent increase in the employer match rate led to a 0.25 percent increase in employee contributions (Engelhardt and Kumar 2003).

The "reverse match" is a policy innovation that places less responsibility on workers and more on employers. With a reverse match, the employer automatically contributes for all covered workers, assuring that all workers covered by the plan receive at least a minimum contribution to their plan. The employee then has the opportunity to contribute to the plan in proportion to the contribution of the employer, which could be on a dollar-for-dollar basis or at a higher employee contribution ratio of two-to-one. This type of option could be encouraged by companies' receiving regulatory relief from nondiscrimination testing. Nondiscrimination testing is required to assure that highly compensated employees do not benefit disproportionately from the pension plan.

Loans. Certain defined contribution plan features besides the match rate may affect the amounts participants contribute. One study found that the ability of plan participants to borrow from the plan increased their contributions by about 1 percentage point (Munnell, Sundén, and Taylor 2000). Another study found that participants in plans that allow borrowing contribute, on average, 35 percent more to their pension accounts than participants in plans that do not allow borrowing (GAO 1997).

Active enrollment. A study of one firm found that active enrollment with no default option, which is enrollment where employees are required to make a decision, improved participation but led to lower average contribution rates (Choi, Laibson, and Madrian 2006). Active enrollment participants had lower contribution rates than standard enrollment participants until the fourth year of participation. The explanation for the lower average contribution rates among active enrollment participants may be that active decisions bring employees with weaker saving motives into participation earlier in their tenure.

Autoescalation. One approach to encourage workers to increase their contributions automatically over time has been given the acronym SMarT—Save More Tomorrow (Thaler and Benartzi 2004). The Save More Tomorrow plan is designed to make it easier for workers to commit to participating in a 401(k) plan, to keep the commitment, and to increase their contributions over time. Under this plan, workers voluntarily agree to save part of their future wage increases—the first payroll deduction occurs a year following the date on which the commitment is made. In the future, today's workers generally will have higher wages than they do currently as they gain more experience, as productivity increases in the economy, and as the price level rises. Therefore, workers will face no absolute reduction in their nominal take-home pay in order to save more, as long as they receive wage increases that exceed the payroll deduction.

Wages increase in both nominal and real terms over time. This plan, however, is not dependent on real wage increases. It assumes that workers are subject to "wage illusion," meaning that they are fooled by inflation and misperceive nominal wage increases as real wage increases that raise their wages above the amount necessary to keep pace with inflation. Workers commit to save part of their nominal wage increase through their pension. Alternatively, autoescalation can occur as an increase in the percentage of wages contributed, regardless of whether future wages increase.

The SMarT approach has five essential aspects: 1) the increased contribution occurs one year following the decision to participate, 2) the increased contribution is taken out of increased income, 3) the increased income of the worker is measured in nominal terms, 4) participation is voluntary, and 5) participation is open to all workers who are eligible to participate in the pension plan.

In the firms that have implemented it, the SMarT approach has succeeded in encouraging workers to participate in 401(k) plans and to increase their contribution rate over time. In its first implementation, 78 percent of the people who were offered the option chose it, 98 percent of the people who took the option remained in it through two annual pay raises, and 80 percent remained in it through three annual pay raises (Thaler and Benartzi 2004).

Investment Choices

With the growth of 401(k) plans, workers' investment decisions play an increasingly important role in determining their retirement income. While traditional defined benefit plans are generally managed professionally, workers have responsibility for managing the investments in their 401(k) plans.

Traditional economic theory assumes that investors are rational wealth maximizers who do not make systematic errors. More recent economic theory and empirical studies, however, increasingly suggest otherwise. Many workers are uninformed about financial markets and lack interest in learning about them. Consequently, they may have biased or otherwise inaccurate information and make predictable mistakes. Not only are they poorly informed, they make irrational decisions when confronted with risk and uncertainty.

These information problems can be addressed by participant education (McCarthy and Turner 2000). However, information provided by financial service providers may be affected by the self-interest of the provider—for example, it may come with little or no discussion of the amount of fees the provider charges and the magnitude of the effect of fees on reducing account balances.

A different information problem is that economists do not agree on what workers should do concerning the management of their pension portfolios. A leading scholar in the field writes, "There is currently no consensus on the optimal asset allocation strategy for investors" (Poterba 2001). For example, most financial planners encourage workers to hold less risky portfolios as they approach retirement, but Bodie (1995) challenges that view.

Financial information may be so complex that, even if it is supplied, pension investors are unable to make rational choices (Barr 2001). This failure may occur in part because the long time horizon for young workers makes it difficult for them to understand the consequences of their choices.

Having a larger number of choices may seem to be desirable. It would better allow workers to find the options that fit their tastes or needs. However, the paradox of choice is that too many choices may immobilize some workers, because the increased number of choices make it difficult for them to decide. One possible explanation is information overload (Agnew and Szykman 2004). With information overload, workers find the problem too complex: there is too much information to understand, and so they take no action. Studies in psychology have shown that having more choices may render people worse off by hampering their ability to identify the option that best suits them (Iyengar and Lepper 2000).

The question arises as to how many options workers should be given in deciding how to invest their pension assets. An example of many choices leading workers to take the default is provided by the experience of the mandatory account system in Sweden. Workers there have a choice of more than 600 mutual funds. Yet only 18 percent of new entrants into the system in 2001 made an active choice; the rest allowed their contributions to be placed in the default fund, which is primarily invested in equities (Turner 2004).

Types of Investment Errors Pension Participants Make

The preceding section discussed reasons why participants in 401(k) plans make errors; this section discusses the types of investment errors they make. Pension investor errors include insufficient diversification and inappropriate portfolio adjustments (Turner 2003b).

Insufficient diversification. Failure to understand the basic principles of diversification may lead to investor errors. Specifically, this lack of understanding leads to insufficient diversification between stocks and other instruments such as bonds, and also to lack of diversification within the stock portion of the portfolio. Lucas (2000), examining the portfolios of 250,000 401(k) participants, found that, typically, participants hold poorly diversified portfolios, focusing mainly on stable value funds, large capitalization stock, and stock in their own company.

Naïve diversification occurs when participants attempt to diversify by dividing their investment portfolios equally among all available investment options offered by a pension provider. Thus, if a pension plan offers three options, participants would split their contributions in thirds. This results in an asset allocation to stocks and bonds that depends on the number and composition of stock and bond funds offered by the sponsoring employer (Benartzi and Thaler 2001). One study explored this pattern and found that only a small percentage of workers appear to manage their pension portfolios this way (Holden and VanDerhei 2001).

Overinvestment in the sponsoring employer's stock is another form of insufficient diversification. When workers invest their pension plans in company stock, if the company goes bankrupt they lose both their jobs and their pensions. In plans that allow employer stock as an investment option, 46 percent of participants (about 11 million employees) hold more than 20 percent of their account balance in employer stock (VanDerhei 2002). This sometimes occurs because the company provides the contribution match in company stock. Providing the match in company stock encourages workers to overweight their portfolios in company stock.

Men and lower-paid employees tend to invest a higher percentage of their portfolios in company stock than women and higher-paid employees (Holden and VanDerhei 2001; Lucas 2000). One study reports that when the employer match is in company stock, employees invest 29 percent of their own contributions in company stock. When the match is in cash, employees invest 18 percent of their own contributions in company stock (Benartzi 2001). This pattern is the reverse of what diversification would indicate employees should do. When employees overinvest in company stock, they take on risk that they otherwise could have diversified away, and that is thus not compensated by a higher expected return.

Some lawsuits have involved pension investment in employer stock. Employees have alleged that employers continued to require or permit investment in company stock, even after they realized that the company was having financial difficulties and its stock was no longer a good investment. Lawsuits have also alleged that employers provided incomplete or misleading information about the future prospects of the company. In some infamous instances, top executives have extolled company stock to their employees while dumping the stock they themselves held.

Inappropriate portfolio adjustments. Overconfidence in one's own abilities as an investor may lead to inappropriate portfolio adjustments. For example, overconfidence may cause some investors to trade aggressively. Barber and Odean (2001) define overconfident investors as those who ultimately lower their returns because of excessive trading. Males, and in particular young adult males, tend to suffer from overconfidence in their ability as investors. This may arise from a feeling by some of superior knowledge concerning the mathematics and concepts of finance (ibid.). Overconfidence tends to increase the amount of trading by individual investors, raising their transaction costs (Odean 1998). A study of trading at a discount brokerage firm (Barber and Odean 2001) found that single men traded 67 percent more than single women, lowering their returns net of trading costs by 1.4 percentage points per year compared to single women.

Inertia causes the opposite problem. It results in some investors not revising their initial investment allocation when their pension plan offers further options or changing to a more conservative portfolio as their expected retirement date approaches.

Inertia may result from workers not being willing to invest the time to learn how to make portfolio allocation changes. The perception that it is a time-consuming process to make changes may be a factor. Samuelson and Zeckhauser (1988) find that most pension participants in TIAA-CREF never make any adjustments to their asset allocation over their entire careers. Ameriks and Zeldes (2000) find that nearly half of TIAA-CREF participants made no changes over a ten-year period.

Failing to adjust one's portfolio can be a manifestation of inertia. Lucas (2000) finds that pension participants typically do not adjust their portfolios as their time horizon shortens. Portfolios are clustered at similar risk levels across age groups from ages 25 to 50. Equity exposure only decreases materially for the portfolio of the typical participant at age 60 and older.

Agnew (2004) examines the question of how pension participants adjust their asset allocation in response to changes in stock market prices. She finds that participants react to changes in the stock market when rates of return are low by moving out of stocks, which is the opposite of the strategy recommended—that of dollar cost averaging, where workers pick an investment allocation for their contributions and stick with it during the ups and downs of the market.

Policy Options

Several possible alternatives exist to having employees managing their own 401(k) plans.

1) The employer could manage the investments of the 401(k) plan. One convenience store chain provides a 401(k) plan for its employees with a trustee-investment structure, where all participants' accounts are aggregated and invested as one pool, and investment earnings are distributed to participants' accounts proportionate to their account balances (Demby 2002). This approach may be desirable in firms with lower-paid employees who may have less experience with and knowledge about investing. However, almost 70 percent of 401(k) participants direct the investment of their entire account balances, and an

additional 17 percent are able to direct the investment of a portion of the assets in their account (USDOL 2004).

2) Some plan sponsors have offered managed 401(k) plans, where employees can pay a fee based on their assets to have professional management of their investments (Maas 2005).

3) Employers can offer a default option, so that workers do not need to make an investment choice.

4) Because of an innovation in mutual funds, some mutual funds adjust their portfolios so that they become more conservative as the worker's expected retirement date approaches. These funds are called life-cycle funds, target-date funds, or age-based funds. These funds have been established to assist workers in managing their retirement funds in a manner that makes appropriate adjustments as retirement approaches. Funds differ in the "glide path" that they take in portfolio adjustments as retirement nears, with some funds being somewhat more conservative than others.

An approach to improving asset allocation in 401(k) plans would be to grant plan sponsors relief from some fiduciary liability if they offered participants alternatives to self-direction of investment choices. This could be done by offering diversified funds that would meet certain standards or by having professionally managed accounts (Gale et al. 2004).

Many workers end up in the default fund in a situation of automatic enrollment. Because of inertia, they then stay with that fund. Thus, the risk and expected return of the default fund warrant careful consideration. Some employers have chosen a low-risk money market portfolio as the default fund because they were afraid of lawsuits if participants lost money. That portfolio, however, would be too conservative for participants over the long run.

The United Methodist church pension fund has a complex default option. It is managed by a computer algorithm, where the default varies depending on the worker's age (single years of age demarcating each group), expected retirement date, and degree of risk aversion (three categories).

This discussion of common errors that individual pension investors make suggests a number of possible pension policy options. These options would restrict the range of investment choices, but such restriction in choice could reduce investor errors. The options are as follows:

1) Limit investment in individual stocks, including employer stocks.

2) Limit investment in mutual funds with narrow market focus.

3) Limit investment in highly risky assets such as high-tech stocks.

4) Offer professional management of pension investments as an option.

5) Educate workers on common investment mistakes.

6) Limit the frequency of investment changes.

7) Provide well-chosen default options that participants can use if they do not want to make an active choice.

8) Provide as an option a low-cost fund that tracks a major index, such as the S&P 500.

Investment and Administrative Fees

Fees in defined contribution plans pay for managing and investing the accounts. Employers typically hire service providers to operate the plans. Participants can be charged fees for establishing an account, contributing to an account, management of assets in an account, switching between funds provided by a single mutual fund provider, assistance from a financial adviser, withdrawals from an account, and termination of an account.

Generally, the largest fees arise from the costs of managing the investments. These fees include fees for active management, fees for transactions, and fees for the administration of the accounts. Fees for establishing and terminating an account are typically flat fees. A plan may be charged a fee for terminating its arrangement with a particular management company.

Because fees are often hidden, many people do not consider the management of a pension account as having a price. While proponents of defined contribution plans sometimes claim that those plans are more transparent to participants than defined benefit plans, the fees charged to participants in defined contribution plans are often far from transparent, and sometimes disclosures are blatantly misleading. An example of blatantly misleading disclosure is the practice of indicating that a number of services are "free," when in reality they are paid for by the participant out of general fees charged. Markets do not perform the function of assuring a competitive price when consumers do not understand the costs and have difficulty comparing across products.

One prominent mutual fund company reports on the account statements of the 401(k) funds it manages that it charges zero fees. Nowhere on the statement is it disclosed that the company is not reporting the fees charged through the expense ratio for the management of mutual funds. When questioned about this misleading reporting, company personnel stated that they did not report the fees charged through the expense ratio because that is disclosed in mutual fund prospectuses.

Pension participants pay billions of dollars in fees annually. The issue of fees would be of no consequence, however, if all mutual funds in which pension participants invested charged the same competitive price. In fact, mutual fund fees vary by an order of magnitude. There is also a wide range of fees charged when comparing across countries (Table 8.1). The wide variability in the level of fees charged for mutual funds, combined with little evidence that high-cost funds outperform low-cost funds net of fees (Choi, Laibson, and Madrian 2006), make adequate disclosure important for pension participants. As retirement income systems worldwide move toward defined contribution plans, the topic of fees becomes increasingly important in terms of its impact on national and individual retirement savings.

Because workers typically do not know how much they are paying in fees (Turner and Korczyk 2004), they are unable to make informed choices in managing their retirement income, resulting in a lack of competitive pressure on fees. With better disclosure of fees, pension participants would be better able to decide whether those fees were justified or whether they would prefer to use lower-fee providers. The excess fees paid, compared to what would be charged in a more com-

Table 8.1 Mutual Fund Expenses, Selected Countries, 2002 (% assets)

Country	Management expenses	Total expense ratio	Total shareholder costs
Australia	1.09	1.17	1.41
Canada	1.96	2.56	3.00
Sweden	1.32	1.37	1.51
United Kingdom	1.07	1.18	2.28
United States	0.62	1.11	1.53

NOTE: Management expenses include charges levied each year for management services. The total expense ratio includes all annual expenses charged against account balances, including investment expenses. Total shareholder costs include all annual expenses plus an annuitized form of loads assuming a five-year holding period.
SOURCE: Khorana, Servaes, and Tufano (2007).

petitive market with better informed participants, amount to money that is subtracted from retirement savings and is permanently lost from the retirement income system.

A principle of fee disclosure is that the nature of the disclosure should depend on the level of financial sophistication of the target audience. Behavioral economics has shown that the level of financial sophistication and interest in financial issues among pension participants with defined contribution pensions is fairly low. Fee disclosure for pension participants thus needs to be different from the disclosure that would be appropriate for professional investors.

Because the fees are paid primarily by participants in defined contribution plans rather than by plan sponsors, plan sponsors have less incentive than they do for defined benefit plans to provide tough oversight of fees. Furthermore, the usual conflict of interest arises between a for-profit service provider and a client. The for-profit service provider is interested in charging fees as high as possible, as is consistent with maximizing its profit.

Investments and Politics

In Chile and elsewhere, an argument has been made concerning individuals investing through defined contribution plans that when individuals invest in the stock market, and in that way invest in companies, it turns workers into capitalists. As capitalists, they are more likely to be pro-business, to be unsympathetic to labor unions, and to vote conservatively. This argument provides an ideological reason to favor or oppose plans such as 401(k) plans.

DEFINED BENEFIT FINANCING ISSUES

With the decline in defined benefit plans, a major issue in defined benefit plan financing is whether the employer decides to stop financing the DB plan.

Plan Freezes

Plan freezes are the most recent aspect of the decline in defined benefit plans. In the 2000s, a number of plan sponsors froze their defined benefit plans. With a hard freeze, which is the most common type (Munnell and Soto 2007), no new benefits are accrued in the plan. A freeze differs from a termination in that the plan is not shut down. A freeze provides the plan sponsor time to continue contributing to the plan to raise its funding, if it is underfunded. A plan freeze is a good alternative for a plan sponsor wishing to stop accrual of benefits but facing a plan that is underfunded. It is expected that frozen plans will be terminated when they have adequate funding. Plan freezes are occurring as a way for plan sponsors to end the financial commitments they have in defined benefit plans.

Sponsors of ongoing plans are required to report the projected benefit obligation (PBO) on their balance sheet. However, if they freeze the plan, they report the accumulated benefit obligation (ABO) on the balance sheet. The accumulated benefit obligation does not take into account pension liabilities arising from future benefit growth, and can be considerably lower than the projected benefit obligation. Thus, freezing a plan can give the impression of considerably improving the financial status of a firm.

Plan Buyouts

A new development in defined benefit plan financing is plan buyouts. Plan buyouts are targeted at frozen plans. A large financial institution, such as a bank, offers to buy the pension assets and liabilities of a frozen pension plan from the sponsoring employer. The financial institution then takes over responsibility for managing the plan.

Accounting Policy

Employers have expressed concern over two aspects of volatility in defined benefit pension financing: volatility in accounting values and volatility in contributions. Accounting policy is much more an issue for defined benefit plans than for defined contribution plans, which are by definition always fully funded. Accounting rule changes have no effect on the underlying economics concerning the costs and the volatility of costs of providing pensions, because accounting rules are just rules for measurement. Nonetheless, they are frequently mentioned as a cause of the recent decline in defined benefit plans. It is argued that investors have not understood the underlying economics of pensions, given the accounting information that has been available. The new accounting requirements apparently have real effects, however, because with the provision of information under the new rules, investors now view pension costs differently from before.

However, just as information in the old accounting rules could be misinterpreted, the same applies for the new rules. Volatility in plan liabilities does not reflect the underlying profitability of a firm. An argument can be made that pension plan volatility should be noted in accounting statements as an extraordinary event that does not affect the long-run profitability of the firm. With this approach, pensions would be listed in accounting statements separately from the accounting for the firm's business activities. This approach would make it easier for investors to evaluate the business performance of the firm without having to take into account the financial performance of the firm's pension fund.

Employer Contributions

Defined benefit pension financing in the United States depends largely on employer contributions. A reason frequently given for why employers have stopped providing defined benefit plans for their workers is the unpredictability and volatility in employer contributions. The unpredictability and volatility are partly the result of investing in risky financial markets, which causes the value of plan assets to vary. But they are also partly the result of government regulations that limit plan sponsors' ability to control the timing of their contributions.

Government regulations prohibit employers from making tax deductible contributions to a pension plan when the plan exceeds a certain level of overfunding. These rules are designed to limit the tax loss to the U.S. Treasury arising from the tax deduction taken for these contributions. Another effect, however, is that firms are prohibited from making contributions when the economy is booming and they have surplus funds to contribute. When the economy is slumping, and the value of the assets in the pension funds has fallen, companies are required to make contributions, even though the contributions come at a time when the companies themselves may be struggling and do not have surplus funds. Thus, the funding rules cause a temporal mismatch between when funding is required and when firms are best able to provide it. By preventing firms from contributing regularly, the rules make it impossible for firms to benefit from dollar cost averaging in funding pension plans.

The volatility of employer contributions could be reduced by allowing employers to contribute, at a minimum, 50 percent of normal cost, no matter what the plan funding level was. This would prevent large swings in contributions, because the floor on allowable contributions would be 50 percent of normal cost rather than zero. The need for this option depends on the extent of overfunding allowed. With the changes in maximum funding rules in the Pension Protection Act of 2006, the need for this option has been considerably reduced.

Employee Contributions

A distinctive feature of the financing of state and local government defined benefit plans is that employee contributions are used for financing, and in fact play a major role. Data from the BLS indicate that in 1998, some 78 percent of state and local government employees in defined benefit plans were in plans that required an employee contribution (BLS 2000).

In contrast, it is rare for employee contributions to be used for financing private sector defined benefit plans. In 2007, it was required for 3 percent of employees participating in private sector defined benefit plans in private industry (BLS 2007). Mandatory employee contributions were more common in the past, but for reasons that are unclear. A survey of the 50 largest pension sponsors in 1979 indicated that seven had defined benefit plans with mandatory employee contributions (Aaronson and Coronado 2005; Wyatt Company 1980).

The explanation for the difference between employee contributions in the private and public sectors is that employee contributions to state and local government plans are tax deductible, while they are not tax deductible for contributions to private sector plans. Thus, employee contributions are tax deductible both for 401(k) plans and for defined benefit plans for state and local government employees, but they are not tax deductible for employees' contributions to defined benefit plans in the private sector.

Employee tax deductible contributions could be allowed on a voluntary basis, so that employees could buy extra years of service to raise their benefit on a tax deductible basis. Alternatively, employers, in designing defined benefit plans, could be permitted to make employee contributions mandatory. Tax deductible employee contributions are permitted in Canada, the United Kingdom, and nearly all other countries with well-developed pension systems. In Canada, employee contributions cannot exceed half of the employee's annual benefit accrual (International Network of Pension Regulators and Supervisors and International Social Security Association 2003).

Mechanisms for Dealing with Imbalances in Pension Financing

In Japan, if a company is facing financial difficulties it can reduce the generosity of its defined benefit plan so long as employees agree to the reduction. This element of flexibility has been credited as being one reason why defined benefit plans have not declined in Japan, where they account for all but a small percentage of pension assets (Webman 2007). In the United States, employers cannot reduce the value of already accrued benefits in defined benefit plans. In reality, however, employers are able to do so when they lay off workers who have not reached the age of eligibility for retirement benefits.

Improving life expectancy among workers causes the increasing pension costs that so many nations face in their social security systems, but it also causes increasing costs for employers sponsoring defined benefit plans. For a defined benefit plan, increasing life expectancy after age 65 raises the costs of providing benefits because retired workers receive benefits for more years. The effect of this change over long periods of time can be large. Employers bear the risk of unexpected increases in life expectancy.

Changes in life expectancy generally occur slowly; perhaps this explains why pension researchers and policy analysts have tended to focus on other issues affecting pension liabilities, where short-term change is more dramatic. In most years, changes in interest rates have a larger effect on pension liabilities than do changes in life expectancy. Over a period of decades, however, the effect on pension costs of the increase in longevity can be considerable, while changes in interest rates generally have little effect because the increases and decreases offset each other. The short-run and long-run importance of the effects on pension cost of changes in life expectancy are thus quite different.

The Effect of Increases in Life Expectancy on Pension Costs

To estimate the effect of increased life expectancy on defined benefit pension costs, a simple calculation can be done. A 40-year-old man in 1980 was expected to live to 73 in the population life table for that year, but was expected to live to 78 in 2002 (Oster 2003). This difference in life expectancy would increase the expected length of retirement from 11 years to 16 years, assuming retirement at age 62—an increase in retirement years of 45 percent.

Making a few assumptions, we can estimate the effect of increased life expectancy on defined benefit pension costs. To calculate for a representative worker, assume a retirement age of 62 in both 1980 and 2002, a 4 percent interest rate for discounting the value of future benefits, and no inflation indexing of benefits past retirement. With these assumptions, the growth in life expectancy since 1980 has increased the nominal cost (measured as the present value of benefits) of providing a defined benefit plan per male participant by roughly 30 percent. A higher interest rate would yield a lower figure, while partial inflation indexing would yield a higher figure. This number is less than the 45 percent increase in years in retirement because of the effect of interest discounting, which reduces the present value of distant future benefits.

Thus, these calculations suggest that defined benefit costs have grown more than 1 percent a year per male participant because of the increase in life expectancy. While this figure is a rough approximation, it indicates the possible magnitude of the effect for a typical defined benefit plan. The "feminization" of some pension plans due to more women in the labor force would further increase cost, since that would further raise the average life expectancy of all participants in the plan.

Life expectancy increases in other countries provide further evidence as to the possible effects on pension plans. In the United Kingdom, the effect of increasing longevity on defined benefit plan costs is thought to be one of the reasons why employers are ending those plans in favor of defined contribution plans (Pensions Policy Institute 2007). According to a British survey, the primary reasons for large numbers of employers terminating defined benefit plans are increased costs due to lower real investment returns and greater longevity (White 2003).

The effect of increases in life expectancy on pension costs is greater in the United Kingdom than in the United States. It is greater because the United Kingdom mandates that pension benefits be price-indexed, which raises the cost of benefits provided to retirees at older ages. However, a similar, though smaller, effect of life expectancy on pension costs also occurs in the United States.

Demographers and actuaries foresee improvements in longevity continuing into the future. Pension policy for the long term needs to consider how defined benefit plans will deal with this increased cost. If nothing is done, increased longevity will result in continued increases in costs for employers.

Employers have a number of options to deal with this problem, though some good options are prevented by pension law (Muir and Turner 2007). Some employers cut future benefit accruals. Some employers are freezing or terminating their defined benefit plans and switching to defined contribution plans, where employer costs are immune to the glacial inevitability of increased longevity.

If pension law were changed so that accrued benefits could be expressed in terms of accrued present value, which is the way employers' liabilities are expressed, rather than as annual benefits, firms would be more encouraged to maintain defined benefit plans. Thus, a possible response to increasing life expectancy—which would require a change in ERISA—would be to index initial benefits received at retirement to increases in life expectancy. With this indexation, workers' lifetime expected present value of benefits would not be affected by increases in life expectancy, but annual benefits at the point of retirement would be cut to take into account life expectancy increases. To shield workers from demographic risk after retirement, no further benefit cuts would occur for improvements in life expectancy occurring during retirement. This approach is used in Sweden for its social security program.

With this proposal, the pension financing risk that, on average, people will live longer is largely shifted from employers to workers. Workers are arguably better able to bear this risk than employers because they are the beneficiaries of the increased life expectancy. They can adjust to the benefit cuts by working longer, which is facilitated by their increased life expectancy. Employers still bear the risk of improvements in life expectancy at older ages that occur after the cohort has reached the early retirement age.

Employers also would still bear idiosyncratic life expectancy risk, which is the risk that a particular worker will live longer than expected. While it is not possible for employers to reduce the cohort life expectancy risk by diversifying across cohorts because all cohorts share in the improvement, plan sponsors can reduce the idiosyncratic risk by diversifying across workers.

A similar approach for dealing with cohort life expectancy risk, which has the questionable advantage of being less transparent to workers, would be to index the plan's normal retirement age to increases in life expectancy. Doing so could also result in a reduction in annual benefits, while maintaining the lifetime expected value of benefits. This change is less transparent because it is presented to workers as an increase in the normal retirement age rather than a benefit cut.

Employer-Provided Plans with Automatic Adjustment Mechanisms

Countries generally have minimum funding requirements for defined benefit plans that require plan sponsors to contribute when the funding ratio falls below a fixed level. The use of other automatic adjustment mechanisms by employer-provided plans is rare but has been done, and may provide useful policy insights.

Iceland. Iceland has mandatory employer-provided hybrid pension plans that cover nearly all workers. Benefits are calculated based on a formula, but the level of benefits is reduced if the plans become underfunded. These plans have been funded by a contribution of 4 percent of wages by employees and 6 percent of wages by employers. In January 2007, the employer contribution was increased to 8 percent. In the past, these plans fixed the contribution rate and occasionally would adjust the generosity of benefits, depending on their funding level. Pension plans that were adequately funded could choose to put part of the contributions into a defined contribution plan. A law passed in January 2007 has made the reduction of benefits automatic when a plan is underfunded. If a plan is underfunded by 10 percent or more in a year or by 5 percent for five years in a row, it must reduce the generosity of its benefits (Social Security Administration 2007).

Netherlands. The ABP plan is the Dutch civil servants' pension fund. It is one of the largest pension plans in the world in terms of assets. It is a privatized plan for civil servants (de Jong and Turner 2001). This plan bases benefits on a benefit formula, as is done in defined benefit plans, but it is a hybrid plan. The plan is financed by contributions from employees and employers. Automatic adjustment occurs through changes in the contribution rate of workers and the indexation rate of benefits in payment for pensioners.

The Board of Governors, which runs the system, changes contribution and indexation rates annually based on the investment performance of the pension fund, using a formula called the contribution/indexation matrix. The calculation of the contribution rates and indexation uses a procedure that smoothes the fluctuations in the rates so that the annual variation is generally small. The formula determines by how much benefit indexation must decline and contribution rates must increase during periods of weak financial performance, and conversely, by how much indexation can increase and contribution rates can decrease during good times. The ABP's Board of Governors is able to take other factors into account besides the matrix, such as general economic conditions and forecast pay trends, so the adjustment is not fully automatic.

United Kingdom. The United Kingdom has a type of plan called a With-Profits Pension Annuity. With this type of annuity, the individual participant chooses an anticipated bonus rate (ABR). If the participant chooses an ABR of zero percent, the participant is guaranteed that each year's benefit in retirement will be no lower in nominal terms than the starting benefit—this, in other words, is the guaranteed minimum benefit. If the underlying investments perform sufficiently well, the participant will receive higher benefits. If the participant chooses an ABR higher than zero percent, the starting benefit will be higher, but the participant risks that future benefits will be reduced at some point, although to no lower than the initial benefit had an ABR of zero percent been chosen. Rather than the plan's payments varying with the rate of return received each year, however, the plan smoothes the benefit payments over time.

The main factor affecting bonuses is the rates of return earned on the fund's assets. The bonuses paid also depend on the longevity experience of the plan's participants relative to assumed longevity experience. The bonuses received are divided into regular bonuses, which change once a year, and additional bonuses, which change more frequently and may change by greater amounts than the regular bonuses. However, both the regular and additional bonuses are affected by the policy of smoothing payments over time. Insurance companies that provide these annuities take an annual charge related specifically to providing the guarantee. One company takes a yearly charge of 75 basis points for the guarantee, with the charge being reviewed annually. Participants are permitted at any time to convert to a fixed income annuity (Aviva 2009).

A different form of self-adjustment plan has been developed recently. In the United Kingdom, employee contributions to DB plans are tax deductible. The new arrangement adopted by some plans ties the level of employee contributions to the improvement in life expectancy at retirement age for participants in the plan (Pension Protection Fund and Pensions Regulator 2006).

CONCLUSION

While coverage in defined benefit plans has declined dramatically in the United States and even more so in the United Kingdom, the decline has been modest in Canada and Ireland. Thus, international experience casts doubt on the view held by many that defined benefit plans are dinosaurs and their decline and extinction is inevitable. In both Canada and Ireland, and indeed in most countries with defined benefit plans, employees make tax deductible contributions to those plans.

A factor that appears to have played a role in the decline in defined benefit plans has been the increase in life expectancy, since the defined benefit plans don't have the flexibility to deal readily with this continued increase in cost. In the United States, some plans have reduced their generosity, but generally they make this change only for new hires, which can make date of hire an important issue for some workers. A possible policy innovation, following the notional defined contribution plan in Sweden, would be to permit life expectancy indexing of benefits at retirement. Thus, each year, the generosity of the plan would be adjusted downward slightly to reflect the trend toward greater life expectancy. Under U.S. law, this innovation would not be allowed because it would violate the anticutback rule. The anticutback rule is defined in terms of annual benefits. If it were redefined to take an economist's perspective and use lifetime benefits as the measure, life expectancy indexing would not constitute a cutback in lifetime benefits.

One of the problems with defined contribution plans that has received little notice in the United States is the persistency of contributions. Many workers do not consistently contribute to their plans, resulting in reduced account balances at retirement. Part of the lack of persistency results from job change, but it occurs even among workers who remain with the same employer.

To reduce the volatility and timing problem of employer contributions for defined benefit plan funding, both the maximum and minimum contribution requirements could be eased. First, plans could be allowed to contribute 25 percent of normal cost in any year, regardless of the level of funding. This proposal would set the floor on contributions allowed at 25 percent of normal costs rather than zero. Thus, plan sponsors would be allowed to contribute every year—the pattern desired for pension plans, which are ongoing entities.

To ease the requirements on the minimum required contributions, plan sponsors could be allowed a longer period over which to amortize unfunded liabilities. For example, they could be allowed a period of 15 years, rather than the current seven years set by the Pension Protection Act of 2006.

9
Pension Benefit Policy

The Search for Lost Pensions and Other Issues

The ultimate goal of pension policy is that workers receive adequate and secure pension benefits. This chapter first considers the payment of benefits from defined contribution plans, then from defined benefit plans. Issues affecting both types of plans, including lost pensions, are discussed last. While defined benefit plans traditionally have provided benefits as annuities, most 401(k) plans do not provide that option. Why they do not, and other issues related to annuitization of defined contribution plans, are considered separately in the next chapter.

DEFINED CONTRIBUTION PLANS

The retirement financing problems facing retirees relying solely on defined contribution plans as their employer-provided pension plan differ considerably from the ones they faced as workers. As retirees, they need to figure out how to manage the spend-down of their assets. During retirement, they are faced with complex issues concerning how to manage various risks. One strategy policy analysts have taken in reforming defined contribution plans is to attempt to make them more like defined benefit plans.

When Congress passed ERISA in 1974, the situation was different. People who were covered by pensions had defined benefit pensions that provided them with annuities. Because their pension was annuitized, they did not face issues about how to manage the spend-down of their pension assets.

Forms of Benefit Payment

Defined contribution plans can pay old-age benefits in any of five basic ways, or in a combination of the five ways: 1) a lump sum, 2) a life annuity, 3) a phased withdrawal (based on annual recalculation of life expectancy), 4) installment (term certain) payments, and 5) ad hoc (unscheduled) withdrawals. A lump sum provides no insurance against the risk of outliving one's resources. An annuity is a financial instrument that converts an account balance into a stream of periodic payments. With life annuities, workers receive periodic payments that continue until death. Life annuities, referred to here simply as annuities, insure workers against running out of money if they live longer than they expect.

With phased withdrawal, workers receive benefits each year that are based on their remaining life expectancy and the amount in their individual accounts. With phased withdrawals, a retiree may wish to receive a fixed real amount each month in order to ensure a steady stream of resources to finance retirement expenditures. A problem with this approach is that when the same amount is withdrawn each month from an equity mutual fund, more shares are sold when the price is low than when it is high. Thus, with periodic withdrawals there is a trade-off between having a steady flow of withdrawals and maximizing the lifetime value of the withdrawals.

With installment or term certain payments, payments are made at a fixed rate (a specified dollar amount) until the account balance is reduced to zero. Alternatively, payments are made for a fixed number of years in an amount that varies with investment performance.

Income Redistribution

A negative aspect of the move toward defined contribution plans that has received little attention is its effect on the inequality of resources for older persons. The growth of defined contribution plans and the decline of defined benefit plans has resulted in a large increase in the inequality of pension wealth holdings among workers (Wolff 2007). This change has occurred in part because lower-income workers who would automatically be included as participants in defined benefit plans are not opting to participate in 401(k) plans. This change has left many older workers unprepared for retirement.

Defined benefit plans that are based on the final three or five years of earnings reward high achievers who rise to the top of their organizations. By comparison, defined contribution plans and career average defined benefit plans are relatively more favorable to low achievers who have less of an increase in earnings over their careers.

Loans

In the United States, plans wishing to do so may provide the option for participants to take loans from the plan. For example, a 401(k) participant could take a loan from his plan, repaying the loan with interest over time. Thus, one of the assets of the plan becomes the interest-bearing loan to the participant. The appeal to the participant is that the loan is generally at a lower rate than he could otherwise obtain. The disadvantage is that the participant's 401(k) account is invested in an asset (the loan) that is paying a low rate of return.

Because of the low rate of return received, and the propensity for participants not to repay the loans, policy analysts often oppose the idea. However, some participants possibly would not have participated without that feature, and a loan from a pension plan may be preferable to carrying an account balance on a credit card.

In other countries, loans generally are not allowed. For example, in Germany the tax subsidy for the pension plan is viewed as being for the purpose of encouraging retirement savings, and not to be used for other purposes. Similarly, loans to participants from their plans are not allowed in Australia or the United Kingdom.

Women's Issues

The pension problems of particular concern to married women are largely benefits issues. These issues arise concerning the spousal benefit rights of divorced women and widows. The assets in 401(k) plans are not automatically split at divorce. The disposition of those assets is the subject of negotiation. Spouses typically are less well protected as survivors by 401(k) plans than by defined benefit plans. Whereas in defined benefit plans the spouse has a right to a joint and survivor annuity unless the spouse waives that right by signing a notarized statement, 401(k) plans provide little protection of survivors. Most 401(k) plans pay benefits as a lump sum, with no benefit rights for spouses. The exception is that they provide survivors' protection for spouses if the participant dies before retirement. In addition, spouses may inherit the remaining account balance or the remaining assets from the lump sum.

Retirement income policy in the United States has not caught up with the growing role of 401(k) plans. It continues to regulate 401(k) plans as though they were supplementary to defined benefit plans, which is how they began in the early 1980s. It treats 401(k) plans as savings plans rather than as pension plans. An example of this policy lag concerns the provision of benefits to women as spouses, including as current spouses, as divorced spouses, and as widows.

The U.S. pension system no longer provides women as spouses the protection it once accorded them when defined benefit plans were prevalent. A worker generally can take the benefit from a 401(k) plan as a lump sum, without the consent of his spouse. A husband anticipating a divorce can shelter his 401(k) assets from division in a divorce settlement by taking a lump sum and spending the money. A widow may receive no benefit from her husband's 401(k) plan because he has taken the money as a lump sum and spent it. This aspect of 401(k) plans may lead to increasing poverty among older women in the future.

A policy issue to be considered is whether all 401(k) plans should be regulated as if they were the primary plan, or whether 401(k) plans should be regulated differently when they are the only plan provided by an employer, as compared to when they are a supplementary plan with a defined benefit plan being the primary plan. Currently, 401(k) plans are regulated more like savings plans than like pension plans.

While husbands and wives in healthy marriages presumably treat their income and assets generally as held in common, pension plans are designed to be held in the name of one person. That could be changed to potentially benefit women through a couple of ways: 1) by allowing spouses to designate their IRA and 401(k) contributions to go into the account of the other person, and 2) by allowing spousal IRAs that would be owned jointly.

DEFINED BENEFIT PLANS

The Progressivity of Benefits

Many lower-income workers participating in defined benefit plans receive reduced benefits because their plan is integrated with Social Security. In 2005, 28 percent of workers in private industry that were participating in a defined benefit plan were in plans that were integrated with Social Security. Integration means that benefits were reduced for lower-wage workers to take into account that their replacement rate from Social Security is higher than it is for higher-income workers (BLS 2007). Integration with Social Security reduces the pension benefits of lower-wage workers and offsets the progressivity built into the Social Security benefit formula.

The private pension system is often viewed as favoring middle- and higher-income workers. Those workers have higher participation rates than lower-income workers, perhaps in part because the tax subsidy they receive per pension dollar is greater because of their higher marginal income tax rates. They are also less affected by integration with Social Security. Viewed this way, the private pension system appears to unduly favor the upper-income segments of society.

However, when viewed within the context of the retirement income system, the picture is different. When Social Security old-age benefits and disability benefits are also considered, the system is considerably more balanced in the way it treats different income segments of U.S. society.

Life Expectancy Indexing of Benefits

A factor that appears to have played a role in the decline in defined benefit plans has been the increase in life expectancy: the defined benefit plans do not have the flexibility to deal readily with this continued increase in cost. In the United States, some plans have adjusted downward their generosity, but generally this change is only done for new hires.

A possible policy innovation, following the notional defined contribution plan in Sweden, would be to permit life expectancy indexing of benefits at retirement. Each year, as another cohort reaches retirement age, the generosity of benefits is reduced slightly to take into account the continued improvement in life expectancy. The adjustment does not reduce expected lifetime benefits.

Life expectancy risk can be divided into the idiosyncratic risk that a particular individual will live longer than expected and the cohort risk that an entire cohort on average will live longer than expected. Annuity providers are able to deal with idiosyncratic risk by pooling it across large numbers of people, effectively diversifying it away. However, cohort risk cannot be pooled. Longevity bonds would provide a hedge, but a market for them has not developed. Longevity bonds have a higher payout when the percentage of a cohort that is surviving is higher. Life expectancy indexing of benefits is one way of dealing with this risk. The idiosyncratic risk is borne by the annuity provider, who can diversify it away. The cohort risk is borne by workers, who are the beneficiaries of the improved life expectancy.[1]

Life expectancy indexing of benefits would shift onto workers the systematic life expectancy risk, which is the risk that an entire birth cohort will live longer on average. The plan sponsor bears the idiosyncratic life expectancy risk, which is the risk that a particular individual will live longer than expected.

An issue arises for plan sponsors as to who would generate the life expectancy index to be used. Department of Labor regulations may need to resolve that issue, setting a required index or a minimum standard.

Under U.S. law, this innovation would not be allowed because it would violate the anticutback rule. The anticutback rule is defined in terms of annual benefits. If it were redefined to take an economist's perspective and use lifetime benefits as the measure, life expectancy indexing would not constitute a cutback in lifetime benefits.

Other Aspects of Benefits

The defined benefit system would have greater flexibility in meeting the needs of workers if they had greater choice in setting the level of their benefits. If tax deductible employee contributions were allowed for U.S. private sector defined benefit plans, that would facilitate another feature whereby employees would be allowed to make voluntary tax deductible contributions, subject to limits, to purchase additional benefits. This arrangement is permitted in Canada. This feature, however, may disproportionately benefit high-income workers.

Without price indexing, inflation erodes the real value of benefits. Few U.S. private sector defined benefit pensions provide price indexing, and those that do generally set a cap, such as no more than a 3 percent increase in benefits per year. An alternative to price indexing benefits is to choose an annuity that provides automatic annual increases in benefits—for example, one that has benefits rising by 3 percent a year regardless of the rate of inflation.

ISSUES AFFECTING BOTH DEFINED CONTRIBUTION AND DEFINED BENEFIT PLANS

The Adequacy of Benefits for the Old-Old

Both defined benefit and defined contribution plans have shortcomings in providing benefits for people who survive to their 80s and older. Pensions that were adequate at retirement often are inadequate at older ages.

Defined benefit plans tend to be inadequate for persons in their 80s and older because they rarely provide cost-of-living adjustments. Thus, their real value is eroded over time by inflation. Even a relatively low inflation rate of 3 percent can have a substantial effect on the real value of benefits over a period of two decades.

Defined contribution plans tend to provide inadequate benefits for people in their 80s and older for two reasons. First, they are rarely annuitized. People who live longer than they expected are particularly at risk of running out of money in their pension accounts. Second, for the relatively few who do annuitize, just as for defined benefit plans, rarely are the annuities adjusted for inflation.

A policy option could be to require that both defined benefit and defined contribution plans provide at least a minimum amount of price indexation. That requirement exists in the United Kingdom. However, it is expensive and may be a reason for employers ceasing to provide plans. When benefit adjustments are flexible, the cost of providing price indexation can be borne by retirees through a reduction in their initial benefits.

Life Expectancy Indexing of Ages in Benefits Law

A number of fixed ages appear in pension law governing the receipt of benefits by workers and retirees. With continued increases in life expectancy, a possible policy option would be to index these ages so that they would increase with increases in life expectancy at older ages.

Workers must begin receiving benefits from Individual Retirement Accounts (IRAs) by April 1 of the year following the year they reach age 70 ½. The 70 ½ rule also applies to other pensions, unless the worker is still working for the employer providing the pension. Workers pay a 10 percent penalty if they begin receiving 401(k) benefits before age 59 ½ while they are still working for the employer providing the pension. Workers cannot receive benefits from a defined benefit plan while still working for the sponsoring employer until age 62.

Recognizing that continued improvements in life expectancy mean that fixed ages occur relatively earlier in the life span, these ages could be indexed to improvements in life expectancy. Such indexing could be a year-for-year increase, but recognizing that retirement is roughly a third of adult life, the indexing could be a two-year increase in pension ages for every three-year increase in life expectancy. That type of partial indexing would keep retirement periods the same length, on average, relative to preretirement periods.

Preretirement Withdrawals for Medical Expenses, Educational Expenses, or Purchasing a Home

Sweden, Chile, Canada, and the United Kingdom prohibit preretirement withdrawals from pension plans. Retirement benefits are locked in until retirement. In the United States, 401(k) plans permit preretirement withdrawals for educational expenses, purchase of a first home, and for high medical expenses. Other things being equal, such withdrawals reduce the amount of retirement savings that workers have. However, it is argued that workers would be less likely to participate in 401(k) plans were such options not available.

Lump Sum Benefits

Lump sum benefits are popular with many retirees. Retirees like the liquidity and financial control that these benefits provide. However, these benefits are not popular with policy experts. Policy experts tend to favor annuities because of the insurance protection they provide against outliving one's resources because of poor planning or from living longer than expected. The two types of benefits, however, are not mutually exclusive. Lump sum benefits can be paid using a part of the funds in an individual account, with the remainder paid as an annuity or a phased withdrawal. Some plans do not provide the option of partial payment, but public policy could be changed, requiring that option to be provided.

Sweden does not permit lump sum benefits to be paid from its mandatory individual account pensions. Chile permits lump sum benefits as an option for taking a part of the account balance. Chilean workers may withdraw a lump sum benefit from their individual account if the remaining amount is sufficient so that the participants can meet one of two conditions: they purchase an annuity at least equal to 120 percent of the minimum guaranteed pension, or they take scheduled withdrawals that are at least 70 percent of the participant's price-indexed covered wages. Few Chilean workers have met these requirements. In Chile, insurance company sales agents in firms charging high sales commissions have provided unofficial lump sum payments of part of the sales commissions, permitting workers to convert part of their individual accounts to a lump sum payment (James, Martinez, and Iglesias 2006).

In the United Kingdom, until 2006 workers had to take the entire account balance of a contracted-out personal pension as an annuity. Since 2006, it has been possible to take up to 25 percent of the account balance as a lump sum, which is consistent with the treatment of other personal pensions.

Lost Pensions

Lost pensions are an issue that affects both defined benefit and defined contribution plans but tends to be more of a problem for defined benefit plans. Over the past two decades, changes in pension law have lowered years of employment required for pension vesting. A worker with a pension plan can be entitled to a benefit after five years or less of full-time covered work. Workers immediately vest in their own contributions. Worker contributions have become increasingly common with the growth of 401(k) plans, and occur in some defined benefit plans, though that is unusual in the United States. Thus, workers who change jobs several times over their careers may be eligible for pensions from several former employers.

In a dynamic economy, each year many firms dissolve, file for bankruptcy, are bought, merge, or change their names. The employer that a former employee had worked for 20 years ago may have moved, may no longer be in business, or may be doing business under a different name. If the company was sold or merged, the pension plan may have been taken over by the new company or may have been terminated. Consequently, when a worker who has worked for more than one employer approaches retirement, he may not know where to apply for the pensions to which he is entitled.

In 1992, in part because of this problem, Congress directed the Administration on Aging to start several pension counseling projects around the country. Established in 1993, the Massachusetts Pension Assistance Project was one of the pilot projects. In 1998, this project expanded its scope to cover all six states in the New England region and became the New England Pension Assistance Project (NEPAP).

Lost pensions are a potentially serious problem for millions of pension participants. As of 1998, 16 million people, even though they had left private sector defined benefit and defined contribution plans that included deferred vested benefits, were not receiving benefits (USDOL 2002). That figure would be higher now because of the growth of the labor market over time. This situation of a person having a deferred future claim on a pension plan from a former employer arises both in defined contribution and defined benefit plans but occurs more commonly in defined benefit plans. In 1998, even though fewer than half as many workers were active participants in defined benefit plans (23.0 million) as in defined contribution plans (50.3 million), more participants who had separated from employers had vested rights in defined benefit plans (9.3 million) than in defined contribution plans (6.9 million) [USDOL 2002]. In addition, for workers changing jobs between

1993 and 1998 the Form 5500 data indicate that 25 percent of the plans in existence in 1993 had terminated by 1998, while another 10 percent of plans had been created and terminated within that period (Perun and Valenti 2008).

No accurate statistics exist concerning the total amount of unclaimed pension benefits in U.S. pension funds. However, evidence suggests that in the United Kingdom it lies within a wide range—from £10 billion to £77 billion, or roughly $18–$140 billion (Maunsell 1998). It is difficult to apply this evidence to the United States because of differences in number of workers, pension coverage rate, and income level, and because of fluctuations in the exchange rate. Nonetheless, this evidence for the United Kingdom, which has a labor force about 20 percent as large as that of the United States, suggests that the amount of lost pension money in the United States could be substantial. Because formal assistance by the government to people seeking lost pensions is greater in the United Kingdom than in the United States (Blake and Turner 2002), we would expect the lost pension problem in the United States to be proportionally larger. As a rough estimate based on the British data, a minimum figure would be about $50 billion in lost pension money in the United States. While it is difficult, if not impossible, to obtain a precise estimate, the total amount lost clearly is in the billions of dollars. Thus, this problem is a serious problem among pension participants who change jobs.

Lost Pensions Policy in the United States

In the United States, it is up to the individual workers who have changed jobs to find their former pension plans. To receive a benefit, the worker needs to contact the former employer to apply for the benefit, but this task may involve tracing the connection back through a complicated series of corporate mergers and bankruptcies.

Employees can start by contacting the Social Security Administration to get a copy of their Social Security earnings record. This record will provide their former employer's federal ID number, which may help in tracking down the plan.

The Pension Benefit Guaranty Corporation (PGBC), which insures most private sector defined benefit plans in the United States, can assist in finding pension plans that are ongoing defined benefit plans paying pension benefit insurance premiums. It also maintains a Pension Search database that will assist workers whose lost defined benefit plans have terminated because of insufficient funding and have been taken over by the PBGC.

Lost Pensions in the United Kingdom

The United Kingdom has established a national pension plan registry so that workers need only contact a single source to trace a lost pension. Workers can make a request by telephone, mail, or the Internet. The Occupational Pensions Regulatory Authority (OPRA) was established to help make sure occupational pension plans were secure for workers. The Pension Schemes Registry (PSR) is now part of OPRA. ("Scheme" is the British pension terminology for "plan.") The PSR is designed to help workers track down their pensions with former employers. Workers in the United Kingdom filing a tracing request form with the PSR are asked information such as the full name and last known address of the former employer. The tracing service then tries to find a current address for the pension fund. It provides this service without fee to persons requesting it. While the British government maintains the PSR on the grounds that it provides an important social service, the cost of the PSR is covered by a levy collected from each of the registered pension plans in the UK.

At regular intervals, the Savings, Pensions, and Share Schemes Office (SPSS) sends the PSR details about new plans that have been granted "exempt approved" status.[2] Active plans are required to provide updated information to the registry at the same time that they pay their annual levy. The two functions are interrelated, in that at the time of collection of the levy, plans are reminded that they should provide updated information to the registry.

The success rate for people contacting the registry varies from year to year but has been uniformly high. Between fiscal years 1991–1992 and 1997–1998, the registry had a total of 74,605 requests, an annual average of almost 11,000. A survey conducted by the PSR indicated that 34 percent of those who used its tracing service received some financial benefit, and the PSR has an 85 percent success rate in tracing contact details (Maunsell 1998, 1999). In fiscal year 1999–2000, the service received 18,000 requests and had a 95 percent success rate in tracing lost pensions. The number of requests increased to 21,000 in 2000–2001, and the success rate was 92 percent.

Lost Pensions in Australia

Australia has taken a different approach. To deal with the lost pension problem, the Australian Tax Office (ATO) maintains a Lost Members Register. Instead of registering plans, it registers members that plans are unable to locate. All regulated pension funds are required to provide details of members with whom they have lost contact. Providers of individual retirement savings accounts (such as IRAs) are also required to register the names of account holders whom they are unable to contact. If a worker is unable to contact a former pension plan, the worker can contact the Australian Tax Office (2001). That worker's plan will presumably have contacted the ATO because of the inability of the plan to contact the worker. Thus, through the Lost Members Register a connection can be made between the worker and the plan. The Lost Members Register database is searched by government bureaucrats on behalf of persons making an inquiry. Plans that are able to contact all members are not required to contact the registry. If a person's pension money has not been claimed by the time he or she reaches age 65, the money is transferred to the Unclaimed Money Register, where it can still be claimed.

Characteristics of People with Lost Pensions

Because little is known empirically about the characteristics of participants with lost pensions, or the relative importance of various causes of the problem, we created a data set to study lost pensions (Bruce, Turner, and Lee 2005). The data set uses three years of pension counseling cases from the New England Pension Assistance Project (NEPAP). To our knowledge, this is the first empirical study of the lost pension problem in the United States.

Characteristics of Clients and Plans

Lost pensions constitute a problem that is more likely to occur for participants in small plans than those in large plans. Changes that caused the employing company to cease to exist under its original name are also an important factor resulting in lost pensions. In 24 percent of lost pension cases, the company had gone out of business. Of the cases in the data set where the company had gone out of business, almost all (32 out of 33) involved a lost pension. In 47 percent of the lost pension cases, the company had been sold or had merged with another company. Lost pension cases are more likely to involve defined benefit plans than defined contribution plans.

How Effective Is Existing Government Policy?

The PBGC seeks people who are eligible for pension benefits due them under plans it has taken over because of the inability of the sponsoring employer to adequately fund the plan. In most of the cases involving lost pensions in the survey data, the PBGC was not involved. The PBGC had taken over the plan, because of the underfunding or termination of the plan, in only 11 percent of the lost pension cases. If the PBGC's efforts to locate plan participants of the plans it administers were effective, then individuals would not seek out pension counseling projects to assist in locating the plans. Since the vast majority of lost pension cases did not involve plans taken over by the PBGC, the data indicate that the limited scope of the PBGC's program to find lost pensioners does not address the full extent of the problem.

People who are eligible for deferred vested pension benefits and who have applied for Social Security benefits should have received two notices that could help them locate their pension. First, when they left their employer they should have received from the employer a notice that they were eligible for a deferred vested pension benefit. Second, they should have received from the Social Security Administration a notice triggered by their application for Social Security benefits that indicated they might be eligible for a deferred vested pension benefit. That notice would contain information about the pension plan's location when they left it.

These notices of entitlement to a pension do not appear to be a significant reason for clients to come to the project for help in finding a pension. The most common reason clients give for looking for a pension is that the client has reached retirement age. While in principle,

100 percent of participants with a lost pension would have received a deferred vested pension notice from their employer, only 16 percent of the lost pension cases report having such a notice in the file. The data do not permit an evaluation of the extent to which people received the notice, nor, among those people, how useful the information was, so it is not possible to judge definitively how useful the notices are. Nonetheless, this percentage indicates the extent to which NEPAP could use the notice to find a lost pension. The delay between the time when this notice is given (when the participant leaves the company's employment) and the point in time when the participant is looking for the pension (retirement age) may account for the apparent lack of usefulness of this notice for people using the pension assistance program.

The data also suggest that government-mandated notice policies in this area have been ineffective in helping the people who use pension assistance programs. In contrast, the pension counseling project was successful in locating pension plans in over 80 percent of the lost pension cases and was able to obtain a benefit in 40 percent of the lost pension cases. The data suggest that individuals can use assistance in locating their pension plans when their former employers have moved or gone out of business.

CONCLUSION

Retirement income policy in the United States has not caught up with the growing role of 401(k) plans. It continues to regulate 401(k) plans as though they were supplementary to defined benefit plans, which is how they began in the early 1980s. It treats 401(k) plans as savings plans rather than as pension plans. An example of this policy lag concerns the provision of benefits to women as spouses, including as current spouses, as divorced spouses, and as widows.

Both defined benefit and defined contribution plans do not provide indexed annuities to deal with inflation. Workers often have the choice of escalating annuities but rarely choose them. The United Kingdom has mandated inflation protection of benefits, up to a minimum level of inflation. These types of mandates protect workers from the eroding effects of inflation, but they are expensive for employers to provide or for workers to choose. When they are an option in defined contribution plans, the worker must accept a substantially lower initial benefit.

The lost pension problem is a problem for workers who are laid off or who change jobs. It can be difficult to track down a pension from a former employer, particularly if that employer has gone out of business. Both the United Kingdom and Australia have gone further than has the United States in assisting people facing this problem. A national registry, perhaps as an expansion of the registry maintained by the Pension Benefit Guaranty Corporation, would be a major improvement in this area.

Notes

1. A study has attempted to quantify the aggregate mortality risk, which is the risk that an entire cohort will live longer than predicted (Friedberg and Webb 2005). The study estimates that a markup of the annuity premium by 4.3 percent would reduce the probability of insolvency from cohort mortality risk to 5 percent, and a markup of 6.1 percent would reduce the probability of insolvency to 1 percent.
2. The role of the SPSS is to grant "exempt approved" status to pension schemes; i.e., it approves pension schemes for the purpose of enjoying tax relief on contributions into the schemes and also approves income and capital gains tax exemption on the assets in the pension fund. The SPSS is part of the Inland Revenue, the UK's tax authority.

10
The Decline in Annuitization
and How to Reverse It

Annuities are generally not provided to participants in 401(k) plans.[1] This is a key shortcoming of 401(k) plans. Annuities are not required in 401(k) plans, making those plans practically indistinguishable from tax-favored retirement savings accounts, rather than making them seem like pension plans. With the decline in defined benefit plans, one of the goals of some policy analysts has been the "DB-ification" of 401(k) plans, meaning that 401(k) plans would be structured so that they have some of the desirable features of defined benefit plans, including providing annuities. Because annuities are a complex subject, they are treated here, in a separate chapter from other benefits issues, which were discussed in the previous chapter.

The goal of pension policymakers is to enable retirees to achieve financial security. With continued increases in life expectancy and poor planning by some, retirees risk outliving their assets. Retirement benefits generally are intended to protect against this risk. This risk can be managed through a life annuity, which provides a guaranteed stream of income that the recipient cannot outlive. While Social Security provides lifetime, inflation-indexed benefits, those benefits do not provide enough income for most retirees to maintain their preretirement standard of living. Defined benefit plans traditionally have provided their benefits as an annuity, but those plans are declining in importance.

This chapter surveys the variety of annuity payout options available in defined contribution systems. It provides examples of payout options from Sweden, the United Kingdom, and Chile and compares those to options in the United States. These countries are chosen because together they provide a wide variety of payout options under different institutional arrangements. The Swedish system, the newest of the three, has been designed with an attempt to learn from the experience of other defined contribution systems. The British and Chilean systems have substantial experience in paying benefits, and those systems have evolved over time.

Defined contribution plans accrue benefits in the form of an account balance and typically in the United States pay benefits as a lump sum or as a series of withdrawals. Thus, with the growth of defined contribution plans and the decline in defined benefit plans, the extent to which workers annuitize retirement income is expected to decline over time, unless workers start obtaining annuities from 401(k) plans. While economists and others have predicted that the growth of 401(k) plans would lead to the growth of the use of annuities (Brown et al. 2001), only 10 percent of individuals with defined contribution plans annuitized their account balances when terminating employment, both at ages 60 to 64 and at ages 65 to 69 (Gale and Dworsky 2006). However, Holden (2007) finds that 23 percent of those having the option to take an annuity do so, while 47 percent take a lump sum, 26 percent defer taking a distribution, and 10 percent take installment payments. Selectivity may affect these statistics, however, as annuities may be offered in workplaces where workers have greater demand for them. A different study (Medill 2008) finds that 11 percent of people in one plan take an annuity when given the option.

ANNUITY BASICS

An annuity is a financial instrument that converts an account balance into a stream of periodic payments. Life annuities provide retirees periodic payments that continue until death. They insure workers against the monetary costs of living longer than expected.

A basic life annuity pays fixed nominal benefits until the annuitant's death. This product combines two features, whose importance varies depending on the age at which the participant takes the annuity. First, annuities provide retirement income, and in this respect they are comparable to other financial instruments, particularly bonds. Second, annuities have an insurance component. They insure against the risk that retirees will outlive their resources. Because retirees tend to spend down their savings, that risk increases with age. Thus, the relative importance of the insurance aspect of an annuity is greater the older the age at which the participant first receives benefits.

Annuities provide insurance against outliving one's resources by pooling mortality risks across individuals. Other risks workers face also can be mitigated by purchasing an annuity. An annuity provides a mechanism for controlling one's level of consumption over time, thus providing a valuable device for self-control and self-discipline (MacKenzie 2007). With an annuity, capital market risks are shifted to the financial institution providing the annuity, usually an insurance company.

Workers purchasing annuities benefit from the "mortality credit," meaning that workers who survive to older ages benefit from the assets of those workers who die earlier. For this reason, annuities typically provide a higher expected return than bonds for workers who live relatively long. However, annuities generally provide a lower expected rate of return than equities, though also with lower risk. Annuities are particularly valuable for women because women tend to outlive the men in their lives, and their risk of poverty at the end of life is greater than for men.

ANNUITIZING 401(k) PLANS

While 401(k) plans generally do not provide annuities, when an annuity is offered by a 401(k) plan, workers generally do not take it. This section investigates why most 401(k) plans do not provide annuities and why most 401(k) plan participants do not take them when offered. It considers changes in policy and in features of annuities to increase the extent to which annuities are offered and to which participants take them.

The Effects of Unisex Pensions

Annuities offered through employer-provided pension plans in the United States must calculate benefits using unisex mortality rates. That requirement is the result of a Supreme Court ruling that using gender-based mortality tables would constitute sex discrimination in compensation. The case *Arizona Governing Committee v. Norris* 463

U.S. 1073 (1983) held that employer-provided pension plans were required to provide men and women the same level of benefits from an annuity if they were the same age and had the same account balance. This means that benefits are determined using the same mortality rates for men and women, not recognizing that women at retirement ages on average live about three years longer than men. Privately purchased annuities do not have this requirement, and are sold on a gender basis in every state except Montana.

Unisex single life annuities are favorable to women but adverse to men, compared to gender-based annuities. The disadvantages to men of purchasing annuities through a 401(k) plan could be offset to some extent because group annuities are priced more cheaply than single annuities in the private market. The disadvantages to men are also offset to the extent that they choose joint and survivor annuities.

Adverse selection occurs when people selecting annuities have information about their life expectancy that the annuity provider does not have. For example, people who choose voluntary annuities on average have lower mortality rates for their gender than the population as a whole. The selection caused by a unisex requirement is not adverse selection because gender and gender differences in life expectancy are common knowledge to both the participant and the insurance company. However, this type of selection has the same effects as adverse selection: it is information about life expectancy that insurance companies are not able to use. Selection increases with the range of mortality rates in the population under consideration, and thus it increases when men and women are pooled together in a single risk pool. Adverse selection either results in insurers raising their premiums or not offering the product at all. Adverse selection concentrates risk, rather than spreading it, and thus hinders the functioning of an insurance market.

The Thrift Savings Plan for government workers allows workers to calculate online how much in benefits they will receive from their account balance. This calculation is done on a unisex basis, and thus is relatively unfavorable to men taking single life annuities. The unisex annuity payable from the Thrift Savings Plan in March 2007 for an account balance of $100,000 with the annuity taken at age 62 was $8,280 annually.

The amount the Thrift Savings Plan provides can be compared to the amount indicated by online annuity calculators that would be available to men in the individual annuity market. An informal survey of online calculators indicates that men participating in the Thrift Savings Plan could receive higher benefits if they purchased an annuity through the individual annuity market, while women would receive lower benefits (Table 10.1).

The level of benefits women receive from the Thrift Savings Plan is higher than what they would receive in the individual market. However, the difference is only a little more than $200 a year, suggesting that most single life annuitants in the Thrift Savings Plan are women, and that the annuity is priced accordingly (Table 10.2). While the Internet survey was not exhaustive, it appears that women could not find a higher annuity in the individual purchase market than the Thrift Savings Plan annuity, while men could.

The Thrift Savings Plan annuity may not be representative of annuities offered by other employers. Because the federal government negotiates for the annuity, it may be that the annuity provides benefits at favorable rates. If that is the case, it further strengthens the point concerning the effect of the unisex requirement on men being able to get better annuities outside the Thrift Savings Plan.

An earlier survey found similar results. The survey of payments from annuities in qualified pension plans (where the unisex requirement holds) and other annuities found that on average the payments from qualified plans were less than other annuities for men, but more for women (Brown et al. 2001, p. 157). However, annuity payments vary considerably, and not every qualified annuity for men paid less than every nonqualified annuity. Payout differences across pension plans may be due to different assumptions for different groups of workers as to mortality experience.

That study found that the annuity benefit payable to men in the Thrift Savings Plan was slightly larger than the average of that payable to men on individually purchased annuities. However, it was somewhat lower than the average for the 10 best nonqualified annuities. It found that the Thrift Savings Plan annuity payable to women was higher than the average of the ten best qualified or nonqualified annuities in the

Table 10.1 Features of Annuities in Mandatory Individual Account Systems in Sweden, Chile, and the United Kingdom

Features	Country		
	Sweden	Chile	United Kingdom
Entitlement conditions			
Entitlement age	61	60 women, 65 men	60
Early benefit receipt before entitlement age with more stringent requirements	No	Yes, based on account balance	No
Benefit receipt while working	Yes	Yes	Yes
Maximum age by which benefit receipt must begin	No	No	75
Annuity acquisition			
Mandatory vs. voluntary annuitization	Mandatory	Voluntary	Until 2006, mandatory starting at age 75; starting in 2006, mandatory at age 75 except for those claiming a religious exemption
Annuity provider	Government	Life insurance companies	Life insurance companies
Factors used in determining annuity value	Age, year of birth	No restrictions	Age, gender, impaired health, year of birth
Fees			
Level and structure of fees for annuitization	Uniform percentage of account balance	Determined by life insurance company	Determined by life insurance company

	Not separately disclosed, bundled with individual account fee	Not separately disclosed, incorporated in net annuity payments	Not separately disclosed, incorporated in net annuity payments
Disclosure of fees			
Benefit forms			
Phased or partial annuitization	Yes	No	Yes
Fixed or variable annuity	Either fixed annuity with some upside variability or phased withdrawal	Fixed but price-indexed	Price-indexed, up to 5% a year
Lump sum benefit allowable	No	Yes, for part of account	No
Disability benefits	Provided separately	Provided separately	Provided separately
Preretirement withdrawals for medical expenses, educational expenses, or for purchasing a home	No	No	No
Minimum period payment guarantees	No	No	No
Minimum benefit guarantee	No	Yes, for workers with 20 years of contributions	No
Benefits for other persons			
Spousal benefit	Worker can contribute to account of spouse	No	No
Benefit for divorced spouses	No	No	Can be negotiated as part of divorce settlement
Survivors' benefits	Optional	Required for men who annuitize their account	Yes, 50% survivors' benefits must be provided

Table 10.1 (continued)

Features	Country		
	Sweden	Chile	United Kingdom
Bequeathable benefits	No	Yes, if taking phased withdrawals	Yes, if taking phased withdrawal before age 75
Risk reduction			
Reinsurance of annuities	Government guarantees annuities	Government guarantees annuities	No government guarantee
Inflation protection	No price-indexing, option of variable annuity	Fully price-indexed annuities	Annuities price-indexed up to 5% a year
Interest rate guarantee for annuitization	Guarantee at minimum of 3%	No guarantee	No guarantee
Taxation and income redistribution			
Taxation	Same as wage earnings	Same as wage earnings	Same as wage earnings
Income redistribution	No explicit redistribution, implicit redistribution through mandatory annuitization	Minimum benefit guarantee provides some redistribution, unrestricted annuity pricing limits redistribution through annuitization	No explicit redistribution, implicit redistribution through mandatory annuitization

SOURCE: Author's compilation.

Table 10.2 Comparison of Monthly Annuity Benefits for a $100,000 Account Balance with Unisex and Gender-Based Pricing, Benefits Taken at Age 62, 2007 ($)

Plan type	Men	Women
Unisex—Thrift Savings Plan (MetLife)	690	690
Gender-based—Annuitybid.com	754	670

SOURCE: Thrift Savings Plan (2009).

Table 10.3 Comparison of a Unisex Annuity Provided through the Thrift Savings Plan and a Gender-Based Annuity Provided to Individuals by the Same Insurance Company, 2007

Annuity source	Monthly benefit ($)	Interest rate (%)
Thrift Savings Plan (MetLife)	888	5.25
Individual purchase (MetLife)	806	5.30

NOTE: This assumes an account balance of $140,000 for a male age 57. The quotations are for March 19, 2007.
SOURCE: Thrift Savings Plan (2009); MetLife agent.

individual market. Thus, this earlier study is consistent with the results of our informal Internet survey.

Table 10.3 compares an annuity for a man obtained through the Thrift Savings Plan to an annuity for a man obtained individually through MetLife. MetLife is the annuity provider for the Thrift Savings Plan, so this comparison holds constant the company providing the annuity. The MetLife annuity quote was obtained from a MetLife agent, rather than from the Internet. The interest rate used for calculating both annuities is slightly higher for the MetLife than for the Thrift Savings Plan. The Thrift Savings Plan annuity is calculated using unisex mortality rates, while the MetLife annuity is calculated using gender-based mortality rates.

The MetLife annuity provides benefits about 9 percent lower than the Thrift Savings Plan annuity, even though the interest rate used is slightly more favorable and the mortality table used is more favorable. The difference presumably is accounted for in part by the commission received by the MetLife agent in the case of the individually purchased annuity.

Adverse selection has the potential for destroying an annuity market. An unintended consequence of the unisex rulings may be that

401(k) plans rarely provide annuities because men can obtain better annuities in the individual annuities market. Selection problems presumably are a more serious problem for 401(k) plans than for private sector annuity providers because of the unisex requirement. Private providers can reduce selection problems by offering different rates to men and to women.

Two Kinds of 401(k) Plans

Recognizing that 401(k) plans generally are no longer mainly supplementary plans, they should be regulated as primary plans. However, an argument can be made that there should be two types of 401(k) plans as far as regulation is concerned. For 401(k) plans that are the primary or sole plan, they would be classified as 401(k) retirement plans. They would be required to provide an annuity as the default option, and to provide spousal protection in the form of a joint and survivor benefit that can be waived only by the spouse signing and notarizing a document. Other 401(k) plans that are supplementary plans, where a defined benefit plan provides the primary benefits, would continue to be regulated as savings plans.

This approach favors extending the requirements applied to defined benefit plans to 401(k) plans. This would mean that 401(k) plans provide annuities as the default option, requiring a spousal waiver if not chosen. That requirement would apply at least for those plans that are the primary or sole pension plan the employer provides. Arguments in favor of this approach include that 401(k) plans now play the role that once was played by defined benefit plans. Also, as a matter of leveling the playing field between 401(k) plans and defined benefit plans, the same requirements should apply uniformly to both. Both the United Kingdom and Ireland require that defined contribution plans provide annuitized benefits.

A different approach would be to require that 401(k) retirement plans offer annuities as an option but that the annuities not be required to be the default option. However, these plans would also be required to provide standard "advice" recommending that an annuity be chosen for at least part of the account balance because that is the only form of benefit that would assure that participants would not outlive their pension savings.

Mandatory versus voluntary annuitization. Some degree of mandatory annuitization may be desirable to assure that workers will not outlive their retirement savings. Mandatory annuity purchases reduce annuity prices by expanding the market to cover individuals regardless of health and life expectancy. Also, mandatory annuities would be less expensive to administer, with greater economies of scale and reduced enrollment costs. However, mandating annuities forces some people to buy them who would be better off not doing so.

Full mandatory annuitization may not be desirable. Full mandatory annuitization restricts the access of participants to their accumulated funds, and for this reason may weaken the argument that defined contribution plans foster an "ownership society." Full annuitization reduces flexibility in meeting unplanned expenses. Instead, a mandate could require that only part of the account balance be annuitized. An alternative policy innovation would be to charge an exit fee when lump sum benefits are taken, and use that fee to subsidize annuities.

Annuitization is a prerequisite to providing survivors' benefits. Thus, the requirement for annuitization is related to providing survivors' protection for widows. Annuitization could be required to be jointly decided by husbands and wives. For example, annuitization could be the default, with other forms of benefit receipt only being allowed if the spouse signs an agreement permitting that.

Perhaps in part because of the interest rate risk associated with converting an account balance to an annuity, many countries with mandatory defined contribution plans do not require that workers annuitize account balances. Seven countries with mandatory defined contribution systems in Latin America allow their workers to choose between an annuity and phased withdrawals throughout retirement, while two countries mandate annuity purchases (Kritzer 2000). Countries that do not mandate annuitization generally mandate that benefits be withdrawn periodically through phased withdrawals.

In Sweden, where the mandatory defined contribution plan is a relatively small part of the mandatory benefits (financed by a 2.5 percent tax rate, out of a total social security tax rate of 18.5 percent), workers must either fully annuitize their account balances or take the benefits as a phased withdrawal. Chile does not require workers to annuitize their account balances, but workers not annuitizing must take their benefits as a phased withdrawal. British workers until 2006 were required to annuitize their account balances by age 75. That requirement has been dropped for those claiming a religious exemption.

Default options. Behavioral finance has suggested that making automatic enrollment the default option can greatly increase the percentage of workers who participate in pensions. However, because of the financial importance of the decision and its irreversibility, if annuities were the default, considerably more people might opt out of the default than has been the case with automatic enrollment. Experience with cash balance plans has indicated that making an annuity the default for receiving a benefit defined as an account balance may have little effect.

Participant education. Participant education is one method for encouraging participants to annuitize. Employees may need to be educated as to the advantages of guaranteed lifetime income, which annuities provide. The U.S. Department of Labor (2005b) has commented that plan communications tend to focus on the accumulation phase rather than on the payout phase. It recommended that the Department of Labor provide guidance as to what constitutes education, as opposed to advice, in providing information concerning benefit options. Such guidance would alleviate concerns that employers have over their fiduciary liability in providing such information to their participants.

Participant education may need to include information about life expectancy. Information concerning life expectancy is the most common way that information about mortality risk is provided. However, approximately half the population will outlive its life expectancy, so information about life expectancy sets a low standard in terms of the number of years that a person should be prepared to finance. It may be more useful in helping participants understand the risks they face to provide information on the probability they will live to age 90, and the higher probability that at least one member of a couple will live to age 90.

Participants are accustomed to thinking of 401(k) plans in terms of their account balance. More participants might annuitize if they think of their 401(k) plans in terms of the amount of annuitized income the account could provide. Thus, it might be desirable for account statements to provide information as to the amount of annuitized income the account would provide if it were annuitized at a fixed age, such as 62. Also providing that information for age 65 would help educate people as to the advantages of postponing retirement.

Participant education is often provided by the institution managing the investments of the participants' accounts. Those institutions generally have a conflict of interest with respect to providing information about annuities. Because they typically do not sell annuities, their income will be greater if participants continue to maintain an account balance rather than purchase an annuity.

Tax incentives. Tax incentives can be used to encourage the choice of annuities by workers. That can occur either by providing more favorable tax treatment to annuities or a less favorable tax treatment to other forms of payment. In 2006, Spain reduced the generosity of the tax treatment of lump sum benefits to encourage workers to purchase annuities (Social Security Administration 2007). To encourage annuitization, the first $10,000 of annual income from an annuity could be exempt from taxation. This proposal, however, would disadvantage defined benefit plans, unless the exemption was also extended to the first $10,000 of benefits received from a defined benefit plan. In that case, the loss of tax revenue would become more of an issue.

Chile, Sweden, and the United Kingdom all do not encourage annuitization. Annuitization could be encouraged by favorable tax treatment, but none of those countries have adopted such a policy. Annuitization could be encouraged by providing preferential tax treatment for annuities, with maximum limits on the level of benefits that would receive preferential treatment to assure some targeting of the tax benefit to lower- and middle-income recipients. However, tax incentives may have relatively little effect on the choices that pension participants make, given what appears to be a fairly strong preference to take lump sum payments.

ANNUITY OPTIONS

A number of options have been developed for annuities in an attempt to make them more appealing by providing pension participants greater range of choice.

Phased or Partial Annuitization or Deferred Annuitization

Phased annuitization offers workers the option of annuitizing their account balance in stages over time. This option facilitates phased retirement by allowing for receipt of partial benefits. Phased or partial annuitization facilitates part-time work with a part-time pension and thus may be a favorable option, particularly for women, because it provides greater flexibility for mixing paid work and family responsibilities. It also is a way of attempting to deal with the interest rate and financial market risk associated with the timing of annuitization.

Sweden and the United Kingdom allow phased or partial annuitization in their individual account systems, while Chile does not. Swedish workers can phase in their annuitization over time, initially annuitizing only a quarter, then a half, and then three-quarters of their account balance, if they wish. Once they have claimed benefits, they can suspend payment or change the percentage of a full payment they receive. Chilean workers may defer annuitization by first receiving benefits as a phased withdrawal and then later annuitize the remainder of their account balance.

Fixed or Variable Annuities

Annuities can provide fixed nominal or fixed real payments, or the payments can vary over time. Among annuities that vary over time, annuities that vary depending on the investment performance of the underlying assets are called variable annuities. Variable annuities offer both the advantages of annuities and the advantages of investments in equities, as well as the risks of investments in equities. Also, frequently insurance companies provide escalating annuities, where the payment increases by a fixed percentage amount each year. With this type of annuity, retirees can attempt to obtain an annuity that mimics an indexed annuity in that it increases over time, though it is not tied to increases in the price level.

Equity-indexed annuities have characteristics of both fixed and variable annuities. Their return varies more than a fixed annuity but not as much as a variable annuity. They combine a minimum guaranteed interest rate with a variable rate that is tied to a market index. The guarantee is backed by the insurance company marketing the product, and is thus only as secure as the insurance company.

When a Swedish participant chooses a fixed annuity, Sweden guarantees a fixed monthly payment for life. The monthly amount may be increased by a bonus, however, depending on the investment experience. When a worker chooses a phased withdrawal, the benefit may vary since the worker's benefit will be affected by the value of the underlying funds. When a worker chooses a phased withdrawal, the funds remain invested with the mutual funds the worker has chosen.

Chilean workers may take their benefit as a price-indexed annuity or as a phased withdrawal, or as a combination of the two. British workers choosing annuities must take price-indexed annuities, but they have the option of a phased withdrawal. Phased withdrawal does not provide longevity insurance, and for this reason it may not be a good option for many workers, especially women.

Benefits for Other Persons

As well as providing benefits to the retired workers who earned them, annuities may pay benefits to other related persons, notably spouses. Doing so, however, generally reduces the benefits received by the retired worker because the extra benefits must be financed out of the account balance.

Providing survivors' benefits for a spouse or domestic partner generally would reduce the benefits paid while both persons were alive by 8 to 20 percent, depending on the ages of the two people (American Academy of Actuaries 2001). Spousal benefits, benefits for divorced spouses, survivors' benefits, and bequeathable benefits are of particular value to women because women are more likely to be economically dependent on their spouses than are men.

Spousal benefits. Spousal benefits are received by the spouse while the retired worker who earned them is still alive. In Sweden, workers can advance-fund retirement income for their spouse by having their contributions deposited into their spouse's account instead of their own. The Chilean and British defined contribution plans do not provide spousal benefits. Dependent spouses must rely on the benefits of their working spouse while that person is alive.

Benefits for divorced spouses. Providing benefits for a divorced spouse from a defined contribution plan is particularly difficult if the worker has remarried and has a current spouse. Any benefits provided to the divorced spouse would reduce the benefits received by the worker and current spouse.

British workers can negotiate rights to pension benefits in divorce settlements. In Chile and Sweden, divorced spouses have no rights to pension benefits of their former spouses. While current spouses, same-sex partners, and dependent children are eligible for survivors' benefits if the participant elects to provide them, divorced spouses are not eligible for survivors' benefits. If a spouse is named as a beneficiary and a divorce subsequently occurs, the divorced spouse loses the right to the future survivors' benefits.

Survivors' benefits. Because workers are not required to annuitize their 401(k) accounts, women whose spouses participate in 401(k) plans are generally denied the form of insurance that an annuity received as a survivor provides.

Survivors' benefits can be a mandated part of a defined contribution system, or they can be provided as an option. In defined contribution systems, providing survivors' benefits results in lower benefits to the couple while both are alive. In voluntary defined contribution systems, participants generally have a choice of level of survivors' benefits—100 percent, 75 percent, 66.7 percent, or 50 percent are common options, though participants generally would not have all those options. An issue when providing survivors' benefits is what happens to the benefit of the participant if the dependent spouse dies first. The participant's benefit could be left unchanged, it could be decreased because there would be only one person for it to support, or it could be increased because there is no longer the need to provide survivors' benefits.

The United Kingdom is the only country of the four (United States, United Kingdom, Sweden, Chile) that requires all married participants in defined contribution plans to provide survivors' benefits. It requires a married participant to provide survivors' benefits equal to 50 percent of the benefits received by the participant.

Bequeathable benefits. Bequeathable benefits take the form of a lump sum payment made to a surviving spouse or other surviving family member or unrelated person at the death of a pension participant. Defined contribution systems may distinguish between deaths that occur before the worker has started receiving retirement benefits and deaths that occur while the worker is receiving benefits.

In the United States, the possibility of accumulating bequeathable wealth through defined contribution systems is considered to be a desirable feature by some people. This possibility allows workers to accumulate wealth that they might bequeath to their heirs, but the trade-off is that annuitized benefits are reduced below what they otherwise would be. Bequeathable benefits generally result when a defined contribution has not been annuitized, and they are eliminated when an account has been annuitized.

If workers die before having annuitized their account balances, the Swedish pension system does not allow the bequest of their account balances. That amount is redistributed among all the participants in the system. When Chilean or British workers die, their account balances are bequeathable to their survivors. If they die during retirement and they have not annuitized their account balances, the remaining account balances are also bequeathable.

INCOME REDISTRIBUTION

When defined contribution plans annuitize benefits without taking into account the longer life expectancy associated with higher income, they redistribute income toward upper-income workers. The use of unisex life tables also causes income redistribution within the system, though the pattern of redistribution is also affected by whether participants choose survivors' benefits for their spouses. Since women and higher-wage workers have on average longer life expectancies than men and lower-wage workers, the system redistributes money in a complex way from men to women and from lower-wage to higher-wage workers. Thus, the criticism by some policy analysts that traditional defined benefit social security programs redistribute income in complex ways (World Bank 1994) also applies—and to some extent for the same reasons—to defined contribution plans that mandate annuitization.

Most of the mandatory defined contribution systems allow workers to avoid the regressive effects of annuitization by taking a phased withdrawal of benefits. Providing this option, however, increases the problem of adverse selection in the annuity market. Adverse selection occurs when long-lived people are more likely to choose an annuity than short-lived people but both receive the same annual benefits for a given account balance.

Because people who expect to be long-lived are more likely to purchase annuities than people who expect to be short-lived, insurers price annuities on the assumption that their purchasers are long-lived. While these prices may be actuarially fair for upper-income workers with long life expectancies, the high price keeps low-income workers out of the annuity market and deprives them of the insurance protection traditional social insurance plans provide against the risk of outliving one's resources. Not requiring annuitization, however, allows low-income workers who die relatively young to bequeath some of their retirement income to their survivors.

An option that has received little consideration for dealing with adverse selection that arises with voluntary annuitization is to levy a charge on persons not annuitizing that offsets the effects of adverse selection. The charge amount would be contributed to the financing of annuities, allowing annuities to be priced as if there were no adverse selection.

Insurance companies in Chile, but not in most countries with mandatory defined contribution plans, use individual characteristics, including income and gender, in determining the level of annuity benefits an account balance provides. Calculating annuities this way limits the regressive income transfers due to annuitization, but at the cost of lower retirement benefits for women than would be the case if unisex life tables were used to calculate annuitized benefits.

Income redistribution can also occur through the way the annuity provider charges fees. The transaction costs to the annuity provider associated with an individual worker purchasing an annuity are largely fixed costs. These costs do not depend on the size of the account balance being annuitized. Thus, these costs have a regressive effect when charged to the individual. They form a larger percentage of small account balances than of big ones, and small account balances tend to be held by people with lower incomes. Vittas and Iglesias (1992) find that annuity charges in Chile are a source of inequality in benefits, as larger commissions relative to annuity payments are often charged to lower-income workers.

MARKET INNOVATIONS: LONGEVITY INSURANCE, LADDERING, AND FRAMING

Longevity Insurance

Much of the utility value of annuitization comes from insuring against the possibility of running out of money if one lives to be older than expected (Brown 2001). An annuity can be used to purchase longevity insurance, while allowing workers control over part of their money. If a worker purchases an annuity with an adequate benefit and a start date that is deferred to age 85, the worker—if he or she lives that long—only needs to manage the spend-down of assets over a fixed period, from retirement to age 85. This strategy greatly reduces mortality risk, while also facilitating the management of the spend-down of assets. The person no longer needs to manage the spend-down of assets over an uncertain period.

Pension-plan tax qualification rules may make it difficult for workers to purchase longevity insurance with start dates at advanced ages. The problem arises with the requirement that minimum distributions from a 401(k) plan start by April 1 of the year following the year the person turns age 70 ½. Changes in these minimum required distribution rules might be considered to encourage the purchase of longevity insurance. Even with such changes, however, it is likely that few people would purchase longevity insurance. People are reluctant to purchase annuities that begin payment immediately. They presumably would be even more reluctant to purchase an annuity that began payment at age 85. With longevity insurance, people have better protection against outliving their resources and ending life in poverty, but the trade-off is that they have less money to spend earlier in life.

Laddering

Another innovation is laddering the purchase of annuities. This process occurs when annuities are purchased in small amounts over time. Doing so reduces the risk related to interest rates. Participants may be more willing to purchase annuities if they do so in small amounts. The purchasing of annuities could be done in the context of a target date retirement plan, where the individual's portfolio becomes more conservative as the individual's retirement target date approaches. Usually this change is done by increasing the share of the portfolio held in bonds. An alternative approach would be to gradually purchase annuities. Participants may be more willing to have annuities in their portfolio if they are purchased by the employer with the employer's contribution. This process could start later in life, for example at age 50.

Framing

An alternative approach to encouraging annuitization would be to require that 401(k) plans report at least once a year to participants the amount of the annuity they would receive at current interest rates if taken at age 62. That approach would encourage employees to think in terms of taking their benefit as an annuity.

CONCLUSION

Several aspects of government policy that were designed to strengthen the protection of workers may have had the unintended effect of discouraging employers from providing annuities. First, the unisex rulings of the Supreme Court that require 401(k) plans to provide unisex annuities may have discouraged employers from providing annuities because often men are able to obtain annuities on more favorable terms by purchasing them individually outside the 401(k) plan. Second, the requirement of a joint and survivor option may have increased the complexity of administering annuities.

A basic policy decision is the extent to which participants will be free to choose from a wide range of options. A wide range of options allows participants the opportunity to structure the receipt of benefits in the way that they prefer. However, in some cases, public policy goals may take overriding importance. For example, should husbands be free to decide whether to provide survivors' benefits for their wives, or should public policy require that those benefits be provided?

Note

1. This chapter draws on Iwry and Turner (2008).

11
Finding Better Solutions

The goals of the pension system are to provide secure and adequate retirement income. In both respects, the U.S. system needs better solutions. With the decline in defined benefit plans and the increasing reliance on 401(k) plans, future retirees will have less secure and less adequate retirement income than current retirees. Some analysts suggest the contrary—that 401(k) plans will provide adequate retirement income for most participants—but their studies do not take into account the developments in behavioral economics indicating all the problems that workers encounter in accumulating retirement savings through 401(k) plans.

This chapter summarizes the main policy implications from the book. It concludes by presenting a proposal for a new type of hybrid pension plan.

PUBLIC POLICY FOR 401(k) PLANS

Since the early 1980s, 401(k) plans have grown from being supplementary plans offered by plan sponsors who also offer a defined benefit plan to being the only plan that most workers have. However, the regulation of 401(k) plans has lagged in recognizing their important role.

One option would be to regulate all 401(k) plans as if they were primary plans, providing equivalent regulatory protection as that provided for defined benefit plans. A less burdensome, but more complex, approach would be to change the regulation of 401(k) plans so that two types of 401(k) plans would be recognized.

First, 401(k) retirement plans would be plans that are the primary or sole plan provided by an employer. These plans would be regulated as retirement plans rather than as saving plans.[1] The policy goal of leveling the playing field between defined benefit plans and 401(k) plans would apply to these plans. For example, these plans would be required to offer annuities, perhaps having as the default that 50 or 75 percent of the account balance would be annuitized as a joint and survivor annuity, or having the option that the annuity would begin at an older age, such as at age 80. These plans would also be required to frame the benefits as an annuity, providing the annuitized value of the account balance for retirement at different ages each time the account balance was reported to the participant. Tax changes could be made to encourage annuitization through 401(k) plans. Such changes could include providing less favorable tax treatment to lump sum payments through 401(k) plans. Alternatively, people choosing a lump sum could be charged a penalty that would be returned to the plan to subsidize the annuities of those taking them. This would be done to offset adverse selection.

The second type of 401(k) plan would be 401(k) savings plans. These would be 401(k) plans offered by employers that also offered defined benefit plans meeting minimum standards as to generosity. These plans would continue to be regulated as they currently are, reflecting their historical roots as secondary plans that are offered to supplement defined benefit plans. Having this two-tier regulation of 401(k) plans could encourage employers to offer defined benefit plans, since that would permit them to offer 401(k) plans meeting less rigorous standards.

A retirement income system based on workers making investment decisions clearly has problems. The U.S. educational system does not prepare most people for making investment decisions. Participants in 401(k) plans tend to make financial mistakes. Many participants lack both knowledge and interest. They fail to contribute, and those who do contribute do not take full advantage of employer matching contributions. They frequently make what appear to be inappropriate investment choices. While defaults relating to workers' choices to participate, contribute, and invest in 401(k) plans may not be optimal for all workers, such as short-tenure workers, they help assure that more workers will accumulate assets in a 401(k) plan, which are then available to finance retirement consumption. The effects of the defaults on women, minorities, and low-wage workers, in particular, deserve further attention.

Some investment experts believe that low-cost index funds are the best choice for many pension participants and other individual investors. According to one proposal, 401(k) plans would be required to offer as an investment option a low-cost index fund.

Participants in 401(k) plans bear the investment costs and typically also the administrative costs of their 401(k) plans. Yet many participants are unaware they are bearing these costs, and most do not know how much they are paying in fees. Fee disclosure to participants would be greatly improved if the fees they paid in dollars for administrative expenses and investment expenses, as well as the expense ratio for investment expenses, were disclosed on their annual and quarterly account statements. This type of disclosure is done in Australia for plan administrative fees and is done by the Janus mutual fund for investment costs.

A problem with defined contribution plans that has received relatively little notice is the persistency of contributions by workers. Many workers do not consistently contribute to their plans, resulting in reduced account balances at retirement. The lack of persistency accounts at least in part for the surprisingly low account balances that many 401(k) participants have at retirement.

A widely recognized problem with 401(k) plans is that few plans provide annuities, and when annuities are offered few participants take them. People may be reluctant to annuitize because a relatively large amount of money is involved in an irreversible decision. Addressing the first concern, one approach that might encourage greater annuitization is the laddered purchase of annuities, meaning that it would occur in small quantities over time. Doing it this way would reduce the interest rate risk, and it might reduce the reluctance of workers to annuitize, because the amounts involved in each transaction would be small. Laddering could be done within the context of a target retirement date plan, where typically the percentage of the worker's portfolio held in bonds is increased as the target retirement date approaches. An alternative would be to gradually purchase annuities as the retirement date approaches. Workers' reluctance to annuitize might be further reduced if that were the default option for the employer's contribution, starting at a fixed age, such as age 50.[2]

An alternative approach to encouraging annuitization would be to require that 401(k) plans report at least once a year to participants the amount of the annuity they would receive at current interest rates if taken at age 62. That approach would encourage employees to think in terms of taking their benefit as an annuity. An additional policy innovation would be to charge an exit fee when lump sum benefits are taken, and use that fee to subsidize annuities, offsetting the effect of adverse selection that occurs when people choose to take a lump sum.

To assure greater participation in 401(k) plans, those plans could be required to provide a reverse match. With a reverse match, the employer would be required to contribute a certain percentage of pay for each worker. Workers could then have the option to contribute to the plan up to a certain matching amount. With this policy, the coverage provided by 401(k) plans would be more similar to that provided by defined benefit plans.

Defaults can be used to improve the outcomes provided by 401(k) plans. They offer the promise of improving participation and having better investment outcomes for workers.

The current approach of tax deductions for pensions favors upper-income workers. An approach that would provide the same amount of incentive per pension dollar would be to provide tax credits.

PUBLIC POLICY FOR DEFINED BENEFIT PLANS

The decline in defined benefit plans is an issue of serious concern. A number of policies should be considered to address that issue.

Private sector defined benefit plans are the only major type of pension plan in the United States that does not permit employee tax-deductible contributions. Employee tax-deductible contributions are permitted for 401(k) plans, and for defined benefit plans for state and local government employees. Extending tax deductibility to private sector defined benefit plan participants would help level the playing field between defined benefit plans and 401(k) plans.

Transition issues arise concerning permitting employee tax-deductible contributions. Employers who instituted employee tax-deductible contributions would effectively be reducing employee compensation if they did not make compensating increases in wages. Nonetheless, employers already have the ability to reduce compensation by failing to provide annual pay increases while inflation erodes the real value of compensation.

While coverage in defined benefit plans has declined dramatically in the United States and even more so in the United Kingdom, the decline has been relatively modest in Canada and Ireland. Thus, international experience casts doubt on the view that defined benefit plans are dinosaurs and their decline and extinction is inevitable. In both Canada and Ireland, and indeed in most countries with defined benefit plans, employees make tax deductible contributions to those plans.

A factor that appears to have played a role in the decline of defined benefit plans has been the increase in life expectancy, as defined benefit plans do not have the flexibility to deal readily with this continued increase in cost. In the United States, some plans have adjusted downward their generosity, but generally this change is only done for new hires. A possible policy innovation, following the notional defined contribution plan in Sweden, would be to permit life expectancy indexing of benefits at retirement. Thus, for each new retirement cohort, the generosity of the plan would be adjusted downward slightly to reflect the trend toward greater life expectancy. Once workers are retired, further adjustments to their pensions for improvements in life expectancy would not be made. Under U.S. law, this innovation would not be allowed because it would violate the anticutback rule. The anticutback rule is defined in terms of annual benefits. If it were redefined to take an economist's perspective and use the present expected value of lifetime benefits as the measure, life expectancy indexing would not constitute a cutback in lifetime benefits.

Continued improvements in life expectancy mean continued increases in the cost of providing defined benefit plans. Sweden in its social security system has a plan, the notional defined contribution plan, where benefits at retirement are indexed for improvements in life expectancy. Each year, as another cohort reaches retirement age, the generosity of benefits is reduced slightly to take into account the continued improvement in life expectancy. The adjustment does not reduce expected lifetime benefits.

Life expectancy risk can be divided into the idiosyncratic risk that a particular individual will live longer than expected and the cohort risk that an entire cohort on average will live longer than expected. Annuity providers are able to deal with idiosyncratic risk by pooling it across large numbers of people, effectively diversifying it away. However, cohort risk cannot be pooled. Longevity bonds would provide a hedge, but a market for them has not developed. The higher the percentage of a cohort that is surviving, the higher the payout longevity bonds have. Life expectancy indexing of benefits is one way of dealing with this risk. The idiosyncratic risk is borne by the annuity provider, who can diversify it away. The cohort risk is borne by workers, who are the beneficiaries of the improved life expectancy.

This feature would shift onto workers the systematic life expectancy risk, which is the risk that an entire birth cohort will live longer on average. The plan sponsor bears the idiosyncratic life expectancy risk, which is the risk that a particular individual will live longer than expected.

With increases in life expectancy at older ages, a number of countries have raised the earliest age at which pension benefits can be received. Doing so has been part of a policy to encourage workers to retire at older ages.

Workers who change jobs or are laid off by their employers and who participate in defined benefit plans suffer benefit losses. They suffer benefit losses because their benefits are frozen in nominal terms at the point of job termination, and the real value of those benefits is eroded by inflation between that point and the point at which they qualify for retirement benefits. Plans can make these workers wait until age 65 to receive benefits. For laid-off workers, the loss of pension benefits can be more serious than the loss of wages, while for employers the loss of pension benefits gives them a bonus for laying off older workers.

One policy option is to require healthy firms that lay off workers in corporate restructuring to price-index the benefits of those workers until retirement. This requirement in a certain sense would not impose a new cost on employers. It just mandates that they pay the benefits to these workers that they had promised to pay.

Funding rules prohibit employers from contributing to defined benefit plans in years when those plans exceed a certain level of funding. These rules have the effect of prohibiting plan sponsors from contributing toward the increased liabilities of their plan in that year. This requirement of zero contributions in some years generally occurs when the stock market and companies are performing well. Because pension plans are long-term commitments and because of the fluctuations in the stock market, at a later date plan sponsors then are required to make contributions. That requirement generally occurs when the stock market and companies are performing poorly. This requirement not only increases the volatility of contributions, it forces plan sponsors to contribute on a time pattern that is exactly opposite of what they would desire.

To reduce the volatility and timing problem of employer contributions for defined benefit plan funding, both the maximum and minimum contribution requirements could be eased. First, plans could be allowed to contribute 25 percent of normal costs in any year, regardless of the level of funding. This proposal would set the floor on contributions allowed at 25 percent of normal costs rather than zero. Thus, plan sponsors would be allowed to make a contribution every year, the pattern desired for pension plans as ongoing entities.

To ease the requirements on the minimum required contributions, plan sponsors could be allowed a longer period over which to amortize unfunded liabilities. For example, they could be allowed a period of 15 years, rather than the current seven years set by the Pension Protection Act of 2006. Underfunding would be less of a problem if the proposal of raising the minimum allowed funding were enacted.

Employers sponsoring U.S. defined benefit plans are responsible for financing any shortfall, but they are unable to tap excess assets in the pension fund should the fund perform better than expected. Allowing employers to withdraw excess assets under certain circumstances would likely increase the willingness of employers to adequately fund plans and could also affect their willingness to offer defined benefit plans. However, it creates the risk that a firm might be taken over for the purpose of withdrawing excess assets from its pension plan.

The tax system could be used to encourage broader coverage through defined benefit plans. For example, to tie the interests of management to those of workers, the allowable maximum income considered for determining defined benefit plan benefits could be raised in plans that provided 100 percent coverage to all full-time workers. Other options linking the interests of management and workers would include the provision that employers that provide a defined benefit plan for management would be required to also provide a similar plan for employees.

In many large companies, the executives have completely different pensions from the workers and have no personal stake in the pension options of the workers. Linking proposals could require that companies that provide defined benefit plans for executives also provide defined benefit plans meeting minimum standards for workers. Similarly, if the company froze or terminated a defined benefit plan for workers, such a stipulation could require that it also do so for executives.

The Pension Protection Fund in the United Kingdom was established with a goal of learning from the experience of the Pension Benefit Guaranty Corporation in the United States. One of its innovations is premiums based in part on the risk of a claim being made.

The lost pension problem is a problem for workers who are laid off or who change jobs. While it is a problem in both defined contribution and defined benefit plans, it is more of a problem in defined benefit plans because they are less portable. It can be difficult to track down a pension from a former employer, particularly if that employer has gone out of business. Both the United Kingdom and Australia have gone further than has the United States in assisting people facing this problem. A national registry, perhaps one created by expanding the registry maintained by the Pension Benefit Guaranty Corporation, would be a major improvement in this area.

PROPOSAL: A NEW TYPE OF HYBRID—THE LIFE-INDEXED DB

Some of the policy innovations just discussed could be incorporated into a new type of hybrid plan called the life-indexed DB. This plan would have three features that would distinguish it from a traditional U.S. defined benefit plan. First, it would permit tax deductible employee contributions. Tax deductible employee contributions are permitted for defined benefit plans in the state and local government sector, and in Canada, the United Kingdom, and a number of other countries. This feature would lower employers' pension costs. To provide some protection to workers during the transition to this plan, the transition could require that employee contributions as a percentage of pay could increase by at most 1 percent in a year and that they could only be made in conjunction with a pay increase of at least 2 percent.

Second, the plan would have life expectancy–indexed benefits. This feature is present in all defined contribution plans and in cash balance plans when account balances are converted to annuities based on current mortality rates. With life expectancy indexing of benefits, when benefits are calculated at retirement age, a life expectancy adjustment factor would be applied to the benefit formula to adjust annual benefits downward so that increases in life expectancy that had occurred before retirement age would not lead to an increased present value of lifetime benefits. This change would shift part of the risk of improvements in life expectancy back to workers. Employers would retain the risk that life expectancy would improve at higher ages after a cohort had reached its early retirement age.

Third, laid-off workers with vested benefits in healthy firms would be protected against the eroding effect of inflation up to the date at which they would be eligible to receive benefits. Their benefits would be price-indexed from the date of layoff to their early retirement age. This change would protect workers and would take away from employers the actuarial bonus they receive when laying off workers. If a worker is laid off at age 51 and cannot receive benefits until age 65, the real value of those benefits is eroded by inflation occurring during that period. With this aspect of the plan, the wages of workers laid off would be price-indexed up to the point of retirement, and the price-indexed wages would be used in the benefit calculation. This way, firms would no longer receive an actuarial bonus for laying off workers.

This is a balanced proposal. The first of the three features would reduce employer cost. The second of the three features would reduce employer risk. The third feature would reduce employee risk.

CONCLUSION

Pension policy is an evolving product of our social institutions and our economy. With the decline in defined benefit plans and the increasing role of 401(k) plans, much remains to be done to improve the way pensions are provided to American workers. One improvement would be to fashion a system that includes new types of plans, such as defined benefit plans with employee contributions and life expectancy–indexed benefits. By making such improvements, steps can taken toward a retirement income system that provides adequate and secure benefits for all Americans.

Notes

1. Issues could arise if an employer offered more than one type of defined contribution plan, such as an employee stock ownership plan (ESOP) and a 401(k) plan. One approach to these types of issues would be to regulate all 401(k) plans as 401(k) retirement plans if the employer did not also provide a defined benefit plan that was not frozen.
2. This innovation was suggested by Mark Iwry in preparation of Iwry and Turner (2008).

References

Aaronson, Stephanie, and Julia Coronado. 2005. *Are Firms or Workers behind the Shift Away from DB Pension Plans?* Finance and Economics Discussion Series, 2005-17. Washington, DC: Federal Reserve Board.

Agnew, Julie R. 2004. "An Analysis of How Individuals React to Market Returns in One 401(k) Plan." CRR Working Paper 2004-13. Chestnut Hill, MA: Center for Retirement Research at Boston College. http://crr.bc.edu/images/stories/Working_Papers/wp_2004-13.pdf (accessed April 29, 2009).

Agnew, Julie R., and Lisa R. Szykman. 2004. "Asset Allocation and Information Overload: The Influence of Information Display, Asset Choice, and Investor Experience." CRR Working Paper 2004-15. Chestnut Hill, MA: Center for Retirement Research at Boston College.

Agnew, Julie R., Lisa R. Szykman, Stephen P. Utkus, and Jean A. Young. 2007. "Do Financial Literacy and Mistrust Affect 401(k) Participation?" CRR Issue in Brief No. 7-17. Chestnut Hill, MA: Center for Retirement Research at Boston College. http://crr.bc.edu/images/stories/Briefs/ib_7-17.pdf (accessed September 3, 2009).

American Academy of Actuaries. 2001. "Annuitization of Social Security Individual Accounts." November issue brief. Washington, DC: American Academy of Actuaries. http://www.actuary.org/pdf/socialsecurity/annuity_nov01.pdf (accessed April 29, 2009).

Ameriks, John. 2002. "Recent Trends in the Selection of Retirement Income Streams among TIAA-CREF Participants." *Research Dialogue* 74(December): 1–19. http://www.tiaa-crefinstitute.org/pdf/research_dialogue/74.pdf (accessed April 29, 2009).

Ameriks, John, and Stephen P. Zeldes. 2000. "How Do Household Portfolio Shares Vary with Age?" Working paper. New York: Columbia University.

Andrews, Emily S. 1992. "The Growth and Distribution of 401(k) Plans." In *Trends in Pensions 1992*, John A. Turner and Daniel Beller, eds. Washington, DC: U.S. Department of Labor, Pension and Welfare Benefits Administration, pp. 149–176.

Arizona Governing Committee v. Norris. 463 U.S. 1073 (1983).

Australian Taxation Office. 2001. *Finding Your Lost Super: Lost Members Register.* Canberra, Australia: Australian Taxation Office. http://www.ato.gov.au/individuals/content.asp?doc=/content/16442.htm (accessed September 5, 2009).

Aviva. 2009. *Important Information: A Guide to Your With-Profits Pension Annuity Investment and How We Manage the With-Profit Fund.* Norwich, UK: Aviva Life Services. www.aviva.co.uk/adviser/product-literature/files/an/an01010c.pdf (accessed September 9, 2009).

Barber, Brad M., and Terrance Odean. 2001. "Boys Will Be Boys: Gender, Overconfidence, and Common Stock Investment." *Quarterly Journal of Economics* 116(1): 261–292.

Barr, Nicholas. 2001. *The Welfare State as Piggy Bank: Information, Risk, Uncertainty, and the Rule of the State.* Oxford: Oxford University Press.

Benartzi, Shlomo. 2001. "Excessive Extrapolation and the Allocation of 401(k) Accounts to Company Stock." *Journal of Finance* 56(5): 1747–1764.

Benartzi, Shlomo, and Richard H. Thaler. 2001. "Naïve Diversification Strategies in Defined Contribution Savings Plans." *American Economic Review* 91(1): 79–98.

Bernheim, B. Douglas, and Daniel M. Garrett. 2003. "The Effects of Financial Education in the Workplace: Evidence from a Survey of Households." *Journal of Public Economics* 87(7–8): 1487–1519.

Blake, David. 1995. *Pension Schemes and Pension Funds in the United Kingdom.* New York: Clarendon Press.

Blake, David, and John A. Turner. 2002. "Lost Pensions, Lost Pensioners: Is a National Registry of Pension Plans the Answer?" *Benefits Quarterly* 18(3): 51–64.

Bodie, Zvi. 1995. "On the Risk of Stocks in the Long Run." *Financial Analysts Journal* 51(3): 18–22.

Boskin, Michael J. 2003. "Deferred Taxes in the Public Finances." NBER working paper. Palo Alto, CA: Hoover Institution.

Brown, Jeffrey R. 2001. "Redistribution and Insurance: Mandatory Annuitization with Mortality Heterogeneity." CRR Working Paper 2001–02. Chestnut Hill, MA: Center for Retirement Research at Boston College.

Brown, Jeffrey R., Olivia S. Mitchell, James M. Poterba, and Mark J. Warshawsky. 2001. *The Role of Annuity Markets in Financing Retirement.* Cambridge, MA: MIT Press.

Bruce, Ellen A., John A. Turner, and Dongsoo Lee. 2005. "Lost Pensions: An Empirical Investigation." *Benefits Quarterly* 21(1): 42–48.

Buessing, Marric, and Mauricio Soto. 2006. "The State of Private Pensions: Current 5500 Data." CRR Issue in Brief No. 42. Chestnut Hill, MA: Center for Retirement Research at Boston College.

Bureau of Labor Statistics (BLS). 2000. *Employee Benefits in State and Local Governments, 1998.* Bulletin 2531. Washington, DC: Bureau of Labor Statistics. http://www.bls.gov/ncs/ebs/sp/ebbl0018.pdf (accessed May 26, 2009).

———. 2003. *Retirement Plans in 2003.* TED: The Editor's Desk. Washington, DC: Bureau of Labor Statistics. http://www.bls.gov/opub/ted/2003/sept/wk5/art05.htm (accessed May 2, 2009).

———. 2007. *National Compensation Survey: Employee Benefits in Private*

Business in the United States, March 2007. Summary 07-05. Washington, DC: Bureau of Labor Statistics. http://www.bls.gov/ncs/ebs/sp/ebsm0006 .pdf (accessed May 26, 2009).

Burman, Leonard, Eric Toder, and Christopher Geissler. 2008. "How Big Are Total Individual Income Tax Expenditures, and Who Benefits from Them?" Discussion Paper No. 31. Washington, DC: Urban Institute.

Butrica, Barbara A., and Gordon B.T. Mermin. 2006. "Annuitized Wealth and Consumption at Older Ages." CRR Working Paper 2006-26. Chestnut Hill, MA: Center for Retirement Research at Boston College.

Chen, Yung-Ping, and John C. Scott. 2003. "Gradual Retirement: An Additional Option in Work and Retirement." *North American Actuarial Journal* 7(3): 62–74.

Choi, James J., David Laibson, and Brigitte C. Madrian. 2004. "Plan Design and 401(k) Savings Outcomes." *National Tax Journal* 57(2): 275–298.

———. 2006. "Why Does the Law of One Price Fail? An Experiment on Index Mutual Funds." NBER Working Paper 12261. Cambridge, MA: National Bureal of Economic Research. http://www.nber.org/papers/w12261 (accessed May 1, 2009).

Clark, Robert L., Madeleine B. d'Ambrosio, Ann A. McDermed, and Kshama Sawant. 2004. "Sex Differences, Financial Education, and Retirement Goals." In *Pension Design and Structure: New Lessons from Behavioral Finance*, Olivia S. Mitchell and Stephen P. Utkus, eds. New York: Oxford University Press, pp. 185–206.

Clark, Robert L., and Sylvester J. Schieber. 1998. "Factors Affecting Participation Rates and Contribution Levels in 401(k) Plans." In *Living with Defined Contribution Pensions: Remaking Responsibility for Retirement*, Olivia S. Mitchell and Sylvester J. Schieber, eds. Philadelphia: University of Pennsylvania Press, pp. 69–97.

Commission of the European Communities. 2002. *Joint Report by the Commission and the Council on Adequate and Sustainable Pensions*. Brussels, Belgium: European Commission.

Congressional Budget Office (CBO). 1993. *Controlling Losses of the Pension Benefit Guaranty Corporation: A CBO Study*. Congress of the United States. Washington, DC: Congressional Budget Office.

———. 2003. *Utilization of Tax Incentives for Retirement Saving: A CBO Paper*. Congress of the United States. Washington, DC: Congressional Budget Office.

Conversation on Coverage. 2007. *Covering the Uncovered: Final Report of the Conversation on Coverage*. Common Ground Proposals to Expand Retirement Savings for American Workers. Washington, DC: Pension Rights Center.

Copeland, Craig. 2001. "Pension Participation: February 2001." *EBRI Notes* 22(12): 1–5.

de Jong, Philip, and John A. Turner. 2001. "Privatizing Government Pensions: The United States and the Netherlands." *Benefits Quarterly* 17(3): 51–56.

Demby, Elayne Robertson. 2002. "Game Plan: Leave It to the Boss." *Plan Sponsor* 2002(September): 60–61.

Elliott, Kenneth R., and James H. Moore Jr. 2000. "Cash Balance Pension Plans: The New Wave." *Compensation and Working Conditions* 5(2): 3–11. http://www.bls.gov/opub/cwc/archive/summer2000art1.pdf (accessed May 1, 2009).

Engelhardt, Gary V., and Anil Kumar. 2003. "Understanding the Impact of Employer Matching on 401(k) Saving." TIAA-CREF Institute *Research Dialog* 76(June): 1–11.

Engström, Stefan, and Anna Westerberg. 2003. "Which Individuals Make Active Investment Decisions in the New Swedish Pension System?" SSE/EFI Working Paper Series in Economics and Finance, No. 527. Stockholm, Sweden: Stockholm School of Economics.

ERISA Industry Committee (ERIC). 2007. *A New Benefit Platform for Life Security*. Washington, DC: ERISA Industry Committee. http://www.eric.org/forms/uploadFiles/ccea00000007.filename.ERIC_New_Benefit_Platform_FL0614.pdf (accessed September 2, 2009).

ESPlanner. 2005. *Tutorial*. Boston, MA: Economic Security Planning. http://www.bu.edu/hr/files/documents/esplanner_tutorial.pdf (accessed September 9, 2009).

Even, William E., and David A. Macpherson. 2008. "Improving Pension Coverage at Small Firms." In *Overcoming Barriers to Entrepreneurship in the United States*, Dianna Furchtgott-Roth, ed. Lanham, MD: Lexington Books, pp. 123–156.

Even, William E., and John A. Turner. 1999. "Has the Pension Coverage of Women Improved?" *Benefits Quarterly* 15(2): 37–40.

Friedberg, Leora, and Anthony Webb. 2005. "Life Is Cheap: Using Mortality Bonds to Hedge Aggregate Mortality Risk." CRR Working Paper 2005-13. Chestnut Hill, MA: Center for Retirement Research at Boston College. http://escholarship.bc.edu/cgi/viewcontent.cgi?article=1107&context=retirement_papers (accessed May 8, 2009).

Gale, William G., and Michael Dworsky. 2006. "Effects of Public Policies on the Disposition of Lump-Sum Distributions: Rational and Behavioral Influences." CRR Working Paper 2006-15. Chestnut Hill, MA: Center for Retirement Research at Boston College. http://crr.bc.edu/images/stories/Working_Papers/wp_2006-15.pdf (accessed May 10, 2009).

Gale, William G., J. Mark Iwry, Alicia H. Munnell, and Richard H. Thaler.

2004. "Improving 401(k) Investment Performance." Issue in Brief No. 26. Chestnut Hill, MA: Center for Retirement Research at Boston College.

Gale, William G., J. Mark Iwry, and Peter R. Orszag. 2005. *The Automatic 401(k): A Simple Way to Strengthen Retirement Savings*. Policy Brief No. 2005-1. Washington, DC: Retirement Security Project.

Gale, William G., J. Mark Iwry, and Spencer Walters. 2007. "Retirement Saving for Middle- and Lower-Income Households: The Pension Protection Act of 2006 and the Unfinished Agenda." Policy Brief No. 2007-1. Washington, DC: Retirement Security Project.

Gebhardtsbauer, Ron, and John A. Turner. 2004. "The Protection of Pension Covered Workers and Beneficiaries: An Analysis of the UK Legislation Establishing the Pension Protection Fund." Unpublished paper. Washington, DC: American Academy of Actuaries and AARP Public Policy Institute.

General Accounting Office (GAO). 1997. *401(k) Pension Plans: Loan Provisions Enhance Participation, but May Affect Income Security for Some*. Report to the Chairman, Special Committee on Aging, and the Honorable Judd Gregg, U.S. Senate. GAO/HEHS-98-5. Washington, DC: General Accounting Office; Health, Education, and Human Services Division.

———. 2000. *Cash Balance Plans: Implications for Retirement Income*. Report to the Chairman, Special Committee on Aging, United States Senate. GAO/HEHS-00-207. Washington, DC: General Accounting Office; Health, Education, and Human Services Division.

Ghilarducci, Teresa. 2001. "De-Linking Benefits for the Single Employer: Alternative Multiemployer Model." Paper presented at the Pension Rights Center conference "Conversation on Coverage," held in Washington, DC, July 24–25.

———. 2008. *When I'm Sixty-Four: The Plot against Pensions and the Plan to Save Them*. Princeton, NJ: Princeton University Press.

Ghilarducci, Teresa, and Mary Lee. 2005. *How Lower Middle-Class Workers Obtain Employer Pensions*. Final Report for Retirement Research Foundation Grant No. 2003-077. South Bend, IN: University of Notre Dame.

Ghilarducci, Teresa, and John A. Turner, eds. 2007. *Work Options for Older Americans*. South Bend, IN: University of Notre Dame Press.

Gillion, Colin, John A. Turner, Clive Bailey, and Denis Latulippe, eds. 2000. *Social Security Pensions: Development and Reform*. Geneva: International Labour Organization.

Gustman, Alan L., and Thomas L. Steinmeier. 1995. *Pension Incentives and Job Mobility*. Kalamazoo, MI: W.E. Upjohn Institute for Employment Research.

Harris, Jennifer D. 1998. *Purchases of Service Credit: Portability for Public-Sector Employees*. Lorton, VA: Public Retirement Institute.

Harrysson, Lars, and Michael O'Brien. 2003. "Pension Reform in New Zealand and Sweden: A Comparative Analysis of Path Dependent Reform Processes." Paper presented at the Fourth International Research Conference on Social Security, "Social Security in a Long Life Society," held in Antwerp, Belgium, May 5–7.

Hermes, Sharon, and Teresa Ghilarducci. 2007. "How 401(k)s and the Stock Market Crash Explain Increases in Older Workers' Labor Force Participation Rates." In *Work Options for Older Americans*, Teresa Ghilarducci and John A. Turner, eds. South Bend, IN: University of Notre Dame Press, pp. 237–266.

Hinz, Richard P., David D. McCarthy, and John A. Turner. 1997. "Are Women Conservative Investors? Gender Differences in Participant-Directed Pension Investments." In *Positioning Pensions for the Twenty-First Century*, Michael S. Gordon, Olivia S. Mitchell, and Marc M. Twinney, eds. Philadelphia: University of Pennsylvania, Wharton School, Pension Research Council, pp. 91–104.

Hinz, Richard P., and John A. Turner. 1998. "Pension Coverage Initiatives: Why Don't Workers Participate?" In *Living with Defined Contribution Pensions: Remaking Responsibility for Retirement*, Olivia S. Mitchell and Sylvester J. Schieber, eds. Philadelphia: University of Pennsylvania, Wharton School, Pension Research Council, pp. 17–37.

Hinz, Richard P., John A. Turner, and Phyllis A. Fernandez, eds. 1994. *Pension Coverage Issues for the '90s*. Washington, DC: U.S. Department of Labor, Pension and Welfare Benefits Administration.

Holden, Sarah. 2007. "Trends and Developments in 401(k) Plan Savings in the United States." Paper presented at the 2007 Mutual Funds and Investment Management Conference, held in Palm Desert, CA, March 25–28.

Holden, Sarah, and Jack VanDerhei. 2001. "401(k) Plan Asset Allocation, Account Balances, and Loan Activity in 2000." EBRI Issue Brief No. 239. Washington, DC: Employee Benefit Research Institute.

Honig, Marjorie, and Irena Dushi. 2003. "How Demographic Change Will Drive Benefits Design." In *Benefits for the Workplace of the Future*, Olivia S. Mitchell, David S. Blitzstein, Michael Gordon, and Judith F. Mazo, eds. Philadelphia: University of Pennsylvania Press, pp. 58–88.

Horack, Sarah, and Andrew Wood. 2005. *An Evaluation of Scheme Joining Techniques in Workplace Pension Schemes with an Employer Contribution: Case Study Findings of Scheme Joining Techniques*. Research Report No. 292. London: Department for Work and Pensions. http://www.dwp.gov.uk/asd/asd5/rports2005-2006/rrep292.pdf (accessed May 12, 2009).

House of Lords. 2003. *Aspects of the Economics of an Ageing Population*. Vol.

1—Report. Select Committee on Economic Affairs. HL Paper 179-I. Session 2002–03, 4th Report. London: Stationery Office Ltd.

Huberman, Gur, Sheena S. Iyengar, and Wei Jiang. 2003. "Defined Contribution Pension Plans: Determinants of Participation and Contributions Rates." Columbia University working paper. New York: Columbia University.

Hutchens, Robert M, and Jennjou Chen. 2007. "The Role of Employers in Phased Retirement: Opportunities for Phased Retirement among White-Collar Workers." In *Work Options for Older Americans*, Teresa Ghilarducci and John A. Turner, eds. South Bend, IN: University of Notre Dame Press, pp. 95–118.

International Network of Pension Regulators and Supervisors (INPRS) and International Social Security Association (ISSA). 2003. *Complementary and Private Pensions throughout the World, 2003*. Geneva: International Network of Pensions Regulators and Supervisors and International Social Security Association.

Iwry, J. Mark, and John A. Turner. 2008. "Expanding the Use of Annuities by 401(k) Participants: Innovations in Policy, Products, Marketing, and Advice." Draft paper. Washington, DC: Retirement Security Project.

Iyengar, Sheena S., and Mark R. Lepper. 2000. "When Choice Is Demotivating: Can One Desire Too Much of a Good Thing?" *Journal of Personality and Social Psychology* 79(6): 995–1006.

James, Estelle. 2005. "How It's Done in Chile: Personal Accounts—with Strings Attached." *Washington Post*, February 13, B:2.

James, Estelle, Guillermo Martinez, and Augusto Iglesias. 2006. "The Payout Stage in Chile: Who Annuitizes and Why?" *Journal of Pension Economics and Finance* 5(2): 121–154.

Kehl, David. 2002. *Superannuation Preservation Rules: A Summary*. Research Note No. 22, 2001-02. Canberra, Australia: Department of the Parliamentary Library.

Khorana, Ajay, Henri Servaes, and Peter Tufano. 2007. "Mutual Funds Fees around the World." Harvard Business School Finance Working Paper No. 901023. Boston: Harvard Business School. http://icf.som/yale.edu/pdf/seminars05-06/Servaes.pdf (accessed May 13, 2009).

Kritzer, Barbara E. 2000. "Social Security Privatization in Latin America." *Social Security Bulletin* 63(2): 17–37.

Kusko, Andrea L., James M. Poterba, and David W. Wilcox. 1998. "Employee Decisions with Respect to 401(k) Plans." In *Living with Defined Contribution Pensions*, Olivia S. Mitchell and Sylvester J. Schieber, eds. Philadelphia: Pension Research Council and University of Pennsylvania Press, pp. 98–112.

Latulippe, Denis, and John A. Turner. 2000. "Partial Retirement and Pension

Policy in Industrialized Countries." *International Labour Review* 139(2): 179–195.

Lichtenstein, Jules H., and John A. Turner. 2005. "Cash Balance Pension Plans and Older Workers." AARP Public Policy Institute Issue Brief No. 78. Washington, DC: AARP Public Policy Institute.

Liebman, Jeffrey B. 2002. "The Role of Annuities in a Reformed U.S. Social Security System." PPI Issue Paper 2002-17. Washington, DC: AARP Public Policy Institute.

Lucas, Lori. 2000. "Under the Microscope: A Closer Look at the Diversification and Risk Taking Behavior of 401(k) Participants and How Plan Sponsors Can Address Key Investing Issues." *Benefits Quarterly* 16(4): 24–30.

Lusardi, Annamaria. 2004. "Saving and the Effectiveness of Financial Education." In *Pension Design and Structure: New Lessons from Behavioral Finance,* Olivia S. Mitchell and Stephen P. Utkus, eds. New York: Oxford University Press, pp. 157–184.

———. 2007. *The Case for Improving Financial Literacy.* Blog entry, December 9. Hanover, NH: Financial Literacy and Ignorance blog. http://annalusardi.blogspot.com/2007/12/case-for-improving-financial-literacy.html (accessed September 9, 2009).

Maas, Angela. 2005. "Managing Retirement—Automatically Managed 401(k) Accounts Appeal to Employers and Employees Alike." *Employee Benefit News* 19(3): 28–31, 49.

MacKenzie, George A. 2007. "In Annuities We Trust: Annuity Markets and Pension Reform." *Contingencies* 2007(March/April): 24–29.

Madrian, Brigitte C., and Dennis F. Shea. 2001. "The Power of Suggestion: Inertia in 401(k) Participation and Savings Behavior." *Quarterly Journal of Economics* 116(4): 1149–1187.

Maser, Karen. 1995. "Who's Saving for Retirement?" *Perspectives on Labour and Income* 7(4): 14–19.

Maunsell, Harriet. 1998. *A View of the Pension Schemes Registry.* OPRA Bulletin, Issue 6. Brighton, East Sussex, UK: Occupational Pensions Regulatory Authority.

———. 1999. *A View of the Pension Schemes Registry: Part 2.* OPRA Bulletin, Issue 8. Brighton, East Sussex, UK: Occupational Pensions Regulatory Authority.

McCarthy, David D., and John A. Turner. 2000. "Pension Education: Does It Work? Does It Matter?" *Benefits Quarterly* 16(1): 64–72.

McGill, Dan M., Kyle N. Brown, John J. Haley, and Sylvester J. Schieber. 1996. *Fundamentals of Private Pensions.* 7th ed. Philadelphia: University of Pennsylvania Press.

Medill, Colleen E. 2008. "Participant Perceptions and Decision-Making

Concerning Retirement Benefits." CRR Working Paper 2008-9. Chestnut Hill, MA: Center for Retirement Research at Boston College. http://crr .bc.edu/images/stories/Working_Papers/wp_2008-9.pdf (accessed September 3, 2009).

Muir, Dana, and John A. Turner. 2007. "Longevity and Retirement Age in Defined Benefit Pension Plans." In *Work Options for Older Americans*, Teresa Ghilarducci and John A. Turner, eds. South Bend, IN: University of Notre Dame Press, pp. 212–231.

Muller, Leslie A., and John A. Turner. 2008. "The Persistence of Employee 401(k) Contributions over a Major Stock Market Cycle." Paper presented at the University of Michigan Institute for Social Research conference "Pensions, Private Accounts, and Retirement Savings over the Life Course," held in Ann Arbor, MI, November 20–21.

Munnell, Alicia H., and Mauricio Soto. 2007. "Why Are Companies Freezing Their Pensions?" CRR Working Paper 2007-22. Chestnut Hill, MA: Center for Retirement Research at Boston College.

Munnell, Alicia H., Annika E. Sundén, and Catherine Taylor. 2000. "What Determines 401(k) Participation and Contributions?" CRR Working Paper 2000-12. Chestnut Hill, MA: Center for Retirement Research at Boston College.

O'Brien, Chris, Paul Fenn, and Stephen Diacon. 2005. *How Long Do People Expect to Live? Results and Implications*. CRIS Research Report 2005-1. Nottingham, UK: University of Nottingham, Centre for Risk and Insurance Studies. http://www.nottingham.ac.uk/business/cris/papers/crisresearchreport 2005-1(summary).pdf (accessed May 18, 2009).

Odean, Terrance. 1998. "Volume, Volatility, Price, and Profit When All Traders Are Above Average." *Journal of Finance* 53(6): 1887–1934.

Oster, Christopher. 2003. "Good News! Insurers Extend Your Lifespan." *Wall Street Journal*, June 24, D:1.

Palmer, Edward. 2001. "Statement of Edward Palmer, professor, social insurance economics, Uppsala University in Sweden, and chief of research and evaluation, Swedish National Social Insurance Board, Stockholm, Sweden: Sweden's New Pension System." U.S. Congress. House of Representatives. Committee on Ways and Means. Hearing before the Subcommittee on Social Security, *Social Security and Pension Reform: Lessons from Other Countries*, 107th Cong., 1st sess., pp. 40–50.

Pang, Gaobo, and Mark J. Warshawsky. 2009. "Reform of the Tax on Reversions of Excess Pension Assets." *Journal of Pension Economics and Finance* 8(1): 107–130.

Papke, Leslie E. 2004. "Individual Financial Decisions in Retirement Saving

Plans: The Role of Participant Direction." *Journal of Public Economics* 88(1–2): 39–61.

Papke, Leslie E., and James M. Poterba. 1995. "Survey Evidence on Employer Match Rates and Employee Saving Behavior in 401(k) Plans." *Economic Letters* 49(3): 313–317.

Penner, Rudolph G., Pamela Perun, and C. Eugene Steuerle. 2007. "Letting Older Workers Work." In *Work Options for Older Americans*, Teresa Ghilarducci and John A. Turner, eds. South Bend, IN: University of Notre Dame Press, pp. 125–163.

Pension Benefit Guaranty Corporation (PBGC). 2003. "PBGC Pension Search Finds 15,000 Owed $61 Million in Benefits; 80 Million Still Unclaimed." News release, January 22. Washington, DC: Pension Benefit Guaranty Corporation.

Pension Protection Fund and Pensions Regulator. 2006. *The Purple Book: DB Pensions Universe Risk Profile.* Croydon, Surrey, UK: Pension Protection Fund; and Brighton, E. Sussex, UK: Pensions Regulator.

Pension Rights Center. 2007. *Pension Policy Statistics: Why Pensions Are Important.* Washington, DC: Pension Rights Center. http://www.pensionrights .org/policy/stats.html (accessed August 19, 2009).

Pensions Policy Institute. 2007. *The Changing Landscape for Defined Benefit Pensions Schemes.* London, UK: Pensions Policy Institute. http://www .pensionspolicyinstitute.org.uk/uploadeddocuments/PPI_Landscape_for_ DB_Schemes_8_October_2007.pdf (accessed May 18, 2009).

Perun, Pamela, and Joseph J. Valenti. 2008. "Defined Benefit Plans: Going, Going, Gone?" Paper presented at the Thirtieth Annual Research Conference of the Association for Public Policy and Management, held in Los Angeles, CA, November 6-8.

Poterba, James M. 2001. "Taxation and Portfolio Structure: Issues and Implications." NBER Working Paper 8223. Cambridge, MA: National Bureau of Economic Research. http://www.nber.org/papers/w8223.pdf (accessed May 18, 2009).

President's Commission to Strengthen Social Security. 2001. *Strengthening Social Security and Creating Personal Wealth for All Americans.* Report of the President's Commission. Washington, DC: President's Commission to Strengthen Social Security.

Profit Sharing/401(k) Council of America (PSCA). 2005. *48th Annual Survey of Profit Sharing and 401(k) Plans.* Chicago: Profit Sharing/401(k) Council of America.

Purcell, Patrick. 2004. *Automatic Enrollment in Section 401(k) Plans.* CRS Report for Congress. Washington, DC: Congressional Research Service.

———. 2006. *Retirement Savings and Household Wealth: Trends from 2001 to*

2004. CRS Report for Congress. Washington, DC: Congressional Research Service.

Reagan, Patricia B., and John A. Turner. 2000. "Did the Decline in Marginal Tax Rates during the 1980s Reduce Pension Coverage?" In *Employee Benefits and Labor Markets in Canada and the United States*, William T. Alpert and Stephen A. Woodbury, eds. Kalamazoo, MI: W.E. Upjohn Institute for Employment Research, pp. 475–496.

Rein, Martin, and John A. Turner. 2001. "Public-Private Interactions: Mandatory Pensions in Australia, the Netherlands, and Switzerland." *Review of Population and Social Policy* 10: 107–153.

Samuelson, William, and Richard Zeckhauser. 1988. "Status Quo Bias in Decision Making." *Journal of Risk and Uncertainty* 1(1): 7–59.

Smith, Karen E., Richard W. Johnson, and Leslie A. Muller. 2004. "Deferring Income in Employer-Sponsored Retirement Plans: The Dynamics of Participant Contributions." *National Tax Journal* 57(3): 639–670.

Smith, Paul A. 2001. *A Longer-Term Perspective on IRA Participation: Evidence from a Panel of Tax Returns*. Washington, DC: Office of Tax Analysis, U.S. Department of the Treasury.

Smith, Sarah. 2006. "Persistency of Pension Contributions in the UK: Evidence from Aggregate and Micro-Data." CMPO Working Paper No. 06/139. Bristol, UK: Centre for Market and Public Organisation, University of Bristol. http://www.bris.ac.uk/cmpo/publications/papers/2006/wp139.pdf (accessed May 22, 2009).

Social Security Administration. 2007. *International Update: Recent Developments in Foreign Public and Private Pensions*. SSA Publication No. 13-11712. Washington, DC: U.S. Social Security Administration, Office of Policy.   http://www.socialsecurity.gov/policy/docs/progdesc/intl_update/2007-02/2007-02.pdf (accessed May 28, 2009).

Society of Actuaries. 2004. *2003 Risks and Process of Retirement Survey: Report of Findings*. Washington, DC: Mathew Greenwald and Associates and Employee Benefit Research Institute.

Technical Panel on Assumptions and Methods. 2003. *Report to the Social Security Advisory Board*. Washington, DC: Social Security Advisory Board.

Thaler, Richard H., and Shlomo Benartzi. 2004. "Save More Tomorrow: Using Behavioral Economics to Increase Employee Saving." *Journal of Political Economy* 112(1): S164–S187.

Thrift Savings Plan. 2009. *Annuity Calculator*. Birmingham, AL: Thrift Savings Plan. http://tsp.gov/calc/annuity/annuity.cfm (accessed September 9, 2009).

Turner, John A. 1993. *Pension Policy for a Mobile Labor Force*. Kalamazoo, MI: W.E. Upjohn Institute for Employment Research.

———. 2003a. "Are Cash Balance Plans Defined Benefit or Defined Contribution Plans?" *Benefits Quarterly* 19(2): 71–75.

———. 2003b. "Errors Workers Make in Managing 401(k) Investments." *Benefits Quarterly* 19(4): 75–82.

———. 2004. "Individual Accounts: Lessons from Sweden." *International Social Security Review* 57(1): 65–84.

———. 2006. *Individual Accounts for Social Security Reform: International Perspectives on the U.S. Debate.* Kalamazoo, MI: W.E. Upjohn Institute for Employment Research.

Turner, John A., and Roy Guenther. 2005. "A Comparison of Early Retirement Pensions in the United States and Russia: The Pensions of Musicians." *Journal of Aging and Social Policy* 17(4): 61–74.

Turner, John A., and Gerard Hughes. 2008. "Large Declines in Defined Benefit Plans Are Not Inevitable: The Experience of Canada, Ireland, the United Kingdom, and the United States." Discussion Paper PI-0821. Report prepared for the Ontario Pension Board. London: Pensions Institute, City University.

Turner, John A., and Sophie M. Korczyk. 2004. *Pension Participant Knowledge about Plan Fees.* Public Policy Institute Data Digest No. 105. Washington, DC: AARP Public Policy Institute.

Turner, John A., Leslie A. Muller, and Satyendra K. Verma. 2003. "Defining Participation in Defined Contribution Pension Plans." *Monthly Labor Review* 126(8): 36–43.

Turner, John A., and David M. Rajnes. 2003. "Retirement Guarantees in Voluntary Defined Contribution Plans." In *The Pension Challenge: Risk Transfers and Retirement Income Security*, Olivia S. Mitchell and Kent Smetters, eds. New York: Oxford University Press, pp. 251–267.

———. 2006. "Fixed Rate Guarantees during Economic Downturns." Unpublished manuscript. Washington, DC: AARP Public Policy Institute.

Turner, John A., and Satyendra K. Verma. 2005. "Extending Pension Participation: The Behavioral Economics of Why Some Workers Choose to Not Participate." Unpublished AARP document. Washington, DC: AARP.

———. 2007. "Why Some Workers Don't Take 401(k) Plan Offers: Inertia versus Economics." CeRP Working Paper 56/07. Moncalieri, Italy: Center for Research on Pensions and Welfare Policies.

Turner, John A., and Noriyasu Watanabe. 1995. *Private Pension Policies in Industrialized Countries: A Comparative Analysis.* Kalamazoo, MI: W.E. Upjohn Institute for Employment Research.

U.S. Department of Labor (USDOL). 2002. *PWBA Needs to Improve Oversight of Cash Balance Plan Lump Sum Distributions.* Report No. 09-02-

001-12-121. Washington, DC: U.S. Department of Labor, Office of Inspector General.

———. 2004. *Private Pension Plan Bulletin: Abstract of 1999 Form 5500 Annual Reports.* No. 12, Summer 2004. Washington, DC: U.S. Department of Labor, Employee Benefits Security Administration. http://www.dol.gov/ebsa/PDF/1999pensionplanbulletin.PDF (accessed May 26, 2009).

———. 2005a. *Private Pension Plan Bulletin: Abstract of 2000 Form 5500 Annual Reports.* Washington, DC: U.S. Department of Labor, Employee Benefits Security Administration. http://www.dol.gov/ebsa/PDF/2000pensionplanbulletin.PDF (accessed May 26, 2009).

———. 2005b. *Report of the Working Group on Retirement Distributions and Options.* Report by the Advisory Council on Employee Welfare and Pension Benefit Plans. Washington, DC: U.S. Department of Labor, Employee Benefits Security Administration. http://www.dol.gov/ebsa/publications/AC_1105A_report.html (accessed May 26, 2009).

———. 2008. *Private Pension Plan Bulletin Historical Tables.* Washington, DC: U.S. Department of Labor, Employee Benefits Security Administration. http://www.dol.gov/ebsa/pdf/privatepensionplanbulletinhistoricaltables.pdf (accessed May 26, 2009).

Valletta, Rob. 2007. "Anxious Workers." *FRBSF Economic Letter* 7(13): 1–3. http://www.frbsf.org/publications/economics/letter/2007/el2007-13.html (accessed May 28, 2009).

VanDerhei, Jack L. 2002. "Prepared Statement of Jack L. VanDerhei: Retirement Security and Defined Contribution Pension Plans: The Role of Company Stock in 401(k) Plans." U.S. Congress. Senate. Committee on Finance. Senate Hearing 107–751, *Retirement Security: Picking Up the Enron Pieces,* 107th Cong., 2d sess., pp. 60–68.

Vittas, Dimitri, and Augusto Iglesias. 1992. "The Rationale and Performance of Personal Pension Plans in Chile." Policy Research Working Paper 867. Washington, DC: World Bank.

Watson Wyatt Worldwide. 2003. *Global News Briefs: New Pension Law in Belgium.* Brussels, Belgium: Watson Wyatt Worldwide.

Webman, Nancy K. 2007. "Japan Could Avoid Path of Defined Contribution Shift; Experts Say That Risk Sharing, Flexibility Could Help Firms Keep Their DB Plans." *Pensions and Investments* 35(26): 50.

Wesbroom, Kevin, and Tim Reay. 2005. *Hybrid Pension Plans: UK and International Experience.* Department for Work and Pensions Research Report 271. London: Department for Work and Pensions.

White, David. 2003. "Employers Support Moves to More Compulsion in Pensions." News release, June 3. London: IPE.com.

Whitehouse, Edward. 1998. "Pension Reform in Britain." Social Protection Discussion Paper No. 9810. Washington, DC: World Bank.

Wolff, Edward N. 2007. "The Transformation of the American Pension System." In *Work Options for Older Americans*, Teresa Ghilarducci and John A. Turner, eds. South Bend, IN: University of Notre Dame Press, pp. 175–211.

World Bank. 1994. *Averting the Old Age Crisis: Policies to Protect the Old and Promote Growth*. A World Bank Policy Research Report. New York: Oxford University Press.

Wyatt Company. 1980. *Survey of Retirement, Thrift, and Profit-Sharing Plans Covering Salaried Employees of the 50 Largest U.S. Industrial Companies as of January 1, 1980*. Washington, DC: Wyatt Company.

Yoo, Kwang-Yeol, and Alain de Serres. 2005. "Tax Treatment of Private Pension Savings in OECD Countries." OECD *Economic Studies* 39: 73–110. http://www.oecd.org/dataoecd/19/0/35663569.pdf (accessed May 28, 2009).

The Author

John A. Turner is director of the Pension Policy Center in Washington, D.C., which provides research and consulting on social security and pension policy. Previously, he worked at the AARP Public Policy Institute in Washington and at the International Labour Office in Geneva, Switzerland. He has also worked in research offices at the U.S. Social Security Administration and at the U.S. Department of Labor, where he served as deputy director of the pension research office for nine years. He has taught as an adjunct lecturer in economics at George Washington University and at Georgetown University in the Georgetown Public Policy Institute. He has lectured and consulted in more than 20 countries and has published 12 books and more than 100 articles. He is the author of three previous books for the Upjohn Institute, including *Individual Accounts for Social Security Reform: International Perspectives on the U.S. Debate*, published in 2006. Turner has a PhD in economics from the University of Chicago.

Index

The italic letters *f, n,* and *t* following a page number indicate that the subject information of the heading is within a figure, note, or table, respectively, on that page. Double italics indicate multiple but consecutive elements.

401(k) plans, 2–3, 19*n*1, 123*n*
  annuities with, 18–19, 98, 104, 107–108, 165, 179, 181
  annuitization of, 183–194
    primary *vs.* supplementary in, 190–194, 203–204, 212*n*1
    unisex pension effect on, 183–185, 189–190, 189*t,* 201
  management of invested funds in, 9, 17, 205
  nonparticipation in, 47, 166–167
    reasons for, 13, 37, 45–46, 142
  participation in, 1, 3, 16, 34, 35, 52–53, 139
    autoescalation and, 144–145
    automatic enrollment and, 5, 38, 40–41, 131
    matched contributions and, 40, 131, 204, 206
  policy about
    government and, 10, 33, 168, 172
    proposals for, 19, 203–206
  risk in, 103, 104–109
  survivor benefits and, 18, 19, 167–168
  taxes and, 1, 8, 14, 84, 88, 89–90, 91*t,* 94, 98
  See also Roth 401(k) plans

ABP plan, as hybrid pension plan in, 16, 125, 126*t,* 129–130, 133, 161–162
Accounting, 30, 154
  benefit accruals in, 27–28, 60, 61–64, 68–71, 110, 126*t,* 160
  as pension policy issue, 2, 37, 155
Actuarial science, 28
  as pension policy issue, 2, 26, 50, 111–113
  See also Life expectancy

Ad hoc payments, defined contribution plans and, 17, 166
ADEA (Age Discrimination in Employment Act), 74
Administration on Aging, U.S., lost pension counseling, 174
Age Discrimination in Employment Act (ADEA), hurdles to flexible employment in, 74
Age of retirement, 77–81
  early, 60, 72, 74, 77–78, 81, 211
  fixed, and pension law, 14, 80, 140
  maximum, 79
  neutrality of, for benefit accrual, 27–28, 58
  pension information at, 178–179
  raised minimum, 79–80, 81, 112–113, 208
Annuities, 1, 4, 118, 181–201
  adjustments for inflation at retirement in, 103, 188*t*
  basic information about, 182–183, 189*t,* 191–193
  benefits from, 86
    notices of value in, 200, 205–206
    pension law and, 183–184, 201
    survivors and, 63–64, 107, 167–168, 187*t*
    trade-off at retirement *vs.* old age with, 122, 171–172
  defined benefit plans and, 112, 125, 127, 170, 180*n*1, 181
  defined contribution plans and, 12, 17, 18–19, 140, 166, 181–201
    featured options with, 186*t*–188*t,* 194–197
    income redistribution with, 188*t,* 197–199
    market innovations in, 199–200

Annuities, *cont.*
  defined contribution plans and, *cont.*
    payout options with, 181–182,
      187*t*, 189, 189*tt*
    pension law and, 10, 18, 19*n*2, 183–
      184, 201
    risk and, 7, 73, 101, 106, 107–109,
      126*t*, 188*t*
    taxation effect on, 88, 93–94, 188*t*,
      193, 204
    See also 401(k) plans, annuitization
      of; *under* 401(k) plans, annuities
      with
Approved Personal Pension, UK, 31
Argentina, pension benefit insurance in, 7
Arizona Governing Committee v.
    Norris, unisex rulings in, 18,
      183–184, 189–190, 201
Australia
  lost pensions in, 18, 177, 210
  pension provision in, 4, 7
    employer mandate for, 24, 33
    job changes and, 18, 60
    mutual funds and, 153*t*, 205
    trustee management of, 139, 205
  social security *vs.* privatized
    retirement income system in, 29,
    79, 167
  tax treatment of pensions in, 87, 92,
    93
Austria, EET pension approach in, 86
Autoescalation, 401(k) plans with,
    144–145

Bankruptcy, 66
  annuities and, 107, 118
  employer declarations of, 7, 8, 113–
    114, 174
  PBGC and probability of, 110, 115–
    116, 119, 123*nn*3–5
Banks, fund management by, 9–10, 155
Behavioral economics, pension systems
    and, 4, 153
Behavioral finance, 2, 16, 46–47
Belgium
  pensions in, 61, 86, 92, 93

raised minimum retirement age in,
    79–80
Benefit payments as pension function,
    85, 126*t*, 154
  adequacy of, and pension policy,
    171–173, 179
  annuities as, 140, 192, 206
  calculation of, 127–128, 131, 211
  receipt of, while still working, 76, 77,
    140, 186*t*
  taxation of, 84, 86–87, 90, 93–94,
    95–96
  types of, 166
  See also Ad hoc payments; Annuities;
    Installment payments; Lump sum
    payments
British Household Panel Survey,
    employee pension contributions
    data from, 34–35, 143
Bush, President George W. ("43"), social
    security proposal by, 23, 25
Business administration, as pension
    policy issue, 2

Canada
  pension provision in, 9, 143, 153*t*
    benefits and, 7, 172
    trends of, 6, 7, 10, 134, 139, 207
  social security in, 96
  tax treatment of pensions in, 6, 86,
    96, 96*t*
    contributions and, 62, 88–89, 91,
    157, 170–171, 210
Capitalism, pension investments and,
    153–154
Career average plans, 2, 110, 167
Cash balance plans, 3, 15, 16, 66
  hybrid nature of, 125, 126*t*, 127–128
  pension portability of, 57, 64–65, 72
  risk in, 7, 125, 126*t*, 128
    employees and, 127, 133–134
    employers and, 105
  shift to, 18, 71, 81
Chile
  government mandates in, 4, 7, 29
    pension benefits in, 7, 79, 93

Chile, *cont.*
  pension benefits in, *cont.*
    inflation adjustments for, 103, 188*t*
    lump sum payment of, 173, 187*t*
    receipt of, while still working, 76,
      186*t*
  pension plans in, 172
    annuities and, 108, 181,
      186*t*–188*t,* 193–197
    investments and, 9, 153–154
China, Hong Kong, IRAs in, 12
Chrysler (firm), downsizing at, 78
Collective bargaining agreements, 76
  multiemployer alliances and, 67–68,
    129
  pensions in, 4, 7, 22–23, 33, 44, 89
  trade-off of wages *vs.* pensions in, 89,
    137
Computer algorithms, fund management
    by, 150
Consumption tax, retirees and, 84
Contracting out of social security,
    extending pension coverage by,
      23–24, 27–28, 30–31, 32*n*2
Contributions as pension function, 84,
    126*t,* 130
  employees and, 41, 87, 88–90, 91*t,*
    156–157, 163, 204
    401(k)s, 84, 87, 142–143, 144–
      145
    IRAs, 34–35, 65, 143
    pension taxation effect on, 87,
      210–211
  employers and, 2, 24, 40–45, 87, 88,
    143, 156, 164, 205–206, 208–209
  government role in, 8, 14, 39, 62,
    91–92, 96–97
  private *vs.* public systems, 8, 27–28,
    62, 84, 87, 98, 157
  tax treatment of, 84, 87, 92, 88, 90,
    91*t,* 157, 170–171, 210–211
Corporate dissolution, 8, 174, 177–178
  failing firms prior to, 121
  takeovers as, 117–118, 138, 155, 174,
    209
  See also Bankruptcy

Current Population Survey (CPS),
    employee pension contribution
    data from, 36, 37
Czech Republic, the, tax treatment of
    pension contributions in, 87

DB(k) plans, 126*t*
  federal authorization of, 3, 15
  policy proposals for, 19, 131, 133
  risk in, 131, 133–134
Defined benefit plans, 2, 12, 19*n*1, 33,
    35, 126*t*
  contracting out of, 30–31
  employer behaviors and, 1, 38, 84,
    138–139, 154–155
  funding of, 154–163
    accounting policy and, 155
    automatic adjustment mechanisms
      for, 161–163
    contributions in, 156–157, 164
    costs and, 10, 15, 80, 112, 113,
      137–138, 158–160
    employer behaviors, 154–155, 204
    imbalances in, 157–158
  investments in, 1, 8
    annuities and, 112, 125, 127,
      167–168
  pension benefits from, 7
    inflation adjustment for, 11, 13,
      70–71, 72
    securing, and pension policy,
      169–171
    See also below under Defined
      benefit plans, portability at
      retirement of
  policy proposals for, 19, 99, 206–210
  portability at retirement of, 55–73
    accrual and transferability rights
      to, 61–64, 68–71
    back-loading in, 64–65
    contrasted, *vs.* defined contribution
      plans, 57–58, 66–68, 72–73
    job changes and, 58–60, 109, 208
  risk and, 1, 3, 6, 11, 14–15, 101–104,
    105, 109–113

Defined benefit plans, *cont.*
  shifts from, 3, 10–11, 17, 30, 71, 81,
    134, 139–140, 207
  taxes and, 87, 88, 89, 90, 91*t*, 92, 94,
    140, 209–210
  See also Career average plans; Final
    salary plans; Hybrid plans
Defined contribution plans, 2–3, 19*n*1
  funding of, 141–154
    contributions in, 142–145, 163
    costs for, 17, 37, 38, 41, 137–138,
      151–153, 153*t*
    financial literacy and, 140, 141
    investment choices for, 145–147,
      204–205
    investment management errors in,
      147–151
    politics and, 153–154
  government role in, 7, 10–11
  pension benefits from, 7, 17
    inflation adjustments for, 11, 13
    portability at retirement of, 57–58,
      65–66, 72–73
    securing, and pension policy, 165–
      168
  pension coverage in, 12–13, 35–37
    extension of, 12–13, 37–47, 50–53
    measures of, 17, 35–36
  pension provision and, 4
    annuities in, 12, 17, 140
    retirement decisions in, 14, 16
  risk and, 1, 3, 6–7, 8, 11, 73, 79,
    101–104, 105
  tax effect on, 87, 88
  See also 401(k) plans; Employee
    stock ownership plan; Hybrid
    plans; Money purchase plans
Denmark, pensions in, 23, 58, 61, 87
Double taxation, 95–96
Dutch plans. *See under* Netherlands, the

Economic Growth and Tax Relief
    Reconciliation Act (EGTRRA) of
    2001, pension rollovers and, 63
EET (Exempt, Exempt, Taxed) stages, 84

EGTRRA (Economic Growth and Tax
    Relief Reconciliation Act of
    2001), 63
Employee behaviors
  investment errors made as, 204
    diversification, 147–148
    inaction, 13, 16, 45–46, 48, 146–
      147, 148–149
    portfolio adjustments, 148–149
  retirement preparation among, 1–2,
    204
    investment portfolios in, 8, 42–43,
      51, 148–149
    mistakes made in, 16–17, 45–46,
      106, 145–146
    plan contributions in, 29, 30, 126*t*,
      142–145
    voluntary participation as, 3, 5, 9,
      12, 13, 37, 141
Employee layoffs, 3, 211
  defined benefit plans and, 1, 11, 13,
    81, 158, 208
Employee Retirement Income Security
    Act (ERISA) of 1974, 3, 41, 70
  flexibility hurdles in, 74, 160
  Industry Committee, and lawsuits,
    103–104
Employee risk
  pension plan type and, 6–7, 15, 105
    hybrid plans, 7, 126*t*, 127, 128,
      129, 130, 132, 133–134, 135, 211
Employee stock ownership plan
    (ESOP), as defined contribution
    plan, 138, 212*n*1
Employer behaviors
  conflicts of interest and, 138–139,
    208, 211
  fund management among, 9, 92
  pension provision as, 4, 9, 37–39,
    139–140, 155, 159–160
    adequate funding of, 116–118,
      121–122, 154, 208–209
    automatic employee enrollment in,
      5, 12, 40–41, 51–52, 131, 140
    differences for executives *vs.*
      workers in, 1, 38, 43, 148, 209–210

Employer behaviors, *cont.*
  pension provision as, *cont.*
    lost, in corporate breakups, 178–
      179
    retirement contributions among, 24,
      40–45, 126*t*, 205
      absence of, 36–37
      joint effort with workers, 2, 40,
        143–144, 206
Employer risk
  hybrid plans, 7, 126*t*, 128, 130, 211
  pension plan choice and, 6, 101, 105,
    110–111
Employment levels. *See* Full-time
    workers; Part-time workers;
    Temporary workers
Enron (firm), collapse of, 8
ERISA (Employee Retirement Income
    Security Act of 1974), 3, 41, 70, 74
ESOP (employee stock ownership
    plan), 138, 212*n*1
ETT (Exempt, Taxed, Taxed) stages, 87
Europe, pensions in, 12
    See also specific countries within
Excise taxes, 94, 117–118
Exempt, Exempt, Taxed (EET) stages,
    pension tax treatment in, 84, 92
Exempt, Taxed, Taxed (ETT) stages,
    pension tax treatment in, 87

Family considerations, 85, 86
  pension coverage and, 34, 89
Federal Insurance Contributions Act
    (FICA), 84
Final salary plans, 2, 102, 128, 167
Financial institutions, 112, 193
  interest rates and, 108–109, 126*t*
  markets as, and risk-bearing pension
    plans, 1, 132–133
  pension fund management by, 9, 106,
    155
Financial literacy
  education needed for, 42–43, 49–50,
    146, 149, 192–193, 204
  as pension policy issue, 2, 141, 149–
    151

Finland, pensions in, 4, 7, 86
Fixed annuities, 194–195
Floor offset plans, UK and, 125, 126*t*,
    128–129, 133–134
France, pensions in, 4, 23, 58, 86
Full-time workers, 174
  government mandates and, 5, 22
  nondiscrimination regulations and,
    37–38
  pension coverage for, 33, 99, 209
Fund management
  costs for, 151–153, 153*t*, 205
  IRAs and, 12, 24
  pension plans and, 9–10, 24, 92
    employee decisions about, 1–2,
      16, 18, 42, 48, 51, 145–147
    errors in, 16–17, 45–46, 106,
      145–146, 147–151
    options provided for, 103–104,
      146–147, 150
  policy options for, 149–151
  types of
    professional, 140, 145, 150
    trusts, 29, 92, 127, 139, 161–162

Gambling behaviors, retirement
    preparation and, 1
Gender differences, 28
  annuities and, 18, 19, 183–184, 189–
    190, 189*t*, 201
  investment decisions among, 16, 48,
    141, 148
  job tenure and, 55–56
  life expectancy among, 50, 184
  pension nonparticipation among,
    48–50, 48*t*, 49*t*
General Motors (firm), downsizing at, 78
Germany
  pension plans in, 86, 87, 167
  pension provision in, 7
    mandates for, 4, 5, 9–10
    trends of, 4, 6
Government role in pensions, 2, 24
  mandatory practices as, 4–6, 7, 12,
    21–32, 83, 101–123, 179
  policy options for, 71–73

Government role in pensions, *cont.*
　regulatory practices, 8, 10, 22, 29,
　　37–38, 91–92, 113, 116, 117
　state and local plans, 156–157, 210
　support as, 4–5, 6, 10–11, 38, 83–99,
　　85
　worker subsidies from, 26, 85, 87,
　　167
　See also under Pension systems, U.S.
　　federal practices
Greece, EET pension approach in, 86
Guaranteed Income Supplement, Canada,
　social security benefits limited, 96

Health insurance, 39, 74–75, 87
High-earnings workers, 121, 144
　life expectancy and, 24, 198
　pension provisions for, 1, 38, 43, 206,
　　209–210
　tax policy and, 83, 85–86, 94, 170–
　　171
Hong Kong, mandatory IRAs in, 12
Hungary, tax treatment of pension
　contributions in, 87
Hybrid plans, 2, 7, 101, 125–135
　international provision of, 4, 125,
　　128–129, 129–130
　proposals for new, 131–132, 210–212
　risk-bearing, analysis of, 7, 11, 15,
　　132–134
　types of, 3, 15–16, 125–130, 126*t*
　See also ABP plan; Cash balance
　　plans; DB(k) plans; Floor offset
　　plans; Life-indexed DB plan;
　　Pension equity plans (PEP)

Iceland, pensions in, 4, 16, 86, 161
Income taxes
　corporate, 84, 88, 94, 116, 117
　personal, 14
　　employee pension contributions
　　　deductible from, 88–89
　　rates of, and pension coverage, 13,
　　　40, 43, 84, 89
　　savings incentives and, 6, 89–90
　　state, 94

Individual Retirement Accounts (IRAs),
　10
　effects of, 4, 41
　employee contributions to, 34–35, 65,
　　89, 143
　mandatory approach to, 24, 172
　privatizing social security with, 12,
　　21–22
　taxes and, 14, 39, 66, 89–90
　types of, 3, 39
　workers' spouses and, 43, 45, 168
Industrial alliances, pensions and, 9, 23
Inflation
　benefits indexed to, 90, 102–103, 171,
　　211
　compensation and, 206–207
　retirement benefits and adjustments
　　for, 11, 13, 14, 70–71, 72, 188*t*,
　　208
　risk of, 101, 102–103, 122, 126*t*
Inland Revenue, UK SPSS and, 180*n*2
Installment payments, defined
　contribution plans and, 17, 166
Internal Revenue Service (IRS, U.S.), 93
　tax code of, 14, 74
　　section 401(k) in, 1, 40, 84
International perspectives on pensions, 11
　annuities and, 186*t*–188*t*
　employer-provided pensions, 4, 5,
　　79–80, 163
　securing lost pensions and, 175–177,
　　210
　survivor benefits and, 79, 102
　tax treatment for pensions, 83, 163
　See also Organisation for Economic
　　Co-operation and Development
　　(OECD) countries; *specific*
　　countries
Investment
　earnings from, as pension function,
　　84, 86, 92
　fund management and, 9–10, 24, 106,
　　145, 204
　　costs for, 151–153, 153*t*
　　employee decisions about, 1–2,
　　　16, 18, 42, 48, 51, 145–147

Investment, *cont.*
  fund management and, *cont.*
    errors in, 16–17, 45–46, 106, 145–146, 147–151
    options provided for, 103–104, 146–147, 149–151
    government regulation of, 8, 29
    mutual funds in, 150, 152, 153*t*
  pension portfolios
    diversification, 147, 150–151
    taxation effect on, 88, 116
  risks of, 3, 126*t*
    financial markets and, 73, 101, 104–106, 110–111, 132–133
IRAs. *See* Individual Retirement Accounts
Ireland
  pension plan trends in, 6, 7, 139, 207
  pension provision in, 59, 86
    mandates for, 4, 5, 61
IRS. *See* Internal Revenue Service
Italy, ETT approach to pensions in, 87

Japan
  contracting out in, 23, 28, 30
  pension provision in, 9, 138
    government cost for, 7, 96*t*
    trends re, 4, 6, 10, 139, 157–158
  tax treatment of pensions in, 86, 93, 94
JCT (Joint Committee on Taxation, U.S. Congress), 96
Job changes, 60, 66, 163
  defined pension plan types in, 56–57, 109, 208
  lost pensions upon, 18, 41, 58–60, 174–175, 210
  portability of retirement benefits upon, 13, 17, 45, 52–53, 58–60, 101
Job tenure, 55–56, 129

Korea, modified EET pension approach in, 86

Labor contracting, extending pension coverage by, 22–23

Labor economics, as pension policy issue, 2
Labor market policy. *See under* Pension plans, portability at retirement of
Laddering, annuities and, 200, 205
Latin America, pension mandates in, 12, 191
Lawsuits, 103, 148
  annuity payouts and, 183–184, 201
Layoffs. *See* Employee layoffs
LI-DB plan, 132, 134
Life expectancy, 14, 24
  gender differences in, 18, 19, 184
  pension costs and, 138, 158–160, 163
  pension policy and, 12, 28, 169–170, 172
  retirement benefits and, 77, 80–81, 166, 207, 211
  risk and, 15, 16, 50, 101, 106–107, 111–113, 126*t,* 128, 133–134, 135, 180*n*1
    idiosyncratic *vs.* systematic, 112, 122, 132, 160, 170, 207–208
Life-indexed DB plan, proposal for, 132, 134, 135, 210–212
Life insurance companies, 9, 189, 189*tt*
Litigation risk, 103–104
Longevity
  financial institutions and, bonds, 112, 208
  insurance for, with annuity purchase, 199–200
  pension risks and, 15, 16, 19, 50, 101, 106–107, 111–113, 126*t*
  pension withdrawals and, 106–107
  resources adequacy and, 166–167, 171–172, 204
Lost Members Register, Australia, 177
Lost pensions
  international perspectives on, 175–177
  job changes and, 18, 41, 58–60, 174–175
  securing benefits of, and pension policy, 173–178, 180, 210

Low-earning workers, 148
  401(k) plans and, 166–167
  pension coverage and, 22, 24, 39,
    43–45, 53
  progressive benefit formula for,
    23–24, 169
  tax treatment of, 5, 83, 90, 94, 99
Lump sum payments, 168
  annuities vs., 88, 93–94, 98, 204,
    205–206
  early retirement and, 78, 116, 121
  life expectancy and, 166, 173
  OECD countries and, 86, 187t, 193
  pension portability and, 17, 70–71
  risks of, 125, 127, 133–134, 166
Luxembourg, tax treatment of pension
  contributions in, 87

Mandatory practices with pensions, 16,
    24
  annuities and, 191–192
  exclusions from, 5, 12, 24
  private pensions and, 4–6, 7, 12,
    21–32, 101–123
  OECD countries with, 29–31
Manufacturing industry, decline in, 140
Massachusetts Pension Assistance
    Project, lost pension counseling
    and, 174
Men in the workforce, 55, 148
  life expectancy among, 50, 115, 159
  pension nonparticipation among,
    48–50, 48t, 49t
  spousal pension coverage for, 13, 45,
    167–168, 187t, 195–196
MetLife (firm), 189, 189tt
Mexico, government mandates in, 4, 7,
    86
Minority workers, pension coverage and,
    53
Money purchase plans, tax treatment of,
    88
Montana, annuities and gender in, 184
Moral hazard, PBGC and, 118–121
Multiemployer alliances
  hybrid plans of, 125, 129

pension plans in, 67–68, 139
pension portability in, 57–58, 72
pension provision by, 9, 114
Mutual funds, 9, 146–147, 150, 152, 153t

National Insurance Board, Sweden, 30
National Insurance contributions, UK,
    27–28
NEPAP (New England Pension
    Assistance Project), 174, 177–178
Netherlands, the
  hybrid pension plans in, 4, 15–16
    ABP plan for government
      workers, 16, 125, 126t, 129–130,
      133, 161–162
    Dutch collective defined
      contribution, 130
    investment earnings in, 86, 92
    pension provision in, 71, 105
      collective bargaining and, 23, 33
      defined benefit plans predominate,
        6, 10
      government mandates and, 4, 23
      multiemployer alliances and, 9,
        23, 58
    tax treatment of pensions in, 62, 86,
      96, 96t
New England Pension Assistance Project
    (NEPAP), lost pension counseling
    and, 174, 177–178
New Zealand, pensions in, 4, 5, 6, 87
Nondeductible contributions, pensions
    and, 90, 91t
Nondiscrimination regulations, 37–38, 144
Norris, Arizona Governing Committee
    v., unisex rulings in, 18, 183–184,
    189–190, 201
Norway, pensions in, 4, 5, 23, 86
Notional accounting system, 57, 127,
    133, 135
  Sweden and, 30, 109, 163, 169–170,
    207

Occupational Pensions Regulatory
    Authority (OPRA), UK, lost
    pensions and, 176

OECD. *See* Organisation for Economic Co-operation and Development countries
Older retirees. *See* Longevity
OMB (U.S. Office of Management and Budget), 96
Organisation for Economic Co-operation and Development (OECD) countries
  private pensions in, 29–31
  tax policy in, 86–87, 88, 96–98, 96*t*
  See also specific countries within

Part-time workers, 38, 77
  government mandates and, 5, 24
  health insurance in phased retirement for, 74–75
Payroll Deduction IRA, 39
Payroll taxes, social security and, 84, 88
PBGC. *See* Pension Benefit Guaranty Corporation
Pension Benefit Guaranty Corporation (PBGC), 114–122, 115*t*
  assets of, 114, 115*t*
  adequate funding and, 116–118, 121–122
  evaluation principles for, 116–120
  lost pensions and, 175–176
  moral hazard policy, 120–121
  plans insured by, 127, 128, 129, 178
  political risk protection and, 121–122
  problems faced by, 15, 18, 114–116, 123*nn*3–5
    lost pensions, 178, 210
    moral hazard, 118–120
Pension coverage
  extension of, 12–13, 17, 33, 37–53
    employee participation encouraged in, 40–47, 50–52
    employer-provided plans in, 37–39, 99
    pathways to, 21–25, 209–210
  measures of, 34–37
Pension equity plan (PEP), 15, 84, 88
  career lump sum in, 125, 126*t*, 128
Pension insurance, 7, 116

PBGC and, 15, 18, 114–122, 115*t*, 123*nn*3–5
Pension law, 65
  benefits and, 70–71, 127, 140, 170, 183–184
  desired amendments to (*see* Pension reform)
  fixed ages in, 14, 80, 81, 172
  as policy issue, 2, 207
  requirements of, 4, 18, 37–38, 51
    employer, in U.S., 5, 22, 36–37, 61, 115, 119, 138, 201, 209
    (*see also by specific country*)
  vesting in, 59, 61–62, 110, 131, 174
Pension plans
  features of, 143–145, 167, 172
  fund management of, 9–10
  funding of, 7–8, 16–17, 126*t*, 137–164, 171–172
    common issues in, 134–140
    defined benefit issues in, 154–163
    defined contribution issues in, 141–154
    employer contributions in, 116–118, 121–122, 130, 211
  participation in, 21, 33, 51–52
    employee refusals for, 13, 36–37, 47–50, 48*t*, 49*t*
  portability at retirement of, 55–81
    defined benefit plans and, 57–58, 66–71
    defined contribution plans, 57–58, 65–66, 72–73
    job change and, 13, 17, 52–53, 58–60, 101
    policy options, 71–73
    transferability of, 61–64, 68–71
    (*see also under* Retirement, phased, and pensions)
  risk in
    (*see* Pension risks; Risk management)
  terminology, 19*n*1, 33
  types of, 25
    (*see also* Defined benefit plans;

Pension plans, *cont.*
  types of, *cont.*
    (*see also* Defined contribution
      plans; Hybrid plans)
  withdrawals from, 14, 17, 86
Pension policy
  effectiveness of current, 178–179
  introduction to, 2–4
  issues in, 4–11, 12, 17, 201
  overview, 11–19
  proposals for, 203–212
  securing benefits through, 165–180
    adequacy of, 166–167, 171–173,
      179
    defined benefit plans and, 169–171
    defined contribution plans and,
      165–168
    lost pensions and, 173–178, 180,
      210
  U.S. development of, 2, 8, 10, 13, 212
    (*see also* Tax policy)
Pension Protection Act (2006, U.S.), 74,
  90
  hybrid plan introduction by, 3, 44, 51,
    131
  maximum employer contributions set
    in, 156, 164, 209
Pension Protection Fund (PPF, UK), 15,
  210
Pension reform, 24
  improving lives of retirees with, 11,
    12, 203, 207
  proposals for, 57, 76, 98–99, 160,
    163, 168, 203–212
  risky employers and, 115–116, 118
Pension risks, 26
  particular plans and, 101, 123n1, 134,
    212
    cash balance, 7, 105
    defined benefit, 1, 3, 6, 11, 14–15,
      105
    defined contribution, 1, 3, 6–7, 8,
      11, 73, 79, 106
    hybrid, 7, 11, 15, 126t
  types of
    annuities, 107–109, 126t

corporate dissolution, 7, 8, 110,
  209, 211
  (*see also* Bankruptcy)
inflation, 101, 102–103, 122, 126t,
  171
investment, 3, 73, 101, 104–106,
  110–111, 126t
litigation, 103–104
longevity/mortality, 15, 16, 19, 50,
  126t
  (*see also under* Life expectancy,
  risk and)
political, 121–122
portability upon job change, 101
regulatory, 113
shared, 15, 105, 110, 125, 134
Pension Schemes Registry (PSR), UK,
  OPRA and, 176
Pension systems
  behavioral economics and interaction
    with, 4, 153
  purposes of, 1, 84, 203
  types of, 8, 22, 62, 90, 157
    private, 4–6, 9, 12, 29–31, 83, 87,
      88, 129–130, 161
    public, 5, 7, 88
    (*see also* Social security systems)
  U.S. federal practices with, 1, 2, 6, 8,
    80, 88, 90
  savings plan and, 48–50
  states preempted by, 2, 51
Phased annuitization, 194
Phased retirement. *See under* Retirement,
  phased, and pensions
Phased withdrawals, defined contribution
  plans and, 17, 106–107, 166, 191
Plain Old Pension Plan (POPP), 126t,
  131–132, 133
Poland, EET pension approach in, 86
Politics, pensions and, 121–122, 140,
  153–154
POPP (Plain Old Pension Plan), 126t,
  131–132, 133
Portugal, modified EET pension
  approach in, 86

PPM (Premipensionsmyndigheten)
    system, Sweden, 30, 45
Premium Pension, Sweden, 30, 45
PSR (Pension Schemes Registry), UK,
    176

Registered Retirement Savings Plan
    (RRSP), Canada, IRA equivalence
    of, 91, 143
Regulatory practices with pensions, 139,
    176
    government role in, 8, 10, 22, 83,
        91–92, 113, 116, 127, 203
    investment portfolios and, 8, 37
    nondiscrimination and, 37–38, 51–52
Retirement
    age and
        (see Age of retirement; Longevity)
    inflation adjustments at, 11, 13, 208,
        211
    phased, and pensions, 73–81
        benefit receipt while working,
            75–77, 186t
        defined benefit plans and, 77–78,
            80–81
        defined contribution plans and,
            78–79
        gradual transition into, 73–75
    preparation for, 1, 14, 50, 53, 83, 167
        (see also Defined contribution
        plans; Savings plans; Social
        security systems)
    strong income system for, 17, 21–22,
        65, 103, 203, 212
    taxes in, 84, 93
Retirement Risk Survey, 73–74
Reversion tax, 117–118
Riester pensions, Germany, 87
Risk management, pension plans and,
    14–15, 114–122
Rollovers, 66, 78
    survivor benefits and, 63–64
    transferability rights of, 62–63, 65
Roth 401(k) plans, taxes and, 3, 14
Roth IRA plans, taxes and, 3

RRSP (Registered Retirement Savings
    Plan), Canada, 91

S2P (State Second Pension) Scheme,
    UK, 25, 31, 32n2
Save More Tomorrow (SMarT),
    autoescalation in, 144–145
Saver's Credit, lower income workers
    and, 5, 44–45, 89–90
Savings Incentive Match Plan for
    Employees (SIMPLE) IRA, 39
Savings, Pension, and Share Schemes
    Office (SPSS), UK, tax
    exemptions and, 176, 180n2
Savings plans, 83, 179
    autoescalation in, 144–145
    tax treatment of, 6, 84, 85–86
    types of
        401(k), 203–204
        SIMPLE, 39
        Thrift Savings Plan, 48–50, 49t,
            184–185, 189, 189tt
SCF (Survey of Consumer Finances), 36
Self-employment, pension taxation effect
    on, 88
SEP plan, 39
SERPS (State Earnings-Related Pension
    Scheme), UK, 25, 30–31, 32n2
Sidecar trusts, 92
SIMPLE (Savings Incentive Match Plan
    for Employees) IRA, 39
Simplified Employee Pension (SEP)
    plan, IRA-based, 39
Single women, pension coverage and,
    13, 34
SIPP. See Survey of Income and Program
    Participation
Slovak Republic, the, modified EET
    pension approach in, 86
Small businesses
    mandates and, 5, 12, 21
    pension plans for, 39, 44, 131
SMarT (Save More Tomorrow), 144–145
Social Security Administration, U.S., lost
    pensions and, 175, 178

Social security systems, 18, 102
  alternatives to, 23–24
    privatized IRAs as, 12, 21
    privatized retirement income
      systems as, 29, 30–31
    (*see also under* Voluntary
      practices with pensions, carve-out
      accounts)
  benefits from, 75, 86, 88, 169
    retirement age and, 77–78, 92
    taxes on, 90, 93, 94, 95–96
  funding of, 84, 88, 95, 191
  life expectancy and, 160, 207
  pension arrangement relationship to,
    24–25
  as state-operated pension, 5, 96
Solvency trusts, 92
Spain, pensions and taxes in, 86, 94, 193
SPSS (Savings, Pension, and Share
  Schemes Office), UK, 176, 180*n*2
State Earnings-Related Pension Scheme
  (SERPS), UK, predecessor of S2P,
  25, 30–31, 32*n*2
State Second Pension (S2P) Scheme,
  UK, contracting out of social
  security with, 25, 31, 32*n*2
Superannuation Guarantee ("Super"),
  Australia, 29, 79
Survey of Consumer Finances (SCF),
  employee pension contribution
  data from, 36
Survey of Income and Program
  Participation (SIPP), pension data
  from, 34, 36, 47–48, 48*t*, 49–50,
  142–143
Survivor benefits, 17, 107
  decline in, 1, 181
  divorced spouses and, 167, 168, 187*t*,
    195, 196
  international perspectives on, 79, 102
  pension law and, 18, 19*n*2, 63
  rollovers and, 63–64
  widows and, 167–168, 196–197
Sweden, 24, 153*t*
  annuities in, 181, 186*t*–188*t*, 193–197

  government mandates in, 4
    IRA provisions in, 12, 24, 29–30,
      45
    notional accounting, 30, 109,
      146–147, 163, 169–170, 207
  pension benefits in, 79
    lump sum payment of, 173, 187*t*
    receipt of, while still working, 76,
      186*t*
    taxes and, 87, 92, 93
  pension plans in, 7, 58, 172
    collective bargaining and, 23, 33
  social security in, 160, 191, 207
Switzerland, 7, 80
  government pension mandates in, 4,
    24, 33, 86

Tax credits, 44, 86
  lower income workers and, 5, 89–90,
    99
  pension savings with, 6, 85–86, 206
Tax deductions, 39, 88
  401(k) plans and, 10, 14, 140
  employee age and, 91–92
  private *vs.* public pension
    contributions and, 8, 62, 84, 98,
      157, 170–171, 206, 210–211
Tax exemptions, 84, 87, 88
  UK and, 176, 180*n*2
Tax policy
  analysis of, 87–98
    contributions, 88–92, 91*t*
    disbursements, 93–94
    implicit taxes, 95–96
    investment earnings, 92–93
    tax expenditures, 85, 96–98, 96*t*
  conclusion, 98–99
  OECD countries and, 86–87, 96–98,
    96*t*
  overview, 84–86
Tax shelters, employers and, 92
Taxation, 78, 84, 94
  government support in pensions
    through, 4–5, 6, 10, 22, 33, 167
  as pension policy issue, 2, 14, 43,
    83–99

Taxation, *cont.*
Roth plans and, 3, 14
See also specifics, e.g., Income taxes
Teachers Insurance and Annuity
Association–College Retirement
Equities Fund (TIAA-CREF),
65–66, 149
Temporary workers, pensions and, 24,
51, 64–65
Thrift Savings Plan, U.S.
reasons for nonparticipation in, 48–
50, 49*t*
unisex annuity payouts from, 184–
185, 189, 189*tt*
TIAA-CREF (Teachers Insurance
and Annuity Association–College
Retirement Equities Fund), 65–66,
149
Trade-offs, 40, 94
investment control *vs.* lawsuits, 103–
104
lower *vs.* higher benefits and
annuities, 122, 197
voluntary carve-out accounts and,
25–28
wages *vs.* pensions, 7, 44, 89, 116–
117, 137
Trade unions, 9, 140
collective bargaining agreements and
pensions, 4, 7, 22–23, 33, 44, 89
multiemployer alliances and, 67–68
Transferability rights, 61–64, 68–71
defined benefit plans and, 68–71
policy options, 61–73
portability as, 63–64, 68–71
reciprocity agreements, 69
rollovers, 62–63, 65
vesting, 57, 61–62
Trusts, fund management via, 29, 92,
127, 139, 161–162
Turkey, modified EET pension approach
in, 86

United Kingdom (UK)
contracting out in, 23, 25, 27–28,
30–31

lost pensions in, 18, 59–60, 175, 176,
210
pension benefits in, 7, 93
inflation adjustments at retirement
for, 11, 102, 171, 188*t*
lump sum payment of, 173, 187*t*
receipt of, while still working, 76,
186*t*
survivors and, 102, 197
pension investments in, 153*t*
annuities and, 181, 186*t*–188*t,*
193–197
pension plans in, 139
employee contributions to, 34–35,
41
hybrids as, 16, 125, 126*t,* 128–
129, 133–134, 162–163
restrictions and, 167, 172
pension provision in
government mandates for, 4, 5, 15,
25, 30–31, 32*n*2, 61, 80, 159, 210
trends of, 7, 10, 134, 139, 159,
207
vesting requirements of, 59, 61
regulation in, 8, 91–92, 176
tax treatment of pensions in, 62, 93,
96*t*
contributions and, 88, 91–92, 162,
210
modified EET approach to, 86,
176, 180*n*2
United States (U.S.)
legislation enacted in, 3, 44, 63, 74,
84, 89–90
mutual fund expenses in, 153*t*
pension benefits in, 7, 11
pension policy development in, 2, 8,
10, 13, 212
default provision and, 51–53, 65,
204, 206
pension provision in, 9
international standards *vs.,* 1, 6,
15–16, 79–81
trends and, 7, 10, 134, 139, 207
securing lost pensions in, 175–176,
210

United States (U.S.), *cont.*
  tax treatment of pensions in, 6
    contributions, 8, 14, 39, 62, 88,
      96, 96*t,* 157
    EET approach to, 86
    See also Pension law; Regulatory
      practices with pensions
U.S. Congress, 96, 174
  PBGC and, 114, 119, 121–122
U.S. Dept. of Labor (USDOL), 3, 127,
  170
U.S. Office of Management and Budget
  (OMB), tax expenditures and, 96
U.S. Supreme Court, unisex rulings by,
  18, 183–184, 189–190, 201
USDOL. *See* U.S. Dept. of Labor

Variable annuities, 194–195
Vesting
  British pension law and, 59, 61
  job changes and, 57, 61–62, 211
  lost pensions and, 41, 174
  pension law and, 110, 131
Voluntary practices with pensions, 21
  annuities and, 191–192
  carve-out accounts, 23, 25–28, 31–32
    trade-off between reduced
      contributions and benefits, 27–28
    trade-off generosity of, 25–26
  employee choice among, 5, 9, 12, 23,
    31–32, 37, 201
  government role in, 4–5, 7, 22, 33, 83
  inertia *vs.* incentive in, 13, 16, 45–46,
    48, 148–149, 204
  private pensions and mandatory *vs.,*
    4–6, 31–32

Wages
  employee layoffs and benefits based
    on, 1, 11, 13, 211
  inflation and, 206–207, 211
  low, and pension coverage, 22, 39
  reduced, and pension trade-offs, 7, 44,
    89, 116–117, 137
  taxes and, 84, 87, 88
With-Profits Pension Annuity, UK, 162

Withdrawals from pension plans, 172
  employer, of surplus funds, 92, 209
  longevity risks and, 106–107
  phased, from defined contribution
    plans, 17, 106–107, 166, 191
  taxes on, 14, 17, 86, 93
Women in the workforce, 141
  job tenure of, 55–56
  life expectancy and, 50, 102, 103,
    122, 159, 184
  pension benefits to, 77, 93
  pension coverage for, 13, 53
  pension nonparticipation among,
    48–50, 48*t,* 49*t*
  spousal pension coverage for, 13, 45,
    187*t,* 195–196
Women's pension issues
  benefits as, 167–168, 185, 189
  coverage as, 13, 34, 53

About the Institute

The W.E. Upjohn Institute for Employment Research is a nonprofit research organization devoted to finding and promoting solutions to employment-related problems at the national, state, and local levels. It is an activity of the W.E. Upjohn Unemployment Trustee Corporation, which was established in 1932 to administer a fund set aside by Dr. W.E. Upjohn, founder of The Upjohn Company, to seek ways to counteract the loss of employment income during economic downturns.

The Institute is funded largely by income from the W.E. Upjohn Unemployment Trust, supplemented by outside grants, contracts, and sales of publications. Activities of the Institute comprise the following elements: 1) a research program conducted by a resident staff of professional social scientists; 2) a competitive grant program, which expands and complements the internal research program by providing financial support to researchers outside the Institute; 3) a publications program, which provides the major vehicle for disseminating the research of staff and grantees, as well as other selected works in the field; and 4) an Employment Management Services division, which manages most of the publicly funded employment and training programs in the local area.

The broad objectives of the Institute's research, grant, and publication programs are to 1) promote scholarship and experimentation on issues of public and private employment and unemployment policy, and 2) make knowledge and scholarship relevant and useful to policymakers in their pursuit of solutions to employment and unemployment problems.

Current areas of concentration for these programs include causes, consequences, and measures to alleviate unemployment; social insurance and income maintenance programs; compensation; workforce quality; work arrangements; family labor issues; labor-management relations; and regional economic development and local labor markets.